Biographical research

BRIAN ROBERTS

Open University Press
Buckingham · Philadelphia

This book is dedicated to Evan and Mary for life, care and memories

Open University Press
Celtic Court
22 Ballmoor
Buckingham
MK18 1XW

email: enquiries@openup.co.uk
world wide web: www.openup.co.uk

and
325 Chestnut Street
Philadelphia, PA 19106, USA

First published 2002

A catalogue record of this book is available from the British Library

ISBN 0 335 20286 1 (pb)   0 335 20287 X (hb)

Library of Congress Cataloging-in-Publication Data
Roberts, Brian, 1950–
    Biographical research/Brian Roberts.
        p.   cm. – (Understanding social research)
    Includes bibliographical references (p. 178) and index.
    ISBN 0-335-20287-X – ISBN 0-335-20286-1 (pbk.)
    1. Biography–Research–Methodology.   2. Biography as a literary
    form.   I. Title.   II. Series.

CT22.R63 2001
808'.06692–dc21   2001021067

Typeset by Type Study, Scarborough
Printed in Great Britain by Biddles Ltd, Guildford and Kings Lynn

Contents

Series editor's foreword   ix
Acknowledgements   xi

1 Introduction: biographical research   1
Biographical research: defining the field   1
The development of biographical research   3
Methodological issues   6
The researcher's role   13
Theoretical approaches   14
Biographical research   15
Recommended reading   17

2 Uses of biographical research   18
Uses of biographical research   18
Disciplines and contexts   22
Education   23
Oral history   24
Health and ageing   25
Feminist research   28
Narratives of the body and sexuality   29
Autobiography and biography   30

Conclusion 31
Recommended reading 31

3 **The life history** 33
The life history 33
Individual lives and social structures 34
Life history data and method 37
Deviance, career, becoming 40
Case studies 42
Types of interpretation 46
Conclusion 50
Recommended reading 51

4 **Autobiography and biography** 52
Autobiography and biography – definitions 52
Genre 56
Issues in autobiography and biography 60
Letters, diaries, memoirs and other personal 'artefacts' 62
Case study 66
Fiction and non-fiction 69
Conclusion 71
Recommended reading 72

5 **Auto/biography and sociology** 73
Auto/biography – definitions and relations 73
Individual experiences and auto/biographical writing 75
Feminism and auto/biography 77
Intertextuality – written and oral texts 78
Hermeneutics, phenomenology and narrative texts 80
Time perspectives – Mead, Schutz and Ricoeur 82
The researcher as an auto/biographer 84
The researcher and the researched subject 87
Individual lives and social lives 88
Case study 88
Conclusion 91
Recommended reading 92

6 **Oral history** 93
Oral history – definitions 93
Uses and types of oral history 95
Origins 97
Development and purpose 99
Ethics 104
Evidence, truth and the researcher 104

Political standpoint 107
Case study 110
Conclusion 113
Recommended reading 113

7 **The narrative analysis of lives** 115
Narrative analysis – definitions 115
Narrative analysis 117
Time and narrative 123
Myth and narrative 124
Case study 128
Other 'models' of life study 130
Conclusion 132
Recommended reading 133

8 **Memory and autobiography** 134
Types of memory 134
The social transmission of memories 140
Case study 142
Family and group memories 144
Public and private memories 145
Methodological issues: recollection and selectivity 147
Conclusion 148
Recommended reading 149

9 **Ethnography and biographical research** 151
Fieldwork, ethnography and participant observation –
    definition and practice 152
Research roles 152
Methodological issues 153
Ethnography and key informants 154
Reflexivity and the researcher's life experience of ethnography 157
Ethnographic texts 160
Case study 162
Oral traditions and biography 164
Conclusion 165
Recommended reading 166

10 **Conclusion** 167
Disciplines 169
The biographical turn 169
Identity 170
Time 171
Memory 172

Researcher's self   172
Methodology   173
New technology   173
Conclusion   174
Recommended reading   175

Glossary   176
References   178
Index   200

Series editor's foreword

This Understanding Social Research series is designed to help students to understand how social research is carried out and to appreciate a variety of issues in social research methodology. It is designed to address the needs of students taking degree programmes in areas such as sociology, social policy, psychology, communication studies, cultural studies, human geography, political science, criminology and organization studies and who are required to take modules in social research methods. It is also designed to meet the needs of students who need to carry out a research project as part of their degree requirements. Postgraduate research students and novice researchers will find the books equally helpful.

The series is concerned to help readers to 'understand' social research methods and issues. This will mean developing an appreciation of the pleasures and frustrations of social research, an understanding of how to implement certain techniques, and an awareness of key areas of debate. The relative emphasis on these different features will vary from book to book, but in each one the aim will be to see the method or issue from the position of a practising researcher and not simply to present a manual of 'how to' steps. In the process, the series will contain coverage of the major methods of social research and addresses a variety of issues and debates. Each book in the series is written by a practising researcher who has experience of the technique or debates that he or she is addressing. Authors are encouraged to draw on their own experiences and inside knowledge.

This new book on biographical method is very timely and very much in line with the goals of the Understanding Social Research series. Brian Roberts has been engaged in biographical research for many years and is therefore able to draw upon a great deal of experience and expertise in writing this book. However, at the time that he began his work in this area, the method was still in a relatively underdeveloped state. This is not to say that the biographical method is new – it manifestly is not, as anyone with just a passing acquaintance with the history of social research will know. The life history method has been with us for decades. But in the last ten to fifteen years, the biographical method (as it is increasingly referred to) has become an extremely significant approach to social research. This surge of interest in the method can be attributed to a variety of factors: a developing disillusionment with static approaches to data collection; a growing interest in the life course; an increased concern with 'lived experience' and how best to express and reveal it; and, of course, the method has shared in the growth in popularity of qualitative research in general.

It is in this sense that Brian Roberts's book is very timely. He brings a great awareness of the different ways in which the biographical method can be executed, but he does so at a time when there is burgeoning interest in what the method entails. His approach indicates a critical awareness of the different ways of doing biographical research. Such an awareness comes about from being steeped in the method in its many forms. He uses many examples to illustrate his key points, including his own research. It is precisely this kind of style that I have been keen to develop in the series – clear expositions of particular methods coupled with the injection of writers' own research experiences into those expositions.

Perhaps one of the biggest difficulties that many of us face when thinking or writing about biographical research is what makes it distinctive. The biographical method draws on materials and ways of conducting research that can be found in many other ways of doing qualitative research, such as the examination of personal documents, conducting interviews, and carrying out a narrative analysis. Readers will find that Brian Roberts makes clear what kind of sensibility a biographical perspective entails and, thereby, what its distinguishing characteristics are. As such, readers will find the exposition in this book clarifies these and many other areas of uncertainty about what makes the biographical method distinctive.

Alan Bryman

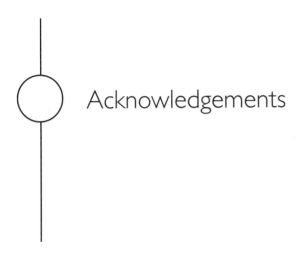

Acknowledgements

During the last ten years I have benefited greatly from discussions on bio-graphical research with friends and colleagues in the following: Auto/ Biography Study Group, British Sociological Association; Biographical Per-spectives on European Societies Research Network, European Sociological Association; Biography and Society, RC38, International Sociological Association; International Oral History Association; and Llafur: Society of Welsh Labour History. I would also like to thank friends and colleagues at Malmö University for their kind invitation to be a visiting lecturer and making me feel most welcome. I am most grateful to Alan Bryman for his encouragement and support and Open University Press for patience and advice. Finally, the greatest thanks are to Mag, Rhiannon and Iwan who have given their unfailing support and encouraged me to finish writing the book.

Introduction: biographical research

Biographical research: defining the field

This book introduces a broad and developing area of study – the collection and interpretation of 'personal' or 'human documents' (Allport 1942; Blumer 1969). It covers a range of disciplines, how they increasingly influence each other and key issues of analysis and method in the study of 'lives'. The book title *Biographical Research* is not intended to be associated with a precise definition but to indicate various, often interrelated, approaches to the study of individuals. Biographical research is an exciting, stimulating and fast-moving field which seeks to understand the changing experiences and outlooks of individuals in their daily lives, what they see as important, and how to provide interpretations of the accounts they give of their past, present and future. Denzin provides an indication of the scope of the field:

> A family of terms combines to shape the biographical method . . . method, life, self, experience, epiphany, case, autobiography, ethnography, auto-ethnography, biography, ethnography story, discourse, narrative, narrator, fiction, history, personal history, oral history, case history, case study, writing presence, difference, life history, life story, self story, and personal experience story.
>
> (Denzin 1989: 27)

The kinds of material that are deemed relevant also cover a wide area: 'personal documents' or 'documents of life' (Plummer 1983) may include diaries, letters, autobiographies, biographies, memoranda and other materials (Denzin 1989). Clandinin and Connelly conclude that these are 'field texts', which may be produced before the research for a different usage (Clandinin and Connelly 1994: 419). They outline oral history, annals and chronicles, family stories, photographs and other personal and family artefacts, research interviews, journals, autobiographical writing, letters, conversations and field notes (Clandinin and Connelly 1994). So, documents may be written for different purposes, for different audiences (including the self) and immediately or much later after the events described. All these different sources and strategies have been adjudged, by opponents and proponents, to raise important methodological issues surrounding reliability and validity (see Allport 1942; Denzin 1970: 219–59; Plummer 1983: 13–38; Golby 1994; Ritchie 1995: 7).

The chapter organization of the book is partly based on disciplinary or sub-disciplinary approaches (e.g. sociology, oral history) to show how biographical research and method developed and the debates within approaches. However, it is increasingly difficult to keep to a simple disciplinary format since there is a growing recognition that methodological and theoretical issues have cross-disciplinary ramifications and common lines of influence (e.g. from feminist research). Writers and researchers are more and more aware of developments in other disciplines and are keen to apply knowledge from numerous sources. Indeed, biographical researchers often actively seek to move over disciplinary boundaries. Thus, the book includes references to work across disciplines, for example, particularly in chapters on memory, narrative and ethnography where interdisciplinary work has explored similar issues. Therefore, the book is intentionally interdisciplinary rather than based on one discipline, to show the wider connections between forms of biographical research. The time is right for the publication of a book with this intent because significant developments are taking place within the rapid expansion of interest in the study of lives.

The book is not a step-by-step guide to doing biographical research but attempts to show the key methodological issues and variety of biographical work. Readers will have an appreciation of this developing field and particular issues, including interpretation, memory, genres of writing, the audience, and the researcher's role.

Biographical research is part of the broader practice of qualitative methods: 'Qualitative researchers tend to espouse an approach in which theory and empirical investigation are interwoven . . . during or at the end of fieldwork, rather than being a precursor to it' (Bryman 1988: 81). Qualitative research has a number of features stemming from its philosophical and theoretical approach to the social world, including remaining close to the experiences and views of the researched. These can be summarized, following

Bryman, as 'viewing events, action, norms, values etc. from the perspective of the people who are being studied'; 'to provide detailed descriptions of the social settings'; 'commitment to understanding events, behaviour, etc. in their context'; 'to view social life in processual, rather than static terms'; 'a research strategy which is relatively open and unstructured'; and a rejection of 'the formulation of theories and concepts in advance' of fieldwork which may 'impose a potentially alien framework' on subjects (Bryman 1988: 61–8). While biographical research shares a common outlook with qualitative research more generally, it also has its own specific challenges. An initial problem in the field of biographical research is the differing use of terms – oral history, personal narrative, biography and autobiography – and their interchangeable use (Reinharz 1992: 129). However, a common distinction is made between life story and life history. A life story

> is the story a person chooses to tell about the life he or she has lived, told as completely and honestly as possible, what is remembered of it, and what the teller wants others to know of it, usually as a result of a guided interview by another . . . A life story is a fairly complete narrating of one's entire experience of life as a whole, highlighting the most important aspects.
>
> (Atkinson 1998: 8)

The life history is usually taken to refer to the collection, interpretation and report writing of the 'life' (the life history method) in terms of the story told or as the construction of the past experience of the individual (from various sources) to relate to the story (see Denzin 1970: 219–59; Fischer-Rosenthal and Rosenthal 1997: 9). Therefore, the term life story is commonly applied to the narrated story by the author while life history infers the later interpretive, presentational work of the researcher. However, such a distinction is difficult to maintain in practice where, for example, the researcher conducts an interview with a participant. In general, in this book, the term 'biographical research' will be used to denote work which uses the stories of individuals and other 'personal materials' to understand the individual life within its social context.

The development of biographical research – the narrativist/biographical turn?

It would appear that the 'cultural and linguistic turn' (including the rise of cultural studies, the 'reading' of cultural phenomena, and so on) in the social sciences is being followed now by a narrative, biographical or auto/biographical turn (Riessman 1993: 5–6; Chamberlayne et al. 2000). For a number of writers this heralds a very significant shift in social study. Stanley claims the study of lives is 'raising central epistemological and thus political issues for all forms of social inquiry and praxis' (Stanley 1994b: 89). Thus, questions are being raised regarding explanation, understanding and interpreting, the determination of individual and group action and assumptions regarding social being.

The self-representation of the individual life or 'autobiography' is not a new phenomenon but has long development as a 'cultural practice' (Mascuch 1997). Even before the eighteenth-century Enlightenment conceptions of political rights, religious discourses from the Protestant Reformation carried notions of introspection. According to Mellor and Shilling, the legacy of a 'cognitive' priority over the carnal can be found in the reflexive aspect of current autobiography (Shilling and Mellor 1994: 125). For Porter, within the Enlightenment 'the traditional Puritan genre of spiritual self-examination was supplemented by more secular modes of confession' (Porter 2000: 278). However, despite philosophical, literary and other explorations of individuality, modern social sciences have tended to omit the 'humanity' of the individual in the pursuit of causal accounts, objective study of the general patterns of human behaviour and standard features of individuals drawn from natural science assumptions, procedures and principles (Rustin 1999: 65). The 'individuality' of individuals and the diversity of human meanings have been either neglected or relegated to a secondary concern (a residue). This is not to say that a 'humanist' or 'idealist' strand of thought has not existed within the social sciences. A complex body of thought from Dilthey's biographical study and Weber's *verstehen*, the phenomenology of Husserl and Schutz, Chicagoan interactionism (Park, Mead and their followers) and Sartre's existential procedure has had a 'subterranean existence' in the social sciences (see Erben 1998b).

In the 1970s there was a change in the way 'science' was being seen – the nature of scientific knowledge and how it was achieved was being put under scrutiny. Within the social sciences, for example, interactionist or subjectivist approaches were being advanced, especially within the sociology of deviance, which were giving a renewed attention to individual meanings and choice. Within sociology a challenge to the dominance of functionalism was being made by Marxian theory, conflict approaches, and subjectivist or humanistic accounts of social life. Meanwhile, cultural studies was beginning to form out of a mixture of literary criticism, popular cultural analyses, social history, new sociologies and additions from Gramscian Marxism, Barthes' semiotics, the structuralism of Althusser and other sources (Rustin 1999). The outcome has been described as a cultural or linguistic 'turn' due to the emphasis on the concerns with language and representation, and the detailed analysis of 'texts'. However, the reading and investigation of cultural forms as texts and the use of 'discourse' to describe bodies of thought and practice produced a diminution or disappearance of the creative, active role of individuals. Even so, the increasing influence of postmodernism with its critique of grand narratives – dominant ideologies and social theories – and a stress on change, diversity, and uncertainty, within cultural studies and the social sciences more generally, have (despite deconstructionism and discourse theory) opened possibilities for new accounts of the individual (see Rustin 1999). The growth of 'narrative analysis' or the advent of a 'narrative turn' has added in further dimensions, for example, of story and time. If we are living in a postmodern or post-traditional world where there is not a shared reality, and identity no longer rests on rituals or given definitions, with resulting risks, uncertainties and doubts (cf. Beck, Giddens), there is also now scope for new types of individuality while the same shifts make the construction of new identities a fraught enterprise (see Shilling and Mellor 1994).

The appeal of biographical research is that it is exploring, in diverse methodological and interpretive ways, how individual accounts of life experience can be understood within the contemporary cultural and structural settings and is thereby helping to chart the major societal changes that are underway, but not merely at some broad social level. Biographical research has the important merit of aiding the task of understanding major social shifts, by including how new experiences are interpreted by individuals within families, small groups and institutions. Perhaps an informative way of understanding the 'biographical turn' in the human sciences is to outline the series of changes in qualitative research during the last century. Denzin and Lincoln (1994c, 2000b) have identified 'five moments' of qualitative research, from the early 1900s and the work of the single fieldworker onwards through various phases after World War II. A crisis of both representation and legitimation has arisen marked by the problem of the connection between experience and the social text compiled by the researcher (usually associated with interpretive, linguistic and rhetorical turns in social theory), and questions of validity, generalizability and reliability 'retheorized in postpositivist, constructionist–naturalistic and interpretive discourses'. Theories are to be understood according to narrative, the concept of the superior researcher is replaced, and action or activist research and local theorization on specific contexts and problems are developed (Denzin and Lincoln 1994c: 7–11). In a possible sixth moment underway, research practice will be multi-voiced and multi-representational (Denzin and Lincoln 1994a) (see Conclusion, this volume).

For some commentators a note of caution is needed when assessing the emergence of the 'narrative turn'. It may not be as progressive or humanistic as it appears. Goodson (1995) places the upsurge in interest in personal knowledge in the genre of narrative or story within the context of cultural restructuring in contemporary society, for example the trend for storytelling, 'human interest' features and personal anecdote in television news. It must be placed alongside the 'attack on many of the existing agencies of cultural mediation and production' (schools, universities, welfare agencies and so on) and the 'overall sponsorship of personal and practical forms of discourse' in cultural production. Noting the power and shifts in the output of a global media, he says 'the life story represents a form of cultural apparatus that accompanies an aggrandising state and market system' (Goodson 1995: 90).

Methodological issues

A reason offered for the traditional lack of use of life stories within sociology and other fields was offered by Becker – that the dominant, 'scientific' hypothetico-deductive method produced the notion that hypotheses were to be constructed for testing and that life stories did not provide the 'findings' that sociological researchers were required to obtain (Becker 1970). Biographical research was alleged to be wanting when measured against criteria of reliability and validity: life stories perhaps provided insights, sources for possible hypotheses before the formulation of 'real' objective research, or more emphasis had been placed on validity rather than reliability. (It may be worth noting here that writers have observed that qualitative methods differ on the balance between reliability and validity; see Kirk and Miller 1986; Perakyla 1997.)

As we have said, the study of lives has become much more accepted and commonplace. However, questions still arise concerning the 'adequacy' or 'quality' of accounts or, putting it rather differently, how far life story research should follow the methodological standards of quantitative research or apply its own qualitative principles. The study of life stories has often taken traditional criteria at least as a starting reference point. However, many writers do argue that the attempt to recognize the meanings given to the social world by individuals requires rather different criteria. For example, Hatch and Wisniewski argue that 'truth' and related epistemological issues can be seen in ways that go beyond the standardized notions of reliability, validity, and generalizability. They also give a range of alternatives used by writers, including adequacy, aesthetic finality, accessibility, authenticity, credibility, explanatory power, persuasiveness, coherence, plausibility, trustworthiness, epistemological validity and verisimilitude and so on (Hatch and Wisniewski 1995a: 128–9; see also Riessman 1993; Denzin and Lincoln 1994a; Blumenfeld-Jones 1995). Here, Silverman provides a warning that there has been a 'romantic' influence on contemporary sociology, which gives the 'experiential as authentic'; he stresses that the interview is collaborative in the construction of the self. More broadly the interview and the appeal of the authentic have a wider presence in society and should be part of explanation 'rather than to be relied upon' (Silverman 1997: 248).

The study of biographical research rests on a view of individuals as creators of meanings which form the basis of their everyday lives. Individuals act according to meanings through which they make sense of social existence. Interpretive, subjective or qualitative approaches to the study of lives have been inspired by Weber's *verstehen*, Schutz's phenomenological perspective, Chicagoan interactionism, Sartre's progressive–regressive method, narratology, literary criticism, and ethnographic analyses in fieldwork, in an attempt to outline the subjective meanings of the 'life' account. Despite their diversity these approaches have some common problems of analysis, such as the 'reality' of events and the meanings attributed to them by life stories, the particular tools or conventions of language used to represent life experience, and issues in the means of interpretation (Denzin 1989: 13–14). While the attention to subjective meanings places biographical research firmly within the orbit of qualitative methods, until recently it has attracted relatively little textbook discussion, being subsumed within ethnographical fieldwork or as allied with and subsumed under in-depth or informal interviewing.

A key debate within much biographical research is 'realism' versus 'constructionism' in the study of lives – it is a debate which has generated forthright views among international sociologists in the field of 'biography and society'. At its most simple realism holds that there is some objective knowledge of reality – an empirical, material basis for individual experience and that stories reflect a lived reality. For realism, the tendency towards a 'constructionist' or 'narrative' position, the reliance on the 'text', the analysis of 'intertextuality' and multiple 'voices' is ultimately a retreat from any idea of reality – interpretation feeds upon interpretation in a swirl of language and symbols. Such a view, it is held, lacks historical insight, political context and a sociological perspective on institutions and structure. For constructionists, at the extreme, the view that life stories reflect reality or empirical truth is simplistic and misconceived – a 'biographical illusion': stories are not simply referential of experience (see Denzin 1989: 14, 20–6). In fact, both the respondents' 'story' and its interpretation by the researcher are shaped by narrative conventions. The emphasis in analysis is also upon how the story is formed, including the 'performance' and collaboration with the researcher. In a more postmodernist vein, there is recognition that interpretation should be attentive to inconsistency and ambiguities in stories rather than assume one story and a simple receptiveness of the audience. Differing textual interpretations are seen as possible, if not desirable (see M. Evans 1993). Focus turns to the processes of 'writing up' of research from the taped stories and field notes – rather than representing an 'objective reality', narrative structures and rhetorical devices become resources for constructing a text (Richardson 1995: 199). These structures provide meanings and thereby define the people and circumstances within the research process. Even scientific writing rests on narrative structures and conventions (Richardson 1995: 199).

Usually, biographical researchers take a pragmatic stance in research practice instead of a firm allegiance to 'realism' or 'constructionism'. There has to be a basis in the material world including the embedded institutions, core structures, and evident bodily realities in which individual existence is situated. Life stories commonly refer to 'real' events and experiences – and often the tellers may be the only witnesses to such happenings but, commonly, their accounts can be checked against other written, visual or oral accounts. Nevertheless, how these events are perceived and selected (even chronologically reordered or changed over time) and placed within understandings of the individual life – by metaphor, myth and so on – are necessary aspects of analysis. A constructionist view can be used to help to analyse how the tellers shape the telling of their experiences of particular events – how the 'reality' (for them) is formed through the account. At base, the common pragmatic view would be that stories or accounts by individuals are central but that they are collected and used in different ways for different methodological and theoretical purposes thus resisting being trapped by realist or constructionist imperatives. For Atkinson and Coffey, the importance of reflexivity and the dependence on conventions of writing and reading in textual practices must be recognized, but they argue strongly that rejections of simple positivist and realist assumptions should not necessarily lead to the 'nihilism' of a textual approach. Writing conventions need to be applied and explored while conveying the diverse lives of others (Atkinson and Coffey 1995: 55). Again, generally, in biographical research a pragmatic orientation is often taken, relying on the similarities in approaches and procedures – the emphasis is on purpose, to gain insights into individual lives as, perhaps, reflecting wider cultural meanings of the society rather than dwelling on differences in methodological and theoretical assumptions (Miller 2000: 18).

A number of important changes have taken place in the discussion of research methods during the past fifteen years or so. Qualitative methodology has risen in relative prominence alongside its quantitative counterpart. In addition, the emphasis on 'methods' has broadened to methodology as the discussion of stages in research have brought a new notion of the research process as involving complex relations between the empirical world, data collection, research design and theorization as the researcher moves between parts of research procedure (Bryman and Burgess 1994b: 1–2). In recent qualitative texts more attention has been devoted to analysing data. Bryman and Burgess (1994b: 3–6) note there have been two main 'general strategies' discussed in these texts: analytic induction and grounded theory.

Florian Znaniecki offered the analytic induction approach to theorization as a contrast to statistical methods (see Hammersley 1990: 163–4). Analytic induction has a number of stages. The researcher outlines a preliminary definition of an area, problem or issue and constructs a provisional explanation. Cases are studied to see if they fit the initial hypothesis. If the data and hypothesis do not match, the hypothesis may require redefinition or the case or cases are rejected. The initial area, problem or issue may need reformulation. As cases are examined the process of hypothesis redefinition continues and more consistency with the data is attained. The process continues with the interrelation between data and hypothesis being scrutinized until a relationship is established as cases that do not fit are no longer found. In summary, in place of statistical sampling a theoretical procedure is applied. Analytic induction is based on a close investigation and comparison of cases – new cases are examined for similarities and differences with existing cases. Analytic induction has the advantages of an intimate interrelation between research observation, conceptualization and theory. On the other hand there are a number of difficulties. Criticisms have pointed to its weakness when compared with causal or enumerative procedures and the great amount of time and effort required (see Denzin 1970: 199; Vidich and Lyman 1994: 39). Analytic induction would seem, at first sight, to be very appropriate for the analysis of life stories since it does not depend on 'pre-existing formulations or large samples': 'Rather, it proceeds from scrutiny of one case to produce a low-level generalisation which then starts to define and characterise a given phenomenon' (Plummer 1983: 125). Unfortunately, the instances of the detailed use of analytical induction appear sparse within qualitative research, possibly due to its demanding procedures.

A second major procedure for relating research and theory generation is grounded theory as offered by Glaser and Strauss (1967). For Charmaz, the procedure can be used across disciplines and is compatible with both interpretive and 'traditional, positivistic assumptions of an external reality that researchers can discover and record' (Charmaz 1995: 30). The intent is to provide a systematic approach to qualitative research which clearly outlines the connection between data and theory and how conceptual development can be achieved and checked. Theory is generated during the research through an ongoing interrelation between a systematic data collection and analysis (Strauss and Corbin 1994: 273). The process is to be open with ideas and conceptualization arising from the data rather than dependent upon pre-existing theoretical approaches. Any other insights from other sources have to be related to the data to avoid 'mismatch'. Grounded theory also challenged a series of assumptions about qualitative research, for instance, as 'impressionistic and unsystematic' and as prior to more 'scientific' methods while showing that data collection and analysis were interrelated (Charmaz 1995: 29).

In the generation of new theory through comparative analysis, verification should take place accurately and as much as possible but it should not overtake generation – theory must be grounded in data (Glaser and Strauss 1970: 34). As Hammersley says, 'empirical fit' is achieved by concepts within grounded theory as 'sensitizing' in providing meaning and 'plausibility' – more than a prior theory; for 'most purposes it is not necessary to go beyond the level of plausibility provided by comparative method and grounded theorizing' (Hammersley 1990: 173–4). Importantly, by theoretical sampling cases are scrutinized until new features no longer arise, or 'theoretical saturation'. As with analytical induction, often grounded theory is referred to in biographical research more as a general stance rather than in detail. Grounded theory provides for a connection between data and theory to be maintained as a procedure for researchers to follow in addressing the complexities of social life but it has also been criticized for the practical problems of the degree of time spent and the detail of analysis. Moreover, a common criticism is that it is often cited in research as a means of giving a respectability to the approach applied. It is also frequently cited as an influence on developments in computer software programs for qualitative research (see Mangabeira 1996).

Grounded theory does attempt to tackle the problem in qualitative research of a tendency towards description due to an avoidance of theory, or reluctance to address it, fearing that the naturalistic commitment to the subject will be compromised. Theory used too early, it is felt, may flatten out social ambiguities and inconsistencies and obscure the views of respondents. Analytical induction, Bryman suggests, may be more prone to this problem than grounded theory with its more delayed use of theoretical generalization; again a tension can be found between greater theoretical concerns and the respondent's view of life (Bryman 1988: 87). In reviewing the subsequent development of qualitative research, Denzin and Lincoln argue that while some 'postpositivist' bases of the grounded theory approach can be challenged the general procedure of accumulating interpretations from detailed observations of social life will remain (Denzin and Lincoln 1994a: 577).

As stated earlier, grounded theory is often mentioned in particular qualitative work, including biographical studies, as informing the procedure used, and commonly a broadly phenomenological or interactionist approach is also cited (Jones 1983). However, frequently how the procedure has been applied is far from easily apparent. While in the study of one life 'theoretical sampling' and 'constant comparison' are not immediately appropriate, multiple life stories could be used in this way (Plummer 1983: 126–7). For Charmaz, there is an 'inherent empiricism' in grounded theory methods 'whether their data sources are autobiographic, published accounts, movies, intensive interviews, case studies, participant observer field notes or personal journals'. There has been a 'realist' orientation (despite initial interpretive assumptions) because of the authority given to the researcher to provide an objective account of the detailed lives and surrounding world of the respondents (Charmaz 1995: 31). Similarly, Miller points to the use of 'saturation' as an important part of a realist/grounded theory approach within some biographical work (e.g. Bertaux) (Miller 2000: 11). Charmaz believes that while grounded theory may be criticized for an 'emphasis on fracturing the data' by analytical categories it does not rule out a concentration on the individual. However, Charmaz later, in responding to criticisms, for instance from narrativists that it breaks up the data and neglects how meanings are constructed by narrator and researcher, points to both objectivist and constructivist 'visions' for the future of grounded theory (Charmaz 2000: 521, 528).

Finally, analytic induction or grounded theory or other observational/interpretive procedures can be seen as forms of reasoning. For instance, Polkinghorne argues that in seeing the relations between data and theory as forms of reasoning, two types can be found: the 'paradigmatic type' is based on 'paradigmatic reasoning' – and applies an analytic process that finds categories in the data, whereas a 'narrative type' based on 'narrative reason' is an analytic process that gives storied accounts (Polkinghorne 1995: 21; see Polkinghorne 1988).

A topic much discussed in qualitative research is the process of 'coding' of data either by hand or via qualitative research computer programs (see Bernard 1995: Ch. 9; Coffey and Atkinson 1996: Chs 2, 6; Miller 2000: 150–3). The notion of 'coding' has been applied in qualitative work in a variety of ways. Generally, it refers to how the data are 'sorted', categorized by 'codes' which summarize or order the material. This is a continuous process as the data are accumulated and scrutinized, and can guide the gathering of future material as well as the initial steps in formulating concepts and theory. The close examination of gathered material provides new insights and ideas, new ways of organizing parts of the materials, forming types and raising new research questions. Coding is a means of relaying these fresh insights to the data. It may take various forms according to the depth and time spent on the contact with the material and research setting – from tentative coding at the beginning to more definite levels and linkages of categories as material is collected and analysed. For example, Bernard distinguishes between coding and indexing when describing 'codes' as encryption, indexing and measurement devices (Bernard 1995: 193). Also, stages in analysis can be identified according to initial work in the collection of materials and, later, fuller attention to coding and building connections. Crabtree and Miller contrast codes in an editing style of data analysis where observations on data are organized into categories or codes with a template style which is a prior coding according to some initial view of the data, previous research, or existing theorization (Crabtree and Miller 1999). Further, various writers have indicated different types of coding according to family relationships, social contexts and other social criteria, or codes which denote explanations, descriptions, and so on.

Another issue prominent in biographical research is the question of size of study – how many stories to collect? Some researchers would rule out a single life story as the basis for a study. An impression at least has been given that early sociological interest in the life history has devoted attention to the single case. This has been due to the famous examples such as the life of Stanley in *The Jack-Roller* (Shaw [1930]1966) and Władek in *The Polish Peasant* (Thomas and Znaniecki [1918–20]1958; see Chapter 3). But while these individuals are presented at length, for instance Władek's 'life-record' is over three hundred pages, it is preceded by around eighty pages of introduction, has seventeen pages of conclusion and numerous explanatory footnotes, there is the claim that the story is shared: Władek is seen as representative of a wider mass and Stanley as typical of hundreds of others. Many sociologists would say that it is not possible to gain an adequate portrait of a culture or to evaluate what is specific to the individual and what belongs to the wider group, institution or society since there is not an appropriate theoretical sample and basis for comparability and representativeness. On the other hand, an individual may be the only direct witness to certain events (although indirect evidence may be available) and may be regarded as representative (an exemplar) of a group, e.g. as in the case of Władek and Stanley, their stories are placed alongside other source materials. In *The Polish Peasant*, groups of family letters (including short excerpts of letters to Władek from his family) are included alongside newspaper reports, official records and other materials. It may also be argued that the research focus is upon particular meanings rather than group regularities. An objection could be offered that a simple individual–society split (the individual as essentially separate) is being offered by ruling out single life stories. Again, usually in biographical research, a pragmatic approach to methodological concerns is evident. As Erben warns, too much emphasis on research techniques can limit an understanding of the connection between the method and purpose of the study (Erben 1998b: 4). The vital issue could be the quality of the theoretical reasoning rather than questions of representativeness and so on. There is also the question of purpose. In *The Polish Peasant* each type of material (e.g. letters, official records, and the life-record) was used to gain information on differing aspects of individual, family and communal change. The intimate detail of the single life history (or a small number), with some commentary–interpretation, allows us to gain a feeling of 'knowing' a life and situation outside common experience and establishes the 'warrant for credibility and authority in the text' (Atkinson 1990: 133). Whereas commonly today multiple lives are given within an analysis of the wider socio-historical context, what is striking about *The Polish Peasant* is the range of materials used to address substantive areas and the breadth of theoretical approach. What was not clear in the classic study – and remains an issue today which may be obscured by taking a 'pragmatic approach' – are the types of conceptualization and uses of personal documents being obtained within the research process: at its simplest, is the purpose to generate or validate theory, gain new conceptual insights or merely illustrate existing theories, or some combination, during collection, interpretation and the presentation of the research?

A final question concerns readership or audience: how the 'text' is read, received, or deconstructed has gained significant attention in recent ethnographic and biographical study. However, the questions of interpretation,

'authenticity' or 'plausibility' of life stories and the construction of life histories is not a new one, as shown by Blumer's evaluation of Thomas and
Znaniecki's *The Polish Peasant* (Blumer 1969: 126). Blumer questioned the
representativeness, reliability, adequacy of purpose and validity of interpretation of the various documents used – the exact connection between the
material presented and the development of conceptualization remained
unclear. Nevertheless, Blumer argued that a number of important contributions had been made including the advocacy of subjective aspects of
social life and the necessity of human documents, and the life record in particular.

The researcher's role

Traditionally in qualitative research commentators in methodological texts
have stressed the empathetic orientation to the 'subject' on behalf of the
researcher, who nevertheless has an 'objective' role as the questioner, interpreter and presenter of the finished research text. More recently the emphasis has shifted to a recognition of the collaborative and reflexive role of the
researcher. Writers have called for researchers to indicate their own relationship to the study – their presence in the research and the influence of social
background, for example gender, race, social class, or religion. However,
there is a difficulty in assessing how much of the personal life of the
researcher should be considered and entered in the text. Sparkes points out
that a 'self-absorption' or 'narcissism' may intrude (Sparkes 1994a: 166).
Atkinson argues that no matter to what psychological, social science or
other uses the material is put (such as for information on community or
family or disciplinary concerns), the interpretations of life stories are either
from a theoretical or personal or subjective basis (Atkinson 1998: 66). Even
so, it seems there is more often some kind of overlap or homology between
the theoretical and the 'subjective' influences (Atkinson 1998: 66). At base,
however, despite these questions and trends in biographical research, the
intention in the study of lives is to gain an understanding of individuals' life
experiences within their socio-historical context.

To place the researcher fully within the research is to recognize that we all
have stories and it seems a fundamental part of social interaction to 'tell our
tales'. In the collection of stories (via interviews), interaction is not only
helping individuals to reflect and give form and structure to their lives (in the
interview situation) but also helping researchers to begin to draw on their
own experiences. How 'collaborative' this relation is in the interview, the
interpretation and the presentation, has been open to much discussion –
whether the power relation is fundamentally unequal and cannot be overcome or whether it can be modified during the full research process. But the
application of terms such as 'power', 'authority', 'empowerment', 'voice'

and 'reciprocity' in regard to relations between researcher and interviewer should be used with caution to describe what is a complex and problematic process (see Sparkes 1997b). For some, biographical and other qualitative research is a means of social intervention that recognizes not only that the research role does affect the context but that it should be involved in aiding personal or collective realization – as consciousness raising, as generating solidarities, or giving those who have not been heard a voice. Even so, a difficult issue remains – a commitment to giving a 'voice' may be insufficient since little is added to their perceptions of the world, which may in turn reflect dominant discourses (Sparkes 1994b: 108).

In summary, discussion of the researcher's role (as a biographical participant) raises not simply the degree to which the researcher should place her/his 'voice' within a socio-political context but methodological and ethical questions concerning the researcher's role. For the researcher, questions arise across the research from collection to presentation regarding subjective interpretations and judgements as new issues or new insights arise. More profoundly, the degree and type of personal 'investment' is in question, e.g. how much to reveal of the self in 'sharing stories', in building trust, establishing 'credibility' or establishing 'solidarity' in the 'field' and in the written study (see Sparkes 1994a: 167; Atkinson 1998: 64).

Theoretical approaches

Qualitative research studies, including biographical research, have drawn on various theoretical approaches – ethnomethodology, phenomenology, narrative analysis, symbolic interactionism, discourse theory, conversational analysis and others (see Silverman 1993; Atkinson and Hammersley 1994: 257–8; Bryman and Burgess 1994a, 1999; Denzin and Lincoln 1994c; Feldman 1995). Bryman and Burgess (1994b) report that some analyses have been based around how language is used drawing, for example, on ethnomethodology, symbolic interactionism or discourse. Other studies, including 'classic' ethnography and life story work, follow a 'descriptive' or interpretive approach. A third strand is marked by a priority given to theory generation, such as grounded theory. Of course, these distinctions are not hard and fast (Bryman and Burgess 1994b: 6). In terms of biographical research, studies tend to cross these boundaries, even if the detail of how they are using grounded theory or symbolic interactionism can be rather thin. Useful comparisons of different 'interpretive paradigms' – positivist, postpositivist, constructivist, feminist, ethnic, Marxist, cultural studies – in qualitative research generally, are given by Denzin and Lincoln (1994c). In biographical work in particular, Miller (2000) outlines three approaches to the study of life stories and family histories. First, the realist approach uses induction, among other procedures, employs 'saturation' (cf. grounded theory) and unfocused interviews, and considers reliability as important. Second, the neo-positivist approach is deductive, theory testing, uses focused interviews and places importance on validity. Finally, the narrative approach sees 'fact' as secondary to an exploration of the ongoing construction of an individual's unique standpoint, uses life or family stories, and emphasizes the interplay between interviewer and interviewee in structuring reality (Miller 2000: 10–14). We can add that the approaches to life stories may vary across, as well as within, the social science disciplines. Different theoretical and methodological approaches may be brought together in types of study or a single study. But commonalities do exist: for example, where interviews are used there is an interactive relationship and, more generally, there is a cross-disciplinary commitment to show the respondents' meanings (Yow 1994: 10). Miller sees both overlaps and tensions between approaches. In terms of theorization, realism and neo-positivism may stress induction or deduction but in practice the research process is more a 'circular' movement between the two, while sharing notions of 'objective truth' and 'factual reality'. In contrast, narrative approaches question the idea of a singular objective reality, and focus on the constructive, relational, 'reality-producing' nature of the interview situation. Nevertheless, all three see some kind of 'tension' between the individuals' subjective view and their perception of social structure (see Miller 2000: 14–17).

Biographical research

The term 'biographical research' is used in this book to encompass a range of types of research (e.g. in oral history, sociology) and biographical data (text, oral, visual, multimedia). The book addresses a number of methodological and other issues, including the epistemological concerns in research, in the use of life stories – from the interview or self-written accounts of lives. While a variety of terms are used to describe work in this general field, for instance in view of its methodology, e.g. the in-depth or life-story interview with those studied (the story-teller, respondent, or the researched), and what is collected and how it is interpreted via the life-story, life history, life cycle and so on, what is very interesting is the growing sense of common purpose. The intent of biographical research in its various guises is to collect and interpret the lives of others as part of human understanding.

Chapter 2: Uses of biographical research – This chapter provides a general overview of how biographical research has been used within a selected number of disciplines and empirical areas. The aim is to indicate the broad range of work now being undertaken and its usefulness in terms of information and insights that would be more difficult to obtain within other methods.

Chapter 3: The life history – This chapter examines the origins of the 'life history' approach within Chicagoan sociology during the 1920s and 1930s where it was applied to understand the processes of immigration and the nature of social problems. The use of 'personal documents' within sociology and other disciplines was subject to intensive reassessment in the 1930s and 1940s, while some revival of use took place in the 1960s. More latterly, the 'life history' approach has undergone further re-examination following the influence of postmodernism and other views.

Chapter 4: Autobiography and biography – This chapter addresses the literary forms of 'autobiography' and 'biography', for instance with reference to questions of genre and the interplay between modes of writing. Questions of 'referentiality', authorship, the fiction/non-fiction distinction and the breadth of autobiographical expression and biography are considered. Writing on the life of Dickens is discussed in relation to how his fiction contained an autobiographical 'statement' and biographical connections.

Chapter 5: Auto/biography and sociology – This chapter examines the study of 'auto/biography' within sociology, as the distinction between autobiography and biography has been challenged due to the influences of feminist, postmodernist and other writing. Again, questions of genre are raised and the role of the researcher's own biography in the collection and writing of the lives of others.

Chapter 6: Oral history – This chapter outlines the development of oral history which seeks to report the past experiences of individuals (and communities and organizations). Oral history has increasingly been affected by methodological and theoretical work in other disciplines on the complexities of understanding life stories, for instance the absences in recollection and the reshaping of the 'past'. Oral history has also challenged 'traditional' history by giving the life experience of those who usually are not heard.

Chapter 7: The narrative analysis of lives – This chapter describes the narrative approach to the study of lives, which takes the idea of story to interpret how individuals construct an account of life. Writers have pointed to various forms of narrative and the part they play in the formation of the self or identity. The narrative often contains a moral evaluation or summary of the life. The chapter also contains various other 'models' of lives that have been applied in the social sciences – for example, the life course and life cycle.

Chapter 8: Memory and autobiography – The question of 'memory' has become more and more central to discussion of the collection of life stories within biographical research. Oral historians, for example, are looking towards other disciplines, including psychology, for greater understanding of the operation and forms of memory, while within psychology some writers are attempting to include more sophisticated notions of the interrelation between the individual autobiography and social context.

Chapter 9: Ethnography and biographical research – Fieldwork has traditionally contained accounts of individual lives, typically in the guise of the 'ethnographic informant'. There have been examples of 'fuller' accounts of individual lives but relatively little attempt to analyse 'life stories' in detail. However, this situation is undergoing change as the interview relation, the researcher's own life and research life, and the researched as 'subjects' are under increasing re-examination.

Chapter 10: Conclusion – For a number of writers the human and social sciences are experiencing a 'biographical' or 'auto/biographical' turn as the importance of the collection of lives and the researcher's own biographical relation to research become more apparent – and raise questions concerning how knowledge is produced. The chapter returns to the problems of definition and practice in biographical research – questions of purpose, and methodological and related issues and, finally, issues of practice including the researcher as auto/biographer.

Recommended reading

Bryman, A. and Burgess, R. G. (eds) (1999) *Qualitative Research*, 4 vols. London: Sage. (These volumes include key articles on issues, methods, and analysis and interpretation.)

Denzin, N. K. and Lincoln, Y. S. (eds) ([1994]2000) *Handbook of Qualitative Research*, 2nd revised ed. London: Sage. (A very comprehensive textbook which addresses important issues in qualitative research including major perspectives, strategies of inquiry, methods of collection, modes of analysis, interpretation, and the future of qualitative research. It contains chapters on biographical method, narrative, interviewing and documents.)

Riessman, C. K. (1993) *Narrative Analysis*. London: Sage. (A short introduction to narrative analysis, which indicates its use (with a wide range of references) across numerous disciplines, raises methodological and theoretical issues and provides 'practical models' of analysis using examples.)

Yow, V. R. (1994) *Recording Oral History: A Practical Guide for Social Scientists*. London: Sage. (This is a practical outline and review of types of research studies in oral history. It contains an interview guide, information on research principles and record keeping, as well as reviews of key texts at the end of each chapter.)

(2) Uses of biographical research

Uses of biographical research

Conventional methodological textbooks in the social sciences have generally ignored biographical research. It has not been seen as part of a particular disciplinary field, or, when acknowledged, has been described as an interesting area but not a 'serious' method, or it has been merely assumed that life stories were 'covered' within the informal, open-ended or extended interview and fieldwork practice. The rise of interest in biography, autobiography, and the collection of life stories has been apparent during the last fifteen years or so – as witnessed by the growth of oral history and the development of narrative analysis; 'the life' has begun to feature as a subject for methodological texts and research discussion. Over thirty years ago Becker commented: 'Given the variety of scientific uses to which the life history may be put, one must wonder at the relative neglect into which it has fallen' (Becker 1970: 117).

An influence on the re-emergence of biographical study during subsequent years has been a return to C. W. Mills's idea of 'the sociological imagination' which

> enables us to grasp history and biography and the relations between the two within society. That is its task and its promise . . . No social study that does not come back to the problems of biography, of history, and of their intersections within a society, has completed its intellectual journey.
> (Mills 1970: 12)

Today, it has been argued that we are on the verge of a deep re-evaluative movement in the human and social sciences as the focus on the collection and interpretation of lives has presented challenges to the epistemological, methodological and theoretical bases of existing disciplines.

Angell reported in 1945 on the uses of personal documents in sociology since the 1920s (Angell 1945). He noted that the dominant trend had been an emphasis on an 'objective' approach which stressed the collection of facts; subjective materials were seen as too unreliable except for some very restricted, preliminary use, perhaps indicating some new avenue for more sophisticated, 'scientific' investigation. Instead, he suggested that personal documents could uncover new facts, aid the formation and verification of hypotheses and inform historical perspectives on individuals and social life. In particular, he argued that the objective approach had neglected the importance of conceptualization and theory construction (Denzin 1970: 254–5; Burgess 1982: 132). In discussions in the 1960s and 1970s the use of 'lives' and its advocacy was often set – at least in sociology – within a broad interactionist framework and as very much providing important dimensions neglected within current methods, as well as a basis for new conceptualization and comparative work (see Faraday and Plummer 1979; Denzin 1989). More specifically, it was said to give the subjective perspectives within institutional life or interpretive meanings in social processes to be placed alongside other data and methods of study (Denzin 1970: 256–8).

Becker, in his re-evaluation of the life history in his introduction to Shaw's republished *The Jack-Roller* (Becker 1966), argued that it delivers information that is a 'realistic basis' for conceptions of 'underlying process' and so 'serves the purposes of checking assumptions, illuminating organization and reorienting stagnant fields . . .' (Becker 1970: 117). In a similar vein to Thomas and Znaniecki ([1918–20]1958) he argued that it provided details on where 'new lines' of individual and collective actions meet and 'new aspects of the self are brought into being' (Becker 1970: 117). Becker gave a number of 'functions' of life history including the evaluation of theory such as relating to the delinquent career and a more fundamental contribution following, Mead's view of the 'reality of social life', in terms of significant symbols and expectations of others: 'The life history, more than any other technique except perhaps participant observation, can give meaning to the overworked notion of *process*' (Becker 1970: 116).

Plummer, in an extensive assessment of the 'documents of life', notes criticisms that allege substantive, methodological and theoretical limitations (Plummer 1983, 1995a). However, his initial response is to outline a number of 'substantive contributions' of the life history to areas commonly overlooked in the field of sociology: 'the subjective reality of the individual'; 'process, ambiguity and change' apparent in everyday life; and the 'totality' of the biographical experience – individual experience as within the context of the group and wider social framework (Faraday and Plummer 1979;

Plummer 1983: 67–9). In terms of the steps in the research process and specific research contribution, Plummer, echoing a traditional view, says that life histories are useful at the 'exploratory' stage as a 'sensitising tool' in areas where information is limited or conceptualization is poor. It can also 'complement', within the research process generally, and have a counter-vailing effect on objective methods with the use of 'tools of subjectivism'. Finally, it aids in 'consolidating, clarifying and concluding' research by providing supporting detail where theorization is complex, which helps comprehension (Plummer 1983: 72–4).

> The central value of life documents – and the job they can best do – lies in the tapping of ordinary, ambiguous, personal meanings . . . With this goal in mind, life documents become important tools in research, in teaching and in political change.
>
> (Plummer 1983: 82)

The features of the theoretical and methodological 'uses' itemized by Denzin, Becker and Plummer relate to the contributions that life histories or stories can make in understanding the meanings people attach to action as part of their lives, how the multitude of events and experience are made 'sense of', and how accounts are made by individuals to define their 'presence' and their social world. In constructing meaningful accounts of our life – our story – in everyday life experience we relate them to our contacts who in turn respond with their own stories. This attribution of meanings in an interactive process with others can help overcome problems or changes in life experience:

> Sharing one's story is a way of purging, or releasing, certain burdens and validating personal experience; it is in fact central to the recovery process . . . Life stories can help other people see their lives more clearly or differently and perhaps be an inspiration to help them change something in their lives.
>
> (Atkinson 1998: 26)

In sociology, the life history approach partly derives from the legacy of the Chicago School and the pragmatist philosophical influence on its work which emphasized the 'democratic' sharing of meanings (see Mills 1966; Roberts 1977). Of course, there are also benefits to the researcher in undertaking research since there are career and professional interests involved. But other personal implications may flow from the research – a reconsideration by researchers of their own interests, a re-evaluation of their own life, a realization that they had chosen the research topic because of an underlying motive or outlook that may become more apparent during the research. These may well influence the conduct of the research, the questions asked, the relationship with the respondent, the research issues that evolve and are pursued, and how the 'story' is edited, commented on and generally presented. In addition, the researcher is also an audience, as a reader of the account or listener to it. The effects on an audience of a life story/history account can be varied and significant. A story may raise questions about a reader's own life (Stuart 1993; Sparkes 1994a: 178). Research relations include biographical processes in which both researcher and researched may well go through a personal transition. Stories can have

> transformative possibilities for an individual in that they challenge the limitations of available narratives by providing new narratives . . . Life history work that provides theoretically framed stories has a part to play in bringing together individuals who, for the most part, stay separated from one another and do not develop a collective identity as an oppressed minority.
>
> (Sparkes 1994a: 178)

There is also the associated vexed issue of the 'interview relationship' and the wider research relations; here are questions regarding the degree to which the researcher is more than a 'researcher' but a collaborator, friend, therapist, or a mix of various types of relationship. A novel approach to narrative is provided by Hollway and Jefferson who examine how the researcher and the researched produce meanings together during research (Hollway and Jefferson 2000). They place 'narratives' at the centre of their interview method but also show how 'free association' should be given priority over narrative coherence. The question of 'voice' – allowing the experiences of groups who are not usually heard to be given (and how this is to be achieved) – has also featured in the use of life stories across disciplines. Women, communal and other groups with a feminist or radical view of research practice connect the notion of voice to the raising of consciousness or the reclaiming of history.

A complex but vital area in qualitative research, including biographical work, is the relation between data and theory (see Chapter 1): at the most simple, is 'theory' found in or generated from the data, or is it applied (and perhaps modified according to new findings)? Rather than apply a theory the emphasis in qualitative research is more towards the development of concepts or theories that remain close to the subjects' accounts. Atkinson (1998) recommends reading life stories in full and judging whether there is a theoretical approach that meets its meaning and movement. Keeping this in mind, the range of theoretical approaches is wide indeed, as Atkinson indicates: personality theories, life cycle, script theory, the use of metaphor, life course, narrative analysis, thematic field analysis and hermeneutical approaches all feature strongly in the analysis of lives (Atkinson 1998: 67–8). There are, perhaps, overarching theoretical issues concerning the nature of 'individuality' and the formation of identity in contemporary society. The analysis of life stories gives us powerful insights into how individuals reshape their sense of past, present and future and their social relations and thus respond to sociocultural and economic changes – for instance, on the important question whether contemporary 'individual identity' is becoming more fragmented or has to be more consciously constructed.

Disciplines and contexts

While each discipline – sociology, literary and cultural studies, psychology, history and so on – has its own theoretical or other assumptions for understanding and making sense of an individual's story of his or her life, the distinctive uses of life stories within particular disciplines or sub-disciplines may be distinguished (Atkinson 1998: 68). For example, within sociology the focus is on the uncovering of the meanings attributed to personal and social relationships and situation, whereas in oral history the concern can be said to be the individual's interpretation of past experiences, or in life course and life review research the emphasis tends towards how accounts relate to a life pattern. However, these distinctions may well be too rigid, especially in practice in specific studies; for example, oral history may well emphasize the 'past' but the experience of the present in forming accounts cannot be ignored. As Yow argues, the boundaries between disciplines become indistinct as writers borrow concepts from different approaches (Yow 1994: 10). What is fascinating and exciting about the growth of biographical research is the cross-fertilization of ideas, methodological issues and perspectives within various types of study.

A number of broad uses for life stories can be identified. For instance, Atkinson distinguishes between psychological (the self, identity development, counselling and therapy, the narrative study of lives), sociological, mystical–religious (anthropology and folklore), and cosmological–philosophical uses (Atkinson 1998: 10–16). A claim is often made that the use of life stories in research has certain advantages by obtaining specific kinds of information:

> The life history may be the best available technique for studying such important social psychological processes as adult socialization, the emergence of group and organizational structure, the rise and decline of social relationships, and the situational response of the self to daily interactional contingencies. It is easy to conceive of life histories carried out on entire organizations, social groups, or even communities.
> (Denzin 1970: 257)

The life story itself may take various singular or mixed forms – from the autobiographical account (written or spoken) to poetry or 'fiction'. It may also be related through a group account. For example, within oral history communal projects have taken a very diverse course in forms of presentation, including published books, theatre and video/CD productions

(Ritchie 1995; Thompson 2000: 214–16). The practice of communal projects provides one usage of life stories found particularly in oral history and feminist research (but at least implicit in much biographical research) – that the study of the lives of others also involves a commitment to social and personal change. There is a further issue relating to life story use: the mode by which life stories are presented to an audience in biographical research. The discussion of biographical research writing has usually described the merits and purposes of forms of editing and commentary on life accounts. Latterly, issues of 'corroboration', 'voice' and theoretical interpretation within the production of texts have intruded. Presentation can, in fact, draw on a range of written, visual, and recorded (e.g. diaries, texts, photographic stills, varieties of family, communal, commercial videos or films) sources and result in single or mixed forms of presentation drawing on the 'spoken', texts, and images recorded on oral/video tape or CD. Again, it can be noted that the 'mere' recounting of a life itself may well alter the life perspectives of the researcher and researched. The problems involved here are very fraught and serious for biographical research and concern the kinds and degree of commitment by the researcher, the relation with the researched and the impact of research on their lives, and the wider social contexts of biographical research. These are issues that form a theme throughout the book.

In the following a variety of disciplinary contributions of biographical research are presented to give an indication of the span of research on individual lives.

Education

The study of biography in education has covered a broad range of topics: schooling experience, teachers' careers and lives, the acquisition of pedagogical knowledge, and adult learning (see for example Goodson 1992; Blake 1995; Hatch and Wisniewski 1995b; Lea and West 1995; Thomson 1995; Erben 1998a; Ward and Jenkins 1999; Goodson and Sikes 2001). In the 'resurgence' of life histories across the disciplines, education has been a field at the forefront (Sparkes 1994a: 165). For example, Erben provides a collection of the very varied work within an 'auto/biographical' perspective in education, including articles on the self and education, choices of adolescent girls, lives of lesbian teachers, learning difficulties, college dropouts, PhD students, historical biographies, and the researcher's own educational development (Erben 1998a; see Chapter 5, this volume). Life or oral history projects within schools undertaken by children of various ages have also developed (see Thompson 2000: 199–204). It would appear that the telling of a story about a life has become an important aspect of practice and research in professional teaching and other settings (Riessman 1993: 5–6).

Of course, life stories have been sought more generally in the study of

---

Box 2.1

Sparkes, A. (1993) Reciprocity in critical research? Some unsettling thoughts, in G. Shacklock and J. Smyth (eds) *Being Reflexive in Critical Educational and Social Research*. London: Falmer Press.

Sparkes's work is an indication of some of the stimulating research in the field of life history and education, in this instance with particular reference to his own life as an educator and student. While for some researchers his commentary on his own self may be too uncomfortably revelatory or self-regarding, he provides illuminating analyses, in this and his other work, which recognize the embodied self of the researcher and the complexities of monitoring his own male, heterosexual identity. Included also in his writings are the collaborative relations with the subject, the mutual reassessment of the research relation, and the introduction of an innovatory technique in the use of 'fictional' life stories in teaching (Sparkes 1993, 1994b, 1997b).

---

occupations; oral history in particular has recounted work experience especially as part of working-class and women's history. In sociology there is a growing awareness of the usefulness of life stories in the study of the life course and work patterns. Dex has noted that both quantitative and qualitative data on life and work histories are flourishing, for instance in relation to policy questions on employment shifts, demographic changes, labour mobility and the employment of women (Dex 1991a: 14). Life accounts have been used in studies of social mobility alongside statistical analyses but perhaps there is a need for more such material to trace experiences of inter- and intra-class transitions (see Goldthorpe 1980).

Oral history

Oral history – the collection of oral accounts of past experiences (see Chapter 6) – has had a significant effect on the practice of history (Perks and Thomson 1998a: ix; see Thompson 1983).

It gives a voice to those who do not leave accounts or have biographers. The 'rise' of oral history has not been without controversy and debate but it has been able to generate material on work, family and other relationships not present in other research. For example, in community or group work, there has been an aim to claim historical experience and empower 'through the process of remembering and reinterpreting the past' (Perks and Thomson 1998a: ix). This work has attempted to move from the traditional assumptions of the history profession to the situated theorizing relating to people in a given context and time (Dunaway 1996). Across a wide range of countries interviews with people whose voice is missing or under-represented in official records have been sought; the experiences and views relating to historical events affecting the working class, various ethnic or religious minorities, indigenous groups and others are now a common feature of research (Bornat 1994c: 163; Perks and Thomson 1998a: ix). Included here are histories of work experience, family transmission, industrial and political struggle, civil rights, and communal projects and activities (see for example Yow 1994; Perks and Thomson 1998b). Of particular importance in the USA (and some other countries) since the 1980s has been the growth of the 'public programme' in oral history practice by libraries, museums and other bodies using various media (Dunaway 1996: 9). In many countries, local and other groups have formed their own community history projects. There is also a broader, 'popular' audience for oral history as shown in TV programmes and books aimed at a wide market, for instance in Britain on memories of war work, child evacuation and emigration or military service (cf. Bean and Melville 1990; Clayton and Craig 2000). A great deal of recent oral history work has taken current major social and political issues such as migration, response to changes in Eastern Europe, the 'reworking' of wartime memories and the transmission of 'memories' to succeeding generations (cf. Passerini 1992b; see Chapters 6 and 8, this volume). Oral history is particularly strong in Central and South America as indicated by participation in the International Oral History Association, and the range of projects, conferences and journals in these areas addressing important social questions (e.g. *Voces Recobradas: Revista de Historia Oral*: Instituto Histórico de la Ciudad de Buenos Aires, Argentina).

Yow argues that the 'open door' of the interview with eyewitnesses, as used across approaches or disciplines, gives answers unobtainable by other methods to questions such as the motivations for particular actions (Yow 1994: 10). For Yow the interview can reveal the informal rules of the group, the 'interweaving' of personal relationships and work, the communal life patterns, the meaning of artefacts in people's lives, and how symbols and images are used in the attachment and ordering of meanings (Yow 1994: 13–14). She argues that the interview shows the 'psychological reality' informing an individual's beliefs and action. In addition to the personal story, the culture and history of the group can be open to investigation (Yow 1994: 15).

Health and ageing

Thompson notes that telling a life story can have a 'therapeutic' effect on the giver – a consequence that may become apparent to the researcher. For instance, an elderly person may be given '. . . a new sense of importance and purpose, something to look forward to, even the strength to fight off an illness and win a new lease of life' (Thompson 1988: 157). Thompson says that 'powerful feelings' may be released when someone, for example, describes the loss of a relative, and usually a sympathetic response is all that is appropriate. More rarely there may be 'unresolved pain' where deep traumas have been experienced within the family or due to war and persecution. Here, Thompson observes that the oral historian is in a more difficult position and help of a professional therapist may be suggested (Thompson 1988: 157). But, 'For most people the pain of the past is much more manageable, lying alongside good memories of fun, affection, and achievement, and recollecting both can be positive' (Thompson 1988: 159).

Attention to life story giving has grown in health, social work and related practices. For instance, investigation has examined how individuals understand their background, current problems, and their personal and familial adjustments and experiences of health and social welfare (cf. Radley 1993b; Yow 1994; Clifford 1995; Martin 1995; Barnard *et al.* 2000).

'Reminiscence' is the term given to types of practice in the biographical field, often associated with older people. It helps the remembering of past experience by valuing the responses people give. The rise of reminiscence work during the 1970s was something of a movement which saw itself as trying to meet a therapeutic or other need (Bornat 1994a, 1994d; 1998; *Ageing and Society* 1996; see also Thompson 1988: 160–5, 2000: 184–9; *Oral History* 1989; Thompson *et al.* 1990). Coleman (1994) points to the links with social gerontology, social anthropology and the psychology of memory. He says that

As they grow older and perspective on past and future changes, many people feel the need to explore and draw out meaning from their

---

Box 2.2

Coleman, P. G. (1991) Ageing and life history: the meaning of reminiscence in late life, in S. Dex (ed.) *Life and Work History Analyses: Qualitative and Quantitative Developments.* London: Routledge.

Coleman reports on a study of 50 people living in sheltered housing schemes. Interviewees reminisced to various extents but reminiscence in itself was not linked to good adjustment to ageing. Some valued reminiscence, some were troubled by it, while others saw no value or avoided it. Coleman also found that many interviewees saw little social use in their life histories. He argues that we should take note of traditional societies where older people have an important role in cultural transmission but for that they need an audience.

life-story . . . Allowing the person to have a voice and the opportunity for genuine self-expression are prerequisites for achieving a sense of control over life . . .

> (Coleman 1994: 8–9; see also Coleman 1991: 128–9)

Box 2.3

Radley, A. (ed.) (1993) *Worlds of Illness: Biographical and Cultural Perspectives on Health and Disease*. London: Routledge.

This series of articles reflects the growing research on the patient's experience of illness and the meaning of health and the implications for treatment. In Radley's own contribution, based on research on cardiac patients, he examines the role of metaphor in the adjustments made by patients to illness. For some, their response has a literal quality – a fight with illness; for others there was a more figural reorientation of their lives, for example one respondent stated: 'There's a point at which you find a crossroads perhaps . . .' (Radley 1993a: 111). Other articles, for example, report from detailed interviews on how 'attitude of mind' relates to resistance to illness (Pollock 1993) and why victims of illness blame themselves (Blaxter 1993).

Studies have identified various types of reminiscence (e.g. those that give coherence or coping) and common themes in such research (childhood, domestic life, health), and numerous handbooks on how to undertake reminiscence work exist. Reminiscence research raises a number of important practical and ethical issues – including the therapeutic role that may arise and how individuals are helped in counselling around negative or upsetting memories such as grief and guilt. Also, while it may be taken as a means of advocacy for those whom society ignores or denies a voice, where is the line between oral history and reminiscence practice in the actions of the researcher? Also, might reminiscence work with a group ignore the negative feelings which may be associated with reviewing the past by encouraging a 'rosy' view of life events (Bornat 1994a: 4)? Further, as Coleman argues, some old people may be reluctant to reminisce while others may reminisce a lot but even so may not be 'happy' in doing so (Coleman 1991: 132). Group reminiscence may not be helpful for these individuals (Thompson 1988: 164). Another important issue may be the difficulty of gaining consent from some older people while the cooperation with carers and other professionals may be problematic. Reminiscence may be a way of involving older people in the way they are cared for, providing status and voice (Bornat 1994a: 4), but it may also run the risk of being patronizing, for example by assuming that older people shared common experiences or hold common beliefs about events in the past.

Biographical research can reveal how ageing is experienced and how individuals 'theorize' about the changes in their lives as they 'age' through a focus on intergenerational cultural transmission and stories across the life cycle (Bertaux and Thompson 1993a; Riessman 1993: 18; Atkinson 1998: 17). For example, Bytheway (1993), in examining the published letters of a couple who had been part of the art world in the early part of last century, observes that biography may help to remedy a lack of theory in the area. He says that there has been confusion in the study of gerontology between the 'autobiographical life review' in the latter years of an individual's life and the biography constructed by someone else. A great deal of gerontological research, he says, starts with the interview which means that the 'relationship between one's age and the on-going construction and reconstruction of one's biography has received little critical attention' (Bytheway 1993: 153). Biographical research can also be used in the study of the consequences of abuse, traumatic events and chronic or other illness on the individual and family and, indeed, in studies across a whole range of health and welfare and crime fields (see for example Bellaby 1991; *Oral History* 1995; Muller, 1999; Chamberlayne and King 2000; Crossley 2000a, 2000b, 2000c; Goodey 2000). Finally, biographical research can be invaluable in uncovering and giving due weight to 'lay perspectives' in medical practice and the experience of training and later careers of various medical practitioners (see Russell 1997). Medical writing using life stories is very diverse in approach, usage and theorization but often there is a common assumption that story telling by the patient to a listening audience is part of the healing process and 'self-renewal' (Manning and Cullum-Swan 1994: 465). As a consequence, biographical research, it is claimed, may enable improvements to be made for those requiring hospital, residential or other care.

Feminist research

Feminist research has had a very significant impact on biographical study across the range of social science disciplines. The emphases on giving a voice, consciousness raising, empowerment, collaboration and attention to meaning and experience have had widespread influence while also being subject to much debate within qualitative methods and much further afield (for example see Personal Narratives Group 1989; Reinharz 1992; Stanley and Wise 1993; Maynard and Purvis 1994; Olesen 2000).

Traditional methodological approaches such as interviewing, oral history, and ethnography were placed under strong re-examination during the 1970s under the impact of feminist contributions. Biographical research, in its various guises, seemed to have a potential affinity with the attempt to portray

---

Box 2.4

Gluck, S. B. and Patai, D. (eds) (1991) *Women's Words: The Feminist Practice of Oral History.* London: Routledge.

Gluck and Patai in their influential book point to how feminist research has sought to go beyond disciplinary boundaries in the collection of lives:

> The contributions of the different disciplines often overlap, revealing the artificiality of the academic division of knowledge. But it was the specific addition of feminist scholarship, frequently transforming these fields and dissolving their boundaries, that led to the multidisciplinary perspective characterizing the essays prepared in this volume.
>
> (Gluck and Patai 1991a: 3)

In the collection, the lives of women are explored in a very diverse range of contexts, traditional research practices are challenged and the ethical dilemmas relating to the structural differences between the interviewer and narrator are addressed.

---

women's experience and history. As Gluck and Patai explain, the insights of the women's movement began to have a transformative effect on fields such as oral history as women's experiences were accorded value and writers began to regard oral accounts as a means for recording women's social and historical experiences (Gluck and Patai 1991a: 1).

Narratives of the body and sexuality

An example of the increasing use of biographical research concerns the meanings, stories or accounts that individuals give in connection with their body and sexual identity (see Connell 1995; Plummer 1995b, 2001). This reflects a wider, growing interest in the body and self in sociological, feminist and other approaches (cf. Turner 1984; Featherstone *et al.* 1991; Shilling 1993). Biographical and other work includes both historical and contemporary dimensions on the formation of perceptions of the self, the individual, sexuality and intimacy in relationships following the writings of Foucault, Giddens and others. For instance, Davis examines the reasons for the current growth of cosmetic surgery for women – the technology for changing the female body – and uses feminist and cultural analyses to explain the recent concern for the body (Davis 1994; see also Davis 1997). An interesting and important aspect of this area of biographical research is

---

Box 2.5

Plummer, K. (1995b) *Telling Sexual Stories: Power, Change and Social Worlds*. London: Routledge.

The collection of life stories or narratives can also show how individuals relate to traumatic events, reveal or change sexual or other identities, or 'adapt' where an identity is not allowed complete expression. Plummer identifies different types of narratives or 'sexual stories' such as abuse and 'coming out' (Plummer 1995b; see also Plummer 1992; Sparkes 1994a).

---

the researcher's own identity in terms of the body and sexuality. Sparkes, as well as interpreting someone else's experience of 'loss of a disciplined body', has detailed his own experiences (Sparkes 1997a, 1997b, 1997c).

Autobiography and biography

The writing of biography as a literary pursuit has undergone a revival in recent years while at the same time it has generated a re-examination of the genre. Biographies and autobiographies (often 'ghosted') of sports stars and entertainment celebrities are particularly popular, as are stories which detail deprived or abused childhoods, business success, fights against illness, or travel adventures. The biographies of literary and other figures have demonstrated increasing detail on all aspects of the subject's life – personal character and habits, the effects of personal life on work, and the intimacies of relationships alongside the minutiae of daily living. These often 'weighty' volumes have also included examples of 'revelation' – how the public image and private life diverged. There have also been experiments in how to present the biography drawing upon various sources and a range of academic disciplines for the investigation of 'character' and the relevance of socio-historical circumstance. Further, under the impact of feminist and postmodern thought the distinction between 'autobiography' and 'biography' has been challenged (see Stanley 1992, 1993; L. Marcus 1994; see also *Auto/Biography*, the journal of the Auto/Biography Study Group of the British Sociological Association). The complex issue of 'genre' is also raised by these discussions in relation to what should be deemed 'autobiographical' – not only letters and diaries (and interview where possible) but also poetry, the novel and new media such as video and e-mails are now under scrutiny. Swindells comments that the concentration on the 'literary autobiography' may give one model while neglecting other kinds of expression

---

Box 2.6

Swindells, J. (ed.) (1995) *The Uses of Autobiography*. London: Taylor and Francis.

In her Introduction to this volume exploring autobiographical writing in a wide range of settings, Swindells draws a parallel between biographical writing and the work of social anthropologists and ethnographers who also use oral and written accounts in their attempts to understand other cultures. She argues that, in various fields, questions regarding how to uncover neglected voices, the nature of interpretation, the reliability of sources, fiction/fact, memory and the 'superior' position of the researcher have come to the fore (see Swindells 1995a: 9–10).

(Swindells 1995a: 9). The traditional format can also disguise the varied modes of expression or mix of genres contained within actual autobiographies.

Conclusion

What is evident from a brief review of the uses of biographical research is the wide range of disciplinary development that is taking place across the social sciences. While life stories may be collected in different ways and for specific research purposes, biographical research is part of a movement to reveal and understand the 'personal' and its interlinking with the immediate and wider social context and political practices. Biographical research has been used to understand numerous fields and issues, for instance the development of careers, as in teaching; the experience of and responses to ageing or ill-health; neglected aspects of social history, to give voice to those who are largely unheard; and to trace the effects of migration and other social upheavals. Biographical research is therefore used for a variety of empirical and theoretical purposes and applicable to both historical research and contemporary social issues.

Recommended reading

The following texts give an indication of the uses of biographical research within a number of disciplines and fields.

Chamberlayne, P., Bornat, J. and Wengraf, T. (eds) (2000) *The Turn to Biographical Methods in Social Science*. London: Routledge.

Erben, M. (ed.) (1998) *Biography and Education: A Reader*. London: The Falmer Press.

Goodson, I. F. (ed.) (1992) *Studying Teachers' Lives*. London: Routledge.
Martin, R. R. (ed.) (1995) *Oral History in Social Work: Research, Assessment and Intervention*. London: Sage.
Radley, A. (ed.) (1993) *Worlds of Illness: Biographical and Cultural Perspectives on Health and Disease*. London: Routledge.

Journals, book series, bulletins: there is an increasing number of national and international journals and book series in biographical research, for example, *Oral History* (UK journal); *Auto/Biography* (UK journal); *The Narrative Study of Lives* (book series, Sage); *Memory and Narrative* (book series, Routledge), *Words and Silences* (members' bulletin, International Oral History Association). The following books have useful bibliographies or reading guides: Yow 1994; Hatch and Wisniewski 1995b; Ritchie 1995; Perks and Thomson 1998b; Thompson 2000; Plummer 2001.

3 The life history

The life history

The use of life stories as a research source has a long history within sociology and is most often associated with the work of William I. Thomas, Robert Park and their colleagues at the University of Chicago during the early years of the twentieth century. The development of the life history or case history method was informed by a commitment to uncover and interpret the meanings attached to interaction and so understand the ordinary lives of individuals and the variety of cultural groups of the city (see Angell 1945; Denzin 1970: 221; Bulmer 1984). As the Chicagoan approach to city life and its patterns of interaction lost favour during the late 1930s and 1940s so the life history method also came under attack. Other methods prospered as attention to criteria of reliability, validity, sampling and representativeness seemed to find the more time-consuming, subjective life history wanting (Denzin 1989: 8). Nevertheless, the use of biography did not die within sociology and from the 1960s the life history method began to revive. In the subsequent interest in life stories, sociological work has not remained immune from outside influences from oral history, feminist theory and research, postmodernism and other sources. In this chapter we examine the early work on life history and its revival from the 1960s to 1980s.

Robert Park, the leader of the Department of Sociology in the University of Chicago in the 1920s and early 1930s saw life documents as a means to uncover cultural meanings and the changes in individual and group experience within the cultural contexts. Students and researchers at Chicago were encouraged to study the city 'at first hand' and so (under a variety of influences such as anthropology, fiction, and reform activities) ethnography and biographical research were pioneered (see Shaw [1930]1966; Becker 1970; Baker 1973; Bulmer 1984). Life history and ethnography approaches came increasingly to the fore in Chicago sociology, although more quantitative methods were also fostered in the department (Matthews 1977). In the rapidly expanding social context of the city these methods could provide a means to see the lives of the new arrivals and provide insights into social issues. Chicagoan studies sought to trace the adaptation of groups to a new social environment – the ghetto, industrial life and the competitive values of American life. The complexity and diversity of the cultures of new groups could be demonstrated. The idea of the 'life history' – as a natural history or stage metaphor of the individual organic life – could also be applied to a whole range of phenomena such as race relations, newspapers, and delinquency as exhibiting processes of adjustment (Turner 1967). The life history complemented the more structural, zonal–ecological model of the 'natural area' and a 'naturalism' – the interest in cultural meanings – in city life (see Matza 1969).

As it developed and renewed the life history not only referred to the use of the written story but also could draw upon diaries, letters or other such 'personal' or 'human' documents. The life story itself could vary in length and could be written at various times and revised. As a method an increasing interest in the role of the researcher has emerged – as initiating the request for a story, as interviewer and in setting its 'agenda' as editor and interpreter of the document, while a recognition has been given to the fact that there are pre-existing stories, diaries and letters which have been composed for other purposes but are nevertheless life history resources as revealing the personal and social outlook, feelings and conceptions of the individual (Denzin 1989: 10).

Individual lives and social structures

From a sociological point of view individual lives should be understood not merely in terms of their uniqueness – recognizing individuality – but also within a social context. The interrelation between individual and society, and how broader perceptions and modes of thought are represented and monitored within the specific situation and outlook of individuals and groups, should be apparent – following the example set by Thomas and Znaniecki in *The Polish Peasant* ([1918–20]1958). In the 1920s and 1930s Chicago Sociology attempted to set life stories via the life history within the social context of neighbourhood or the 'human ecology' of the city. There

Box 3.1

Baker, P. J. (1973) The life histories of W. I. Thomas and Robert E. Park, *American Journal of Sociology*, 79(2): 243–60.

These life histories are of particular interest because they are given by Thomas and Park, pioneers and advocates of the method. Several hundred sociologists were contacted in 1927 to gain information on the history of sociology and autobiographical accounts in response to a set of 16 questions on topics such as educational background, intellectual influences and research projects. Thomas felt he had lived in three centuries in his life as he moved from an isolated area of Virginia to the modern urban life of Chicago, while Park describes life in Minnesota in an area of Scandinavian immigration. Both stress great enjoyment in outdoor activities. They outline their varied studies, occupations, intellectual influences and their important meeting, which brought Park to the University of Chicago. Both give some interpretation of their lives including an important shift in intellectual outlook in later life. Park describes himself as awkward and romantic as a boy, leading a vagabond life, an image he repeats when he says that later in adulthood he realized he could have a romantic outlook and also solve a problem. Thomas says it was not until around 40 years old that he began to take a critical view of opinions and books. He concludes by saying his main sociological interest has been in new concrete 'types' and describes himself as an extrovert having an introvert life – and any conflicts in his life have been between these tendencies. There are interesting parallels here with Thomas and Znaniecki's classic analysis of Wladek's life-record in *The Polish Peasant* ([1918–20]1958) and the social formation of bohemian, philistine and creative types (Smith 1988: 107–9).

followed a series of evaluations of the use of life history in sociology and other disciplines and a decline of the method. During the 1960s and 1970s the dominance of the functionalist approach to the 'society–individual relation' was challenged by a range of approaches, which criticized its consensual or structural features and its societally ascribed view of individual roles. These 'new' views (interactionism, ethnomethodology and phenomenology) sought to change the emphasis of analysis to the subjective reality or the social interaction of daily life – more particularly, for some, the key question for study was 'the meaning of personal life' (e.g. as in motivations, accounts and situational definitions; Stone and Farberman 1970: 1). In the refocusing of sociological endeavour, attention turned to the conceptions of the individual and everyday life, and Mead's symbolic interactionism and

Schutz's phenomenology, alongside other influences such as Sartre's pro-gressive–regressive method, were being examined (Mead [1934]1967; Sartre 1968; Schutz 1971; see Laing and Cooper 1971; Fisher and Strauss 1979; Wolff 1979). In addition to these sources, biographical research has also been influenced by Mills's views on 'sociological imagination' and the con-nection between biography and social structure. C.W. Mills advocated the placing of the individual life in the broader public sphere, without subsum-ing individual characteristics and relational patterns:

> We have come to know that every individual lives, from one generation to the next, in some society; that he [*sic*] lives out a biography, and that he lives it out within some historical sequence. By the fact of his living he contributes, however minutely, to the shaping of this society and to the course of its history, even as he is made by society and by its his-torical push and shove.
>
> (Mills 1970: 12)

Mills's view became increasingly influential from the late 1960s and early 1970s and were joined by the writings of Peter Berger who was also seeking to bring a biographical dimension to sociological study (see Berger 1966; Berger and Luckmann 1971; Berger and Berger 1975). Sociologists were also turning to an autobiographical reflection on their own lives, although

---

Box 3.2

Whyte, W. F. (1970) Reflections on my work, in I. L. Horowitz (ed.) *Socio-logical Self-images*. Oxford: Pergamon.

Whyte, summarizing his career (its interests and influences), assesses the impact of his work as follows:

> Up to this point, I feel that I have had little impact upon the development of general theory in sociology. I have contributed more to methodology in writing about field methods and the role of the participant observer. Perhaps the publication of *Street Corner Society* helped to set off the boom in small group research. I have certainly played a role in shaping the field of industrial sociology or organizational behavior, through my writing and through the students who have worked with me.
>
> (Whyte 1970: 46)

Whyte's article and others in the volume deal mainly with professional or institutional life (a fuller CV) rather than more intimate biographical relations in research and teaching or 'personal life' outside academia.

usually rather narrowly focused on their academic influences, career path and some comments on their own work. For example, Horowitz collected accounts from prominent figures such as Homans, Lipset, Whyte and Etzioni by asking questions on their type of sociology, intellectual influences and the impact of their work (Horowitz 1970b). His intention was to show the subjective processes in research and institutional practices – and how science is produced (Horowitz 1970a: 9). He concluded: 'The process of becoming a sociologist is intimately linked to the sociologist becoming a person. Perhaps this simple, yet elusive truth is what most characterizes these papers' (Horowitz 1970a: 12).

However, during the last twenty years or more the discussion of sociological and other research practices (e.g. anthropology) has explored the research relationship and the biography of the researcher (under the impact of feminist research practice and other influences) in a much more sustained and interrogative manner.

Life history data and method

During the late 1930s the 'life history method' came under increasing scrutiny at a time when quantitative methods were rapidly developing. As the survey became increasingly prominent, interview techniques and experimental methods developed criteria and procedures. The life history appeared inadequate according to scientific standards and relatively expensive, long-winded and cumbersome; surveys could provide more accurate, representative information in a much shorter time. In particular, the method appeared deficient according to standards of reliability and validity. The life history became part of a debate on the merits of the 'case method' when judged according to 'scientific' criteria, what kinds of materials should be included and what the differences were in life 'cases' as required for academic and various professional purposes, such as social work (see Burgess 1925; Hammersley 1990).

Commonly, until recently, the 'life history method' was assessed from a traditional, positivistic point of view or at least as its starting point, first by examining issues regarding process – practical methodological questions – and second, by a general assessment of the purpose of the method. Much of the methodological discussion around the life history method by its proponents was intended to establish its status and credibility (alongside qualitative methods generally) by applying or adapting traditional methodological principles, criteria and procedures while attempting to remain true to individuals' meanings. Plummer in his assessment and advocacy of the method gave a procedure for life history research (Plummer 1983: 86–116; see Plummer 1995a). This included the choice of subjects with reference to methodological and theoretical intent rather than the usual procedures of sampling; collection of lives by the informal interview – a procedure which lies between the conversation and the closely structured interview; and organization of materials – usually by tape transcription but also including a variety of written and visual materials. Also noted are the inspection of data by 'careful' attention to questions of reliability and validity, and the writing and editing of the story for presentation. The latter, he says, is generally overlooked due to the assumption of the 'privileged reporter' existing in the world of objectivist, positivist social science. On the purpose of the life history, Plummer suggests a distinction can be made between case history and case study; in the former, personal documents can be presented for their own intrinsic worth and theorization is inductive whereas, in the latter, there is a more general theoretical purpose and theory is used to join the analysis documents (Plummer 1983: 107).

Denzin (1970) also lays out organizational and other problems in the construction of the life history document as a series of steps – hypotheses to be explored, selection of the subject(s), recording the subject's experiences of objective events, obtaining the subject's interpretations of events as they take place, analysis of materials collected according to internal and external criticism and validity, establishing the 'priority of sources for subsequent hypothesis tests', testing hypotheses, the initial draft of life history and its delivery to subjects for reactions. There follows the redrafting of the life history in its 'natural sequence', the presentation of hypotheses that have been upheld, and comment on the theoretical relevance of the report. He adds that these should not be seen as 'inflexible steps', rather as the appropriate criteria for evaluating life histories. Further, there is a bias here towards theory in organizing materials and he adds that life histories can be used in both theory generation and validation (Denzin 1970: 253–4; see Denzin 1995: 116). Even so, the researcher attempts to provide an account, which does not lessen the 'authentic meanings' given by the respondents (Plummer 1983: 111).

The questions of reliability and validity have figured extensively in discussions of the life history method. Validity has to do with the measurement instruments (e.g. questions, scales) used – in the production of data and the development of explanations (Plummer 1983: 101). Reliability concerns whether the same instrument provides the same measurement each time. Against the collection of personal documents the charge is made that individuals can not only 'make up' stories or respond according to passing recall but also propound untruths and deceive themselves as well as the researcher. Life history researchers have appeared to be in a quandary in responding to the view that they lack methodological rigour and criteria. One response is to follow quite closely traditional methodological principles, another is to find modifications or alternatives. Another response is to throw back the criticism by arguing that generally methodological procedures have attempted to meet criteria of reliability rather than validity. For Plummer, validity becomes more attainable where the study of a topic remains close to an actual context (Plummer 1983: 101). He adds that the subject may be asked to comment on the document produced, or a comparison might be conducted with other similar documents (e.g. of criminals) or witnesses (friends, relatives or others) for areas of confirmation and difference. Additionally, checks for validity can be made with reference to official records of biographical details, although the latter also have limitations (Plummer 1983: 104–6). A distinction has also been made between internal and external validity. Denzin says external validity requires that the case used for generalization is representative of the population and that restrictions of time and place are taken into account. He adds that, for continuity to be achieved, researchers must note the surrounding 'historical conditions' in relation to the subject when the life story was given (Denzin 1970: 241). In terms of internal validity, Denzin argues that internal validity gives particular difficulties due to the reactive effects and the surrounding changes that take place as the subject reappraises life experiences. The researcher also has an influence on research as the person who usually requests an account and conducts the life story interview. However, Denzin advises that the personality of the researcher must not interfere. He suggests the writing of a logbook covering the research so that other sociologists can evaluate the ultimate objectivity and validity of the final study (Denzin 1970: 241–4). Further, he recommends that the 'observer' notes the subjective shifts the individual is undergoing. The person researched may be recalling very old events and memory may have faded and be fallible; he or she may also have falsely interpreted happenings at the time (Denzin 1970: 245).

Writers using life accounts began to look for alternative criteria of evaluation. For Atkinson, writing more recently, quantitative criteria are not required for the interpretation of life story interviews. Instead, the interview is very subjective since it is an interpersonal encounter influenced more by the interaction than theoretical application. He argues that a 'multiplicity of perspectives' is possible and the accuracy of the record of a person's life is not the issue – it is whether the story is 'trustworthy'. Further, in place of Denzin's 'internal validity' Atkinson says: 'Internal consistency is a primary quality check that can be used by both the interviewer and the storyteller to square or clarify early comments with recent insights, if they appear to be different' (Atkinson 1998: 60).

What is being argued is that individuals 'inherently' connect events and experiences and thereby ensure meaning – giving life a certain 'sequence and directionality' – and hence it 'makes sense' to the provider and reader. Instead of Denzin's 'external validity' we have 'external consistency' or what we know about the person, and the giver's experience, rather than 'historical truth'. Here, Atkinson notes that the research on lives by narrative study pays attention to internal coherence – the individual's experience; truth or validity according to external criteria are not stressed to the same degree

(Atkinson 1998: 60–1). We could add here that inconsistencies are also important in themselves – signs of tension or change in interpretation. What appears important in many recent accounts is 'authenticity' – a certain 'adequacy' at the level of meaning.

Two further measures are given by Atkinson which have similarities with Plummer's discussion – corroboration (see Gottschalk 1945) and persuasion: the former refers to the reading of the transcribed account by authors and whether it supports their earlier account – it allows the subjects to feel content with what is given. Here the basis of the change is also of interest – they have had a chance to think about the original and provide new meanings and interpretations. Atkinson adds that those close to the subject could also be part of the process but in the end the story is that of the original teller (Atkinson 1998: 61). He argues that, ultimately, the life story interview is founded on a collaboration. Interviewers do have their own interests but these become less important due to ethical considerations (Atkinson 1998: 61). The discussions of Denzin and Atkinson show continuing perceived difficulties in use of life stories – the extent to which quantitative criteria are applicable, and the degree to which alternative criteria can be formulated which are in keeping with the special nature of individual experience.

Box 3.3

Atkinson, R. (1998) *The Life Story Interview*. London: Sage.

Atkinson provides a very useful introduction to life story interviewing, including definitional issues, the functions and uses of life stories, and generating data. He argues that the approach can be scientific but carried out as an art by the individual interviewer. The text gives a practical guide on planning, conducting and interpreting the interview and includes numerous possible questions under a range of headings such as family, cultural background, education, love and work. Under 'major life themes' he argues the interview may include questions which help reflection on life as a whole, e.g. 'What were the crucial decisions in your life?', 'What has been the happiest time in your life?', 'What matters the most to you now?' (Atkinson 1998: 51–2). A detailed life story example is included, which in this case shows the individual moving from present to past, and then to the present in the story.

Deviance, career, becoming

In addition to the revival of Chicagoan interactionism and ethnographic empirical studies in the 1960s a number of sometimes related 'micro-sociologies' came into prominence such as phenomenological and ethnomethodological approaches. Much empirical work from these approaches concentrated around the study of the construction of 'deviance' and the ideas of labelling, social reaction and social process (see Downes and Rock 1995). The notion of career was a central concept in this work and appeared in various guises – as moral career, becoming, drift, and primary and secondary deviation (Becker 1963; Matza 1964, 1969; Lemert 1967; Goffman 1968). The underlying view was that individuals enter deviation as part of social interaction and an interrelation between 'deviance' and social control. There was a clear legacy in the sociology of deviance of Chicagoan empirical studies, such as the work of Clifford Shaw on delinquent careers (Shaw [1930]1966), the theorization of G. H. Mead on the self, symbols and the generalized other (Mead [1934]1967), and Park's formalism and methodological approach.

Research on deviance and other forms of career continued to be influenced by interactionist, phenomenological and other approaches in the 1970s onwards. In particular, the important issue of identifying 'turnings', 'transition' points, 'epiphanies' or trajectories in 'careers' in deviance, work and other areas, remained: but how are such points defined at the time and in retrospect according to the relations between the inner life, social relationships and the events (ordinary or major) in life?

Box 3.4

Matza, D. (1969) *Becoming Deviant*. New Jersey, NJ: Prentice-Hall.

Matza provided perhaps the most sophisticated 'career' theory of 'becoming deviant' during the 1960s. Following an account of previous Chicagoan and Functionalist approaches and the emerging deviancy perspective, he attempted, by drawing on the 'complexity' and 'appreciation' of deviance, to combine ideas on 'affinity', 'affiliation' and 'signification' (loosely, area, group and labelling) to deviance. He offered a 'naturalistic' perspective on 'becoming' within which the individual deviant travels between 'humanism' and 'determination' – a perspective influenced by previous sociological theories on crime but also from phenomenology and other sources. Thus, the deviant is portrayed as exercising choice while subject to the effects of 'ban' or social control. *Becoming Deviant* can be seen as extending the motivational accounts in his earlier work in *Delinquency and Drift* (1964) and elsewhere, especially ideas on techniques of neutralization, subterranean values, drift and will in understanding individual careers in crime and deviance.

Case studies

Two classic case studies, W. I. Thomas and F. Znaniecki's *The Polish Peasant in Europe and America* ([1918–20]1958) and C. R. Shaw's *The Jack-Roller* ([1930]1966), demonstrate the origin of the life history method and its associated assumptions and issues. These studies, while influential, went through a long period of being noted and referenced but rarely used, until the 1960s and then again over the past twenty or more years due to a renewed interest and reassessment within the development of biographical research.

Case study 1
Thomas, W. I. and Znaniecki, F. ([1918–20]1958) *The Polish Peasant in Europe and America*, 2 vols. New York: Dover Press (originally published by Gorham Press, 5 vols).

The early status of the 'life history' was achieved by W. I. Thomas and F. Znaniecki's massive study *The Polish Peasant in Europe and America* which was originally published in five volumes (1918–20) and was the first major empirical study completed within the Department of Sociology at Chicago (Bulmer 1983: 470). It was regarded as a key theoretical and methodological achievement at the time and has been subsequently called a 'classic' within the discipline. While still frequently cited, especially in biographical work as a founding example, it remained rather a 'neglected classic' (Bulmer 1983). Its rather daunting size might be some reason for the reluctance to consult it. Although subsequently published in fewer volumes it still contains over 2000 pages. *The Polish Peasant* deals with a major social question – the arrival of immigrants in the context of the public discussion of the restriction of immigration and the influence of national, racial and eugenic assumptions (Bulmer 1983). The study sought to show that the problems of the immigrant community were due to the transition from a very different society, which required a series of communal adaptations to the new situation.

Of particular interest for biographical research is the publication of the life story of Władek, a Polish immigrant, which runs to over three hundred pages. Within his story is a description of his early life and movement from a village community to his life and fortunes in America. The account is intended to provide an illustration of how the individual may undergo 'disorganization' in such changes. The story was an inspiration for subsequent examples of the use of the life history in Chicagoan sociology. A wide range of other materials is present in the study. Over 700 letters between immigrants in America and families in Poland are arranged in family series of 50; there are accounts from Polish newspaper archives and an emigration bureau, and records from a number of social work, court and Polish–American organizations (see Bulmer 1983; Plummer 1983: 41–2). Each of these sources had a purpose in showing the features of Polish family and communal life and the difficulties and disruptions produced by migration to a large industrial city in America. The study also reveals how an adaptation or communal reorganization was taking place with the formation of Polish–American organizations, despite pressures towards social demoralization and breakdown (Bulmer 1983). *The Polish Peasant in Europe and America* stimulated a widespread debate surrounding case and statistical methods, questions of interpretation between theory and data, and the reliability and validity of 'personal documents', particularly life stories. Ranged against the life history or case method was the view, for example from Lundberg, that its use could not be scientific (Plummer 1983: 45–6).

Thomas and Znaniecki believed that the life-record could be used to explain the appearance of new individual attitudes and new social values by looking at the interplay of existing attitudes and values. While the individual's attitudes and view of values are unique, they argue, individual differences can be ignored for the purpose of scientific generalization; but in the study of mass phenomena the life histories of individuals are needed. However,

> . . . in order to be able to use adequately personal life-records for the purposes of nomothetic generalizations social science must have criteria permitting it to select at once from a mass of concrete human documents, those which are likely to be scientifically valuable for the solution of a given general problem.
>
> (Thomas and Znaniecki [1918–20]1958: 1834)

Thus a few representative cases are required to produce results as close as possible to the rest of the cases identified while criteria are drawn from a theory of 'human individuals as social personalities'. Thomas and Znaniecki begin with the idea of 'typical lines of genesis' which refers to the development of attitudes and values and then outline a number of other ideas: the distinction between temperament and character; ideas of life-organization, rules, types of situations; types of personal evolution – philistine, bohemian, creative individual; the desires of new experience and stability; mechanism of suppression; the principle of sublimation; and emotional and rational morality. These are provided to inform the reading of Władek's life-record: he is a 'typical representative of the culturally passive mass'; his personal evolution draws on certain social conditions; and many of its elements have a significance 'beyond his milieu and his time'. Władek described his search for work, his daily adventures and family relationships in great detail. He ends with his path to America and the subsequent birth of a son but also his disappointment with the new life on being dismissed from the stockyards and the resulting hardships being faced by him and his wife. Thomas and

Znaniecki described Władek's personality as oscillating between bohemianism and philistinism in his life, but tending towards an economic type of the latter.

The status of *The Polish Peasant* was demonstrated by an evaluation of the study, under the auspices of the SSRC (Social Science Research Council), as a work that had made a major contribution to the discipline of sociology (Blumer [1939]1969; Plummer 1983: 46). Herbert Blumer, a follower of G. H. Mead, carried out the appraisal, and he produced a finely detailed and intensive critique. Starting with theory, Blumer was puzzled as to where the study's theoretical ideas come from. It appeared that not all the theorization (or even major elements) came from the sources or materials collected. The interpretations seemed to be 'plausible', adding 'significance' to the materials and making theorization more 'understandable' (Blumer 1969: 121). Blumer concludes: 'Perhaps, this is all that one can expect or should expect in the interpretative analysis of human documentary material' (Blumer 1969: 121–2). Here he poses a problem: while studies restricted to 'objective' factors are not adequate since we need an understanding of human experience, there is the issue of how to judge interpretation. For instance, single documents can easily be questioned on scientific criteria of reliability, adequacy, comparability and representativeness. But to reject them would be a mistake because life-records can be of great benefit (Blumer 1969: 125). The theoretical contribution of *The Polish Peasant*, he argues, is due to a number of conceptual developments, especially in the areas of attitudes and values where it is commended for the ability to balance attitudes, meanings and experiences with objective characteristics of cultural values as found in social institutions. Thus, Blumer argues, this allows analysis to graduate from the small-scale analysis of primary groups to institutional contexts.

The study of a life-record, such as Władek's, enables Thomas and Znaniecki to investigate the 'disorganizing effects' of the passage between forms of social organization. Such a record is used to assess a social evolution or adaptation – in temperament, character and life organization – and the formation of the 'typical lines of genesis' (Thomas and Znaniecki [1918–20]1958: 1840, 1860). Thomas and Znaniecki famously stated: 'We are safe in saying that personal life-records, as complete as possible, constitute the *perfect* type of sociological material . . .' (Thomas and Znaniecki [1918–20]1958: 1832). They see life histories as aiding the classification of types of social personalities, to indicate how attitudes and acts are related over time, and to use individual experiences to form more general 'laws of social becoming'. They add that since the life stories of all the individuals within a context cannot be used, a few representative cases are applied despite the difficulties of selection.

For Martin Bulmer *The Polish Peasant* has a high place within the history of sociological research:

The Polish Peasant has a lasting significance as one of the most important methodological contributions to the establishment of *the social* as a
distinct and legitimate area of enquiry. It rejected entirely any element
of biological reductionism and sought to explain ethnic social behaviour in terms of sociological and social psychological categories.
(Bulmer 1983: 474)

Similarly, Coser regards *The Polish Peasant* as a 'monumental achievement'
and a 'major landmark' in the early history of American sociological
research (Coser 1977: 511). Nevertheless, there remained some conceptual
ambiguities: 'Too often, conceptual distinctions that appear clear-cut in the
methodological discussion become blurred in concrete exposition. Even
such key concepts as attitude and values . . . often come to be used almost
interchangeably' (Coser 1977: 518).

At the centre of *The Polish Peasant* study are basic issues of interpretation
and analysis in life documents – the relationship between generating and
verifying theory: whether generalizations are being made from the range of
documents or whether they are used to support pre-existing theorization.
Nevertheless, in *The Polish Peasant* there is a persuasiveness at the level of
human experience in the interpretations and theorization outlined even
though, as Blumer observed, the connection between the materials collected
and theorization used is not always clear.

Blumer's ([1939]1969) 'appraisal' of *The Polish Peasant* was one of a
number of reviews of life or personal documents in the social sciences carried out in this period. Dollard (1935) reviewed the use of the life history
and set out a number of principles regarding the value of such materials and
of this approach. Allport (1942) carried out a review of the types and benefits of the life or case approach within psychology, and Gottschalk *et al.*
(1945) reviewed such work in history, anthropology and sociology.

Case study 2
Shaw, C. R. ([1930]1966) *The Jack-Roller: A Delinquent Boy's Own Story*,
revised edition Chicago, IL: University of Chicago Press.

Clifford R. Shaw utilized the stories of youths alongside a range of other
material in his studies of delinquency. *The Jack-Roller* (1930) is regarded as
a 'classic' early sociological example of the 'life history'. It is one of several
texts written on delinquent lives by Shaw (*The Natural History of a Delinquent Career* 1931; *Brothers in Crime* 1938). Stanley's story has become one
of the most famous 'lives' in sociology and was later updated when he was
elderly (Snodgrass 1982).

The Jack-Roller draws on quite an amount of detail regarding the collection
of Stanley's life, including the interviewing, the written accounts by Stanley

and the range of official records (police, social work) consulted and used to compare with the events described. It seems that Shaw had known Stanley a number of years previously as a settlement worker. Burgess provides a methodological overview in which he argues for the case method against the charge that it cannot meet scientific criteria. It was published in the context of a debate on the relative merits of the case method (life history, community studies) and statistical data (Hammersley 1990: 93–4; see Burgess 1925).

The charge can be made that Chicagoan work was caught by the attempt to conform to 'objective' or 'scientific' criteria (as outlined by Blumer) – reliability, validity, representativeness and means of theory and hypothesis construction – while realizing that the outline of subjective meanings may not provide 'truths'. In overall presentation, as Denzin notes, on the one hand the 'objective' stages in the delinquent career (e.g. entering the institution) are outlined and on the other the responses of Stanley (Denzin 1989: 52). Denzin, in a later detailed evaluation of *The Jack-Roller*, argues:

> The classic, natural history approach . . . confuses the flesh-and-blood, textual, empirical and analytic versions of the subject. It presumes that 'an objective' record of a life can be given, and that this objective report lies in documents and records which detail the life in question. It fails to consider the possibility that these other documents are themselves social constructions, social texts which create their own version of the subject, in this case Stanley and his life history . . . This approach sees in a life materials for the testing and development of scientific hypotheses about human behaviour.
>
> (Denzin 1995: 118)

Again, here the traditional scientific criteria are questioned concerning the way in which the document is produced and the individual life is related (see Plummer 1983: 105–6). Further, Denzin alleges that *The Jack-Roller* contains a romanticized view of the subject, informed by a social realism in the text, upholding the political status quo by an 'over-identification with society's undesirables' – an emotional illusion cannot change what requires an economic solution (Denzin 1995: 122). A connection can be made here with Mills's earlier sustained critique of the assumptions of adjustment/maladjustment and situational reformism found in pragmatism and 'liberal practicality' (Mills 1966, 1970: Ch. 4).

Types of interpretation

Life stories within the life history method may be edited and presented in a number of ways. At the broadest they may be generally left to 'speak for themselves' with little apparent editing and interpretation. What is given appears or is claimed to be a full presentation, perhaps with some brief introduction or summary. Even here we may say that some pre-editing of the language or style will take place as the written text is examined or the oral account is transcribed into the written format and are later published. This is apart from the influences on how the story is initially requested or otherwise obtained. Another model is where the interpretative framework is prominent and the life story is presented in an interspersed, abridged fashion in conjunction with editorial comment and analysis. Life stories as presented may also be related to various other documentation. So, in terms of interpretation, at the extremes, life stories may be given as (or claimed to be) more or less unmediated by the researcher or adopted as merely illustrative of some theoretical and analytical perspective.

Distinctions can be made according to a life story's subject matter and comprehensiveness – whether it is a period in a life, a 'career', or meant to be the 'full' life. Again, there are questions concerning the degree of editing, abridgement, commentary and analysis. Allport (1942) offered three main forms of life history writing: the edited, the topical, and the complete. The edited may be on a particular theme, like the topical, and may be interspersed with commentary or accompanied by a short interpretive/descriptive account. It may also be an editing of a 'complete' life story, which gives the 'full' life of the individual. Following Dollard's 'criteria' for the life history, a commentary may not only include an interpretation of the subjective aspects of the development of the individual's life but also the links with

---

Box 3.5

Bertaux, D. (ed.) (1981) *Biography and Society*. London: Sage.

This classic text by an international group of writers marked the re-emergence of the life history in the social sciences and examined methodological issues, examples of life history research, and oral history. Bertaux in his Introduction points to a 'new wave' of sociological studies using life stories and a key theoretical issue in the volume – 'the relationship between individual and collective *praxis* and sociohistorical *change*'. The studies employ a very broad range of theorization including interpretive sociology, Sartrian and other forms of Marxism, social psychology, and socio-historical perspectives. Papers include Bertaux and Bertaux-Wiame's study of French bakers; Elder's work on cohort/life course research on the Depression; Gagnon on historical consciousness in Quebec; Hankiss on myths and the life story; and Ferrarotti on the biography of the primary group. The papers demonstrate for Bertaux how macrosociological questions, such as social mobility, class formation and migration, can be addressed by a method deemed at best only suitable for micro sociological analysis.

family and the wider cultural context (Dollard 1935). The purpose of the commentary is usually to draw out the key aspects of the story but for some later writers (see especially Chapter 4) should include the reflection by the researcher on the research process and personal life.

Recently, as in Denzin's (1995) views on *The Jack-Roller*, with the expansion of biographical research, attention has been turned again to questions of interpretation and presentation of the life: the construction of the 'story', and the internal features of the personal document. A whole range of terms is now to be found in the study of life stories including biography, narrative and life history. The term 'story' appears to presume a narrative fiction with main and lesser characters and a discernible plot structure around which the given of elements of the story, as written or told, fit. Differences in stories may be found according to the presence of the 'personal' in the document – the amount of inner reflection, motivations, feelings, personal beliefs, on the one side, and the extent to which the group (community, organization) is the focus on the other (Denzin 1989: 43–4). As in other forms of qualitative research, such as ethnography, the editing and writing of the research document brings within it certain styles and complex processes of interpretation, involving insight and imagination (see Erben 1998b). The writing of research can be likened to a literary exercise in expression which can take various forms – descriptive, analytic, fantasy, comic, realistic, romantic, philosophical and so on – of presentation (see Bruyn 1966: 245; Atkinson 1990: 8). These modes of expression have not been noted as much as they should – how they may represent different voices, time shifts, and the overall construction of the 'research narrative' of the researcher. The focus on the 'writing' of the text is now very much part of the discussion of life story work. In fact, this is part of a wider movement in the interpretation of culture and the questioning of the notion that the 'reality' of the individual life is simply represented in the biographical research text. There is the charge that traditional approaches assume a chronology within stories and fail to recognize that individuals' interpretations of experience are located in particular time periods and ideological formations (Denzin 1989: 9). In the traditional 'realist' account the voice of the researched is deemed paramount. Critics have pointed out not only that the ultimate decisions on what is presented are the researcher's but also that the researcher is influenced by current conventions or codes of writing and interpretative schemas. For Van Maanen:

> Basically, the narrator of realist tales poses as an impersonal conduit who, unlike missionaries, administrators, journalists, or unabashed members of the culture themselves, passes on more-or-less objective data in a measured intellectual style that is uncontaminated by personal bias, political goals, or moral judgements. A studied neutrality characterizes the realist tale.
>
> (Van Maanen, cited in Atkinson 1990: 33)

Van Maanen (1995a) argues that following a 'heightened self-consciousness' or 'ethnographic introspection' alternatives to 'ethnographic realism have emerged' – in which the 'voice' of the researcher has a different position. Van Maanen identifies confessional ethnography giving the field-worker's difficulties; dramatic ethnography which relies more on literary techniques and personal statements than documentary methods; and critical ethnography where the local culture is placed in a wider historical or social setting beyond the participants' references. Finally, there are 'self-' or 'auto-ethnographies' where researchers' own groups are passionately reported and the researcher–researched distinction collapses (Van Maanen 1995a: 8–10). In biographical research a parallel reappraisal of the researcher's modes of presentation and complex biographical relation with the 'subject' and the research context has been taking place.

The re-emergence of biographical research in sociology was heralded by Bertaux (1981) and Plummer (1983). By the time of Denzin's (1989) work a wider range of influences outside sociology were beginning to have an effect. Denzin notes that there are a number of approaches to life history, autobiography and biography. His preference is for a literary and socio-logical analysis that produces specific portraits of individuals within their historical settings as against typological or generic forms which canonically trace back current work to an original classic study (e.g. *The Polish Peasant*) (Denzin 1989: 34–5). He argues that forms and rules of genre are implicated in the writing of a life. He also criticizes forms which see the autobiography as an accurate, truthful reflection of reality – a common-sense approach, which conforms to positivistic assumptions of text-life – rather than lives as narrative fictions ideologically located (Denzin 1989: 37). Unfortunately, the issues involved here can be too crudely polarized into a question of 'real-ism' vs. 'representation' by a simple postmodern view instead of a sense that while texts are not 'purely' referential, they are constructed within or medi-ate 'reality'. Much care must be taken with this question of 'representation': the term has various meanings. As Hutcheon says:

> Postmodern representation is self-consciously all of these – image, narrative, product of (and producer of) ideology . . . in literary and art critical circles there is still a tendency to see postmodern theory and practice either as simply replacing representation with the idea of tex-tuality or as denying our intricate involvement with representation, even though much postmodern thought has disputed this tendency . . .
> (Hutcheon 1989: 31)

There is also the argument that 'knowledge' is related to particular circum-stance and time, and to privilege the text, as 'constructed', therefore demotes 'reality' to a resource.

Within sociology there have been examples of sociologists, as mentioned earlier, giving accounts of their lives or lives of other sociologists (in addition to accounts of work 'in the field'). These professional lives often remain within chronological description, and genre constraints of 'beginnings' and 'turning points' (Denzin 1989: 40). Horowitz's and other texts on the careers of sociologists usually give prime influences, sociological work undertaken and so on (Horowitz 1970b). However, Merton's (1988) discussion of 'sociological autobiography' advocates the use of sociological approaches, ideas and procedures to form a narrative story of a life in its social and historical context (Stanley 1993). Merton argues that we are in a unique position, since it is our own life, as our own participant–observer who has access to our specific hidden experiences (Stanley 1993: 43). Another, but much less detailed, example of 'sociological lives' is provided by Morgan whose editing of a book on social research unusually contains, at the end of each author's chapter, a biography which gives some early background alongside institutional career and some reflections on academic influences and instances of life–career links (Morgan 1983). The examination of the sociologist's own life and its relationship to work undertaken (under the impact of feminist and other writing) has raised important issues in biographical research (see Chapter 4). For example, in studying the lives of others are we also researching and constructing ourselves?

Conclusion

The life history within sociology underwent extensive development during the 1920s and 1930s followed by debate, appraisal and critique. Its decline was marked by the relative rise of other methodologies, including the growth of statistical techniques, and a turn to 'macro' theory. Some revival of the method took place with the rise of new 'micro-sociologies' in the 1960s and, in particular, through the sociology of deviance, with its notions such as career, and an ethnographical approach to sociological study. Early assessments in sociology and other disciplines considered the assumptions of the method, types of data, collection of materials, and general guidance required on the research process. More specifically, questions of reliability and validity were at the fore of discussion, issues that reappeared when the method again began to find favour in the 1970s and 1980s. What is apparent today is that the variety and breadth of life history data – becoming wider – and the discussion of evaluative criteria, such as authenticity and plausibility, are still prominent. Questions regarding the relationship between data and theory are still current, but with additional issues: the challenge to so-called 'realist' accounts of individual lives and context, the issue of the visibility of the researcher's own biography and relation with the research context and the researched, and the process of reading by an audience.

Recommended reading

Berger, P. L. and Luckmann, T. (1971) *The Social Construction of Reality*. Harmondsworth: Penguin. (This eclectic text on the 'sociology of knowledge' draws on phenomenology and a diverse range of sociological theory. It addresses society as both a subjective and objective reality and was influential on later biographical researchers in sociology.)

Bertaux, D. (ed.) (1981) *Biography and Society: The Life History Approach in the Social Sciences*. London: Sage. (This volume helped to revive the life history in the social sciences, especially within sociology and oral history. It contains articles by international writers and research from a wide range of countries; methodological issues are prominent and subjects covered include the life course, cohort analysis, autobiography, and migration and social change.)

Denzin, N. K. (1989) *Interpretive Biography*. London: Sage. (This study of biography provides a short but comprehensive introduction to the range of definitions and approaches to the life history and related areas.)

Plummer, K. (1983) *Documents of Life*. London: George Allen and Unwin (revised edition, 2001, Sage). (A wide-ranging review of the diversity of 'life documents', the foundation of the method in the Chicago School, the uses of life histories, and a guide to doing, writing and theorizing.)

(4) Autobiography and biography

Autobiography and biography – definitions

Autobiography and biography are commonly considered within literary study and criticism as genres of writing by the self or about another. But if considered a little more deeply as 'life writing' the literary canvass becomes very broad, including memoirs, autobiographies, diaries, case studies, profiles, journals and other documents, each of which indicates a degree of difference in purpose (Smith 1994: 287). Even so, there are connections between these forms of writing and sources and also between interpretative life work across disciplines. For instance, the practice of oral history and the writing of biography have many similarities. Also, as literary biographical writing itself has developed it has drawn on psychology and other disciplines to explore the influences on the individual's perceptions of life and interactions with others (Yow 1994: 167).

The similarities between literary autobiography and biography and oral history are worth pursuing further. Usually, the oral history is dependent on the face-to-face interview whereas the biographer may not have met the subject but may rely on interviews with 'significant others' and any diaries, letters or other personal writing – including any autobiographical account – by the individual. Whereas the oral history of an individual is based on an interactive, collaborative encounter, the biography need not be so. There is also the issue that biographies tend to be singular in orientation, although they may be joint or even of a group (usually, a literary or other artistic grouping). Oral histories or sociological life story studies may present 'exemplars' but they tend to be oriented towards the social grouping in its historical or contemporary setting. While it is apparent that these distinctions are not hard and fast, some sociologists would rule out the 'single' life story study, and literary biographers might wish to retain 'biography' as simply a form of literary pursuit. A further objection to overlap may be raised that 'biography' is more edited and 'authored' by the writer/researcher whereas the oral history or sociological life history approach is more inclined to enable the individual subject to 'speak'. The view would be that the latter practice is based on interaction with the individual: there is more guidance and focus by the researcher by framing the collection of life accounts in ways not always applied in biography (see Yow 1994: 169).

Turning to autobiography, Yow makes an interesting comparison with oral history in terms of presenting a self. Both have an audience – if only the self – and the subjects are in fact forming a view of themselves continuously before, during and after interviewing, even if questions are formed in a particular way by the interviewer (Yow 1994: 169–70). In terms of the practice of oral or life history and autobiography there is a similar interpretative attempt – commonly to grasp the life as a whole (or a major part) in all its inconsistencies and contradictions. The intention is to present a perspective

---

Box 4.1

Sisman, A. (2000) *Boswell's Presumptuous Task*. London: Hamish Hamilton.

Sisman's biography of Boswell presents a detailed portrait of his life and character, and his relationship with Johnson. Boswell wrote notes on Samuel Johnson for years and gathered recollections and letters from others after his friend died. Sisman shows that Boswell was not simply part of Johnson's life as a friend of an older mentor but that the latter knew of Boswell's biographical writing and helped to an extent in the task. Boswell's contribution to biography in the *Life of Johnson* (following Johnson's own biographical work) was to challenge prevailing sensibility that written lives of great people should be uplifting; rather, he gave a portrait which included Johnson's private conversations including his observations on friends and others and his human failings (see Anderson 2001: 37–8). Sisman is very informative on Boswell's method: his ability to memorize and record conversations, and the ethical questions raised in reporting Johnson's views of others and using private materials – questions which remain salient to biographical writing.

upon it but one which may alter during the research as information is gained, the relationship with the individual or the material alters and interpretation proceeds. The life story teller or autobiographer seeks an audience just as the listener/reader seeks comprehension and human connection. Within the forms of communication between giver and receiver are sets of expectations and conventions which make understanding and rapport possible although still subject to variable interpretation (see Tonkin 1995).

Biographical writing has gone through a number of significant changes during its history, as marked by particular well-known works. For example, the commonly cited are Dr Johnson's exploration of the life of Savage; Boswell's *Life of Johnson*; and the later work *Eminent Victorians* written by Lytton Strachey who attempted 'through the medium of biography, to present some Victorian visions to the modern eye . . . to be of interest from the strictly biographical no less than from the historical point of view' (Strachey [1918]1948: 9–10; see Erben 1993: 21–3; Holmes 1994; Sisman 2000). Today, we seem to be in a period of particular interest in biographical and autobiographical writing, by biographers, novelists and literary critics, as witnessed, for instance, by the work of Ackroyd (1991), Forster (1996, 1999), Byatt (2000a), Holmes (2000), Holroyd (2000) and many others. As Mary Evans argues (commenting on Holroyd's influential biography of Strachey), there has been a 'reinterpretation' of the 'code of biography' which has made private details behind public actions the focus of assessment (M. Evans 1993: 8; see also Evans 1999). In observing the 'lucrative nature' of biographies about the famous, as evidenced by the piles of best-sellers in the bookshops, she argues that the form has until recently been very conservative or conventional with a chronological pattern of life delivered with some general assessment.

Box 4.2

Holmes, R. (2000) *Sidetracks*. London: HarperCollins.

Richard Holmes, a prominent contemporary biographer who has contributed much to the reshaping of biographical writing (with work on Coleridge, Shelley and others), interestingly comments on the relation between the biographical writer and the subject. He examines the impulse of the biographer; empathy with the subject; the degree to which the biographer creates a fictional subject; and the intense interest in the detail of the subject's life (see Holmes 1985: 2000; *Auto/Biography*, 1996). He argues that biographical writing is a connection across time – an exercise in human solidarity and love, and finding of a self in the other.

Box 4.3

Holroyd, M. (2000) *Basil Street Blues*. London: Abacus.

Holroyd, acclaimed for his biographies of Shaw and others, describes a 'concealment' of his identity (even from himself) which formed his biographies of others until he began replacing this 'invisibility' in an account of his own family and autobiography following the deaths of his parents. *Basil Street Blues* (2000) is a detective-like quest for his family history that is connected to his own autobiographical exploration. There have also been recent examples of prominent novelists and literary critics directly exploring their own family histories and relationships (cf. Forster 1996, 1999; Sage 2000).

Complex and important questions found in other fields of biographical research are now being encountered in 'literary' life writing concerning the relation between the autobiographer or biographer and the audience, and issues such as the importance of the biographer's self, the bases of interpretation, and the types of writing and presentation. For example, on autobiographical writing, Sheridan (following Lejeune) asks questions regarding the 'autobiographical impulse' which touch on the area of motivation – is such writing to provide a confirmation of self or even of existence itself? To require a listener? To influence or be flattered by an audience? (See Sheridan 1993: 30–1). In fact, a complex range of motivations may lie behind an individual's autobiography and the writing process and text can also have important and varied effects on authors (Gullestad 1995). Such questions can also be posed in relation to biographical writing.

Many other writers have interrogated (especially recently) the problematic nature of the connection between author, text and reader. De Man, for example, from a 'deconstructionist' or 'theory or reading' viewpoint starts with the relation between philosophy and literature (see Norris 1991: 104; see also Anderson 2001: 12–16). Philosophy, he argues, like any other form of writing is constrained by language (e.g. the use of metaphor). When reading texts different understandings are possible (aporia). Thus 'reading' contains limitations, which actually reside in the text. In a 'deconstructionist' view there are a number of meanings in a text which may be in opposition, rather than an assumption that there is a complete or a singular definitive understanding. The nature and place of authorship is contested as the place of the variety of meanings of the text and the role of readership is brought under scrutiny. The challenge to the traditional, taken-for-granted understandings of texts has been influenced by forms of (post)structuralism and later postmodernist writers who relegate or dispense with the 'author' and contest the author's privileged cultural role. The attention to shaping 'structures' or discourses (cf. Foucault) replaces the identity (motivations, informing influences) of the author by a focus on the reading of the text and how texts are related to wider practices (Sim 1998: 221–2).

Genre

The idea of 'genre' is a vexed area since commentators and writers have identified various influences and differing criteria which shape expression, such as 'subject setting theme authorial attitude genesis purpose occasion structure effect' (Hawthorn 1987: 47; see also Walder 1995). In addition, according to Hawthorn, 'psychological and sociological factors' and 'historical specificity' have also been identified, specific works have been placed within genres according to differing elements and designations may be given prior to or allocated later to a work (Hawthorn 1987: 50–1). Recent writers have commented on the ambiguities, shifting basis and mixed nature of autobiographical writing as a genre not merely in terms of fact–fiction but also as subject–object and public–private, and also as related to self and identity (Marcus 1995: 13–14).

For Olney, autobiography should be considered not so much on formal criteria or as evolving historically; instead autobiography may be expressed through history, psychology, political economy, poetry, or natural science. The individual will be shown in the personal essay, poem or scientific work (Olney 1972: 3; see also Olney 1980). Raymond Williams observes that while 'genre' has been associated with classification, in an attempt to have an historical reference a wider conception emerged; however, this element was subsequently eroded, leaving rather abstract formulations (Williams 1977). He outlines a number of basic elements of genre: stance (traditionally, the narrative, the dramatic and the lyrical), mode of composition, and appropriate subject matter. Of course, he says, these are subject to variation according to social, cultural and historical context but analysis has to begin with them (Williams 1977: 183–4). Chamberlain and Thompson argue that the complicated topic of 'genre' has a very long history deriving from the Greeks' differentiation between the epic, dramatic and lyrical forms of literature and later nineteenth-century distinctions between styles of painting or novel according to purpose and form (Chamberlain and Thompson 1998a: 1–2). They observe that the generation of taxonomies, if too prescriptive, becomes a problem, although generally in the literature there has tended to be a vagueness – genre has been defined by form, mood or content, or a type of text, or element of text: a recent trend has been to stress the role of expectations and conventions in communication in shaping autobiography (Chamberlain and Thompson 1998a: 1–2). Agreement has been difficult because genre definitions insufficiently overlap.

The discussion of the features of literary genres has spread across the social science disciplines. In a postmodern, deconstructionist vein some historians have argued the writing of history to be as much a literary genre as a practical method for establishing the truth of the past (Munslow 2000: 73). White, in his well-known deconstructionist approach which sees the practice of history in terms of narratives given to the past, offers a complex analysis of the 'historical imagination' through tropes or figures of speech (e.g. metaphor), emplotment types (e.g. comedy), kinds of argument (e.g. formist), and ideological connections (e.g. conservative) (Munslow 2000: 225–6; see White 1973).

Smith likens the writing of biography to a 'craft' whose practice features uncertainty and complexity but this ambiguity is all within the delights and frustrations of completing biographies (Smith 1994: 289). He describes a procedure for biographical writing – choice of subject, creating an archive, developing a theme or conception of the subject and the form and shape of the writing (Smith 1994: 292). Smith also presents a form of typology (drawn from Clifford) – the objective biography, the scholarly historical, the artistic–scholarly, narrative biography and the fictional biography. There is a kind of continuum from fact collection to character construction as dialogue and settings become closer to fiction (narrative biography) and, eventually, to where writing becomes close to the historical novel with little reference to detailed research (fictional biography) (Smith 1994: 292). Obviously, as he recognizes, no biography can be completely 'factual' and we can also add that biographies tend to use a mix of these approaches as fact, interpretation and construction takes place. Biographical writing has also changed with contemporary writers experimenting with the use of fictional dialogue; dual, group or family biography (cf. Hattersley 1999); the recovery of 'hidden' lives and relationships (Tomalin 1991); different forms of writing (e.g. types of novel), and fictionalized periods in life (cf. Ackroyd 1997). Similarly, autobiographies may be categorized into 'sub-genres' according to field of interest, for instance within the study of labour and political history various types of previously published autobiographies or oral histories of workers have been collected (Burnett 1994; Thompson 2000: Ch. 3). Scott (from Vincent's historical work) points to two main ones – the 'spiritual' and the 'oral tradition' autobiography: the former arising from seventeenth-century religious conflict and the latter being written accounts drawn from a ballad and storytelling tradition. A third type (taken from Burnett's researches) is the 'political or radical autobiography' of individuals within the labour movement (Scott 1990: Ch. 8). However, the many typologies and classifications may reflect deeper issues.

Marcus argues that in some recent discussion autobiography is itself seen in opposition to generic classifications as it 'transcends' boundaries and highlights the differentiation and complexity of literary work in general. Further, the autobiography can be seen as a 'precondition or guarantor of a remedy for the fractured identity of modernity' (Marcus 1995: 14). Thus, autobiography connects with broader questions; it is a 'microcosmic version' of a wider crisis, which it represents and articulates: 'Autobiographical consciousness, for example, has been held up as a mode of healthy self-awareness which could heal some of the wounds of the nineteenth-century spirit' (Marcus 1995: 14).

It appears that there are more autobiographies and memoirs of working men and women during the nineteenth and early twentieth centuries than has been realized until recently. Such writings, although largely by men, 'provide valuable information about the family, work and leisure experiences' of the time (Golby 1994: 103). The fact that many were meant for publication shows a rising literacy and popularity in such materials, and that cheaper publication had become available during the period. Golby notes that autobiography 'is one of the few historical sources in which we can learn of the direct experiences of individuals' (Golby 1994: 103). As Golby observes, there has also been the recent feature of the local publication of life stories becoming popular as part of the local oral community history movement and interest in family history (Golby 1994: 104; see Blatchford 2001).

Traditionally, published autobiographies have been generally by men since the means and 'scripts' were not so available for the telling of lives of eminent women (Smith 1994: 300). Swindells, examining the position of women in autobiographical writing, says women have traditionally been in a 'negative' cultural position and outsiders even in published autobiography, but have sought (along with others) to resist this designation (Swindells

---

Box 4.4

Marcus, L. (1994) *Auto/biographical Discourses: Theory, Criticism, Practice*. Manchester: Manchester University Press.

Marcus uses a very wide variety of theoretical and literary work to examine biographical and autobiographical writing. She argues that genres and disciplines have histories and boundaries that are always open to contestation and adds that autobiography can be seen as a 'topic, a resource and a site of struggle' (Marcus 1994: 9). The book includes discussion of the 'new biography' of Woolf and Strachey, science, literature and auto/biographical writing, historical consciousness and autobiography from Dilthey onwards, feminist discussion, autobiography and ethnicity, and recent literary criticism and related writing on autobiography (cf. Olney, Lejeune and De Man). Marcus's intent is to demonstrate the place of autobiography and biography in the current re-examination of subject–object, fact–fiction, public–private distinctions.

1995a: 5). The contribution of feminist writers has enhanced the new attention to autobiographical writing and criticism and has aided a refocusing
of work in oral history and other biographical research (see Stanley,
1992; Chamberlain and Thompson 1998a: 4–5). Women writers (historians, literary critics, and sociologists) have brought a 'methodological
self-consciousness' to the study of women's lives and have challenged existing disciplinary boundaries. They have addressed issues concerning identity,
forms of writing, and the interplay of discourses (Reinharz 1992: 157). For
example Carole Boyce Davies describes the intention of her book *Black
Women, Writing and Identity* as follows:

> Black women's writing . . . should be read as a series of boundary cross-
> ings and not as a fixed, geographical, ethnically or nationally bound
> category of writing . . . marginalized in the terms of majority–minority
> discourses . . . [It] redefines its identity as it re-connects and remembers,
> brings together black women dis-located by space and time.
>
> (Davies 1994: 4; see also Birch 1994)

Box 4.5

Steedman, C. (1986) *Landscape for a Good Woman*. London: Virago.

Steedman's influential study presents an interlinked autobiography of her
1950s south London childhood and biography of her mother who grew up
in Burnley, a textile town in northern England. In trying to understand
these stories she refers to historical research, psychoanalysis, feminist,
political and cultural interpretation, and studies of working-class life (e.g.
Hoggart 1958). What emerges is the uniqueness of stories – the 'irre-
ducible nature of all our lost childhoods' – and a challenge to dominant
assumptions found in other accounts of the lives, attitudes and aspirations
of working-class women. It is concerned with family silences,
mother–daughter relations and the marginality of certain voices (see also
Fraser 1984; Heron 1985; Walkerdine and Lucey 1989).

The use of autobiographies or life stories within biographical research
practice involves the interconnection between genres. Alessandro Portelli
highlights some of the complexity of the use of genre with reference to oral
history. He regards oral history as a 'cluster of genres' which includes what
oral historians listen to and what they write, as well as the dialogue of the
interview situation (Portelli 1998: 23). A life story may contain a memoir,
poems, theses, reportage and so on (see Gullestad 1995). The writing of biography may not include contact with the subject (who may not be available)

but may well include interviews with those who knew or know him or her and refer to all kinds of personal writings (autobiography, novels, memos and so on) and official records. Various writers see autobiography (and we may add biography) as being an unstable genre since, in 'blurring' the distinction between fiction and non-fiction, it challenges assumptions of positivism – the collection of measurable, observable facts, notions of objectivity and validity, and a deductive procedure – by raising questions regarding the nature and construction of knowledge, the emphasis on the subjective dimensions of social life, the reference to alternative evaluative criteria (e.g. authenticity, credibility), and the recognition of the poetic or literary in interpretation and presentation of lives (Smith 1994: 288). It also has a more general significance as a central part of recent 'paradigmatic shifts' in social thought (Smith 1994: 288).

Issues in autobiography and biography

There has been a growth in the collection and critical attention given to the autobiography, paralleled by a challenge to the notion that it is the 'actual' life which is presented and the idea that the 'autobiographical act' is individualistic since individuals can be detached from their surrounding milieu (Swindells 1995a: 1). Swindells argues that the Western European individualistic tradition is not only 'male' in authorship and commentary but gives a certain notion of the connection between the individual and society. Such autobiographies claim to 'speak authoritatively' but: '. . . this way of analysing autobiography fails to accommodate any sense of tension, struggle, contestation, or outright conflict between consciousness and environment, between people and their surrounding ideological world' (Swindells 1995a: 2).

Smith (1994) in his comprehensive review of 'biographical method' gives 'autobiography' as an example of a 'special case of life writing'. Additionally, following Lejeune, we can identify various forms of autobiography including the oral history interview, the autobiography in the third person and the radio interview (Thompson 1988: 245). Commentators (such as Olney 1972; Eakin 1985, 1999b; Lejeune 1989) address a number of central issues on autobiography and biography: how the reader evaluates and interprets, how the autobiography is an individual's assessment of life at a particular time and subject to reassessment, and how the autobiographical–biographical distinction when challenged also 'disrupts' boundaries such as present and memory, self and other, public–private (cf. Stanley 1993). For example, Eakin (1985) believes that contemporary writers no longer consider that imagination and memory frame the autobiography as connected to some unmediated 'truth' of the past – the act of autobiography is in the present. Taken to an extreme, autobiography could be said to be

---

Box 4.6

Gullestad, M. (1996) *Everyday Life Philosophers*. Oslo: Scandinavian University Press.

The Norwegian anthropologist Marianne Gullestad explores the central values by which individuals organize their lives – the relationship between wider values in major institutions and the individuals' attempts to make sense of their particular circumstances – in other words, the question of what individuals take from others and how they adapt values and beliefs by an active reconstruction. She is interested, therefore, in the transmission of values in Norwegian society and how, at a time of uncertainty regarding broader social narratives, autobiography or other forms have an importance in guiding moral life. Gullestad provides four autobiographies taken from 630 stories (often very different in form) from a life story competition held between 1988 and 1989 (see Gullestad 1995). Eakin concludes his reading of Gullestad's study: 'We are always out of sync with our selves, always lagging behind, always trying to catch up retrospectively, for the self we seek turns out to be a self *in process*' (Eakin 1999a: 39–40).

'made up' descriptions of experiences as they may have occurred; such a recognition of the fictive nature of individual writing is not new but is often now accompanied by a new theoretical justification after postmodernism (Roos 1994: 6).

Realist, modernist and postmodernist views on life story analysis are often more similar on specific issues or approach than often appreciated (see Stanley 1992: 11–18). For example, while proclaiming the 'death of the author' (or a version of authorship) as someone with a superior position in relation to determination and interpretation of the text, Barthes also wrote an autobiography *Roland Barthes by Roland Barthes* (1977). This has been called a 'whimsical' piece since it plays with his former intellectual positions (Sim 1998: 192). Yet, for Hutcheon, it 'is hard to imagine a text that would address the issue of representation-as-construction more directly than this postmodern autobiography' (Hutcheon 1989: 41). He describes this stance, the 'simultaneous use and abuse of both realist reference and modernist self-reflexivity' as 'typically postmodern'. He argues that it was the modernist reaction to an assumed 'transparency' that showed photography and fiction to be intimately coded and passed this view of representation as construction rather than reflection on to postmodernism (Hutcheon 1989: 41).

Questions for autobiographical and biographical practice remain. Are there disciplinary differences regarding autobiography and biography? Should they be seen as distinct or exclusive or are the movements between disciplines – interdisciplinarity – to be seen as strength by linking issues of culture and memory, self and group identity, socialization and power? Such disciplinary 'flexibility' provides a problem, in terms of how it is perceived in such a multiplicity and away from the reassurance of categories of genre and the histories of particular forms of endeavour and interpretation and appreciation as within literature (see Marcus 1995: 16). Finally, as biographical researchers interested in the lives of others, we should be cognisant of our own individuality, our own stories, and how we relate to and construct the lives of others. There is a sense that our own autobiography, as Bakhtin argues, is always incomplete; we do not know its outcome (Dentith 1995: 7–8). But, the telling of 'our story' may be connected to the pursuit of 'authenticity' or an attempt to establish our individuality (see Widdicombe and Wooffitt 1995: 157).

Letters, diaries, memoirs and other personal 'artefacts'

Within the area of 'personal documents' a wide range of materials can be placed – letters, diaries, photographs, jewellery, old birthday cards and notes – a kaleidoscope of artefacts from life which can signify personal attachments to relationships in time and place. Individuals may specially store these, or often (as in the case of photographs of major life events) have a particular place on a desk or wall in the home (Clandinin and Connelly 1994: 420; see Pryce 1994). These materials revive memories and stories which we can retell about ourselves, and may intimately connect with self-identity. Even other forms of writing, which are not usually taken for examination, such as the curriculum vitae or the Internet web page, may be considered 'autobiographical practices' (Miller and Morgan 1993; Lee 2000). In writing autobiographies, letters and diaries, 'factual information' is given but detail of values and beliefs of individuals are also present (Golby 1994: 105). More generally the study of the 'visual' within qualitative practices such as biography and ethnography and the interpretation of documents within wider 'material culture' are undergoing increasing examination (see Harper 1994, 2000; Hodder [1994]2000; Lee 2000).

Within sociology letters have been used for their merits but have quite rarely been given detailed attention. It has been largely within historical and literary practice that they have been applied and assessed (see Scott 1990). Letters have commonly been drawn upon within biographical and autobiographical writing. For example, H. G. Wells presents various 'exhibits in evidence' in his autobiography to show the 'tone and quality' of his relations with his family and others (Wells 1934). One moving usage, in historical work, is Francis's study of Welsh miners who had fought in the Spanish Civil War which places their oral evidence of involvement alongside a selection of letters sent home at the time (Francis 1984). However, private letters were used by the Chicago School, for instance in Thomas and Znaniecki's *The Polish Peasant in Europe and America* ([1918–20]1958) where they were examined for material on personal life within marriage, family and the community of Polish immigrants to connect with generalization on the effects of migration and industrial/urban life in America. Thomas and Znaniecki organized over 760 letters according to 50 family groups and identified five general types: ceremonial, informing, sentimental, literary and business. Of course, letters can take many forms, and fulfil many purposes – business letters, family letters, love letters, fan mail, the anonymous threat and so on. They can vary between the more formal and informal, say according to business and friendship, are usually between a specific sender and recipient, and often a reply is expected. Also, usually they are not intended for publication but may be published later, for instance commonly after the death of the famous individual (as in Boswell's *Life of Johnson*) or open to the public in an archive. Private letters generally have opening and closing conventions, which indicate the relationship between sender and receiver. They are also a way of sharing meanings and providing accounts of experiences and ourselves (Clandinin and Connelly 1994: 421).

It may be argued that there has been a qualitative decline of written communication with the rise of oral and visual telecommunication but, in any case, diaries (which are relatively uncommon) and correspondence may still not give the inner motivations and feelings of the writers (Wallot and Fortier 1998: 367). In one view letters do not commonly have an appropriate focus to be of use; in addition, when the researcher edits such materials certain kinds of undeclared selection may operate (Plummer 1983: 24). More recently, letters have become more discussed in sociology as a qualitative resource and as sociologists have broadened their interests in other disciplines and materials. Letters may also be exchanged between researchers and between researchers and participants in a study (Clandinin and Connelly 1994: 421). It is difficult to construct a convincing 'taxonomy' of 'private' letters, say according to intimacy, types of relationship or form, although there are also types which appear to be becoming more common, such as the circulated Christmas letter between families, and 'newer' forms brought by the Internet. Generally, the distinctions between public/private and informal/formal are not always easy to maintain and conventions of writing are subject to change as wider social influences (modes of address, expression of sentiment, or imagery and myth) have an effect (see Golby 1994: 105).

The publication of diaries has become something of a vogue. The popularity of the 'diary' form of autobiography is increasing (at least in Britain) – whether fictive as in the case of the volumes tracing the lives and troubles of Adrian Mole and Bridget Jones, or 'factual' as in the best-selling political diaries of MPs Tony Benn and Alan Clark. In the case of Tony Benn, his nightly recordings on tape of the day's proceedings run into millions of words over the years and have been published and aired on radio. The public fascination with diaries seems to be for the insight into the inner lives and actions of individuals, especially those in power, that are not 'public'. In addition, television has brought the video diary where 'ordinary' members of the public record their thoughts and daily lives for later public consumption. Here, we can also mention the tradition of documentary film and fieldwork filming, and the later rise of TV 'faction' programmes. An extension of this may be the 'docu-soap' or filming of the working lives of people at an airport, hotel, or on the street as traffic wardens, or training to be doctors or veterinary surgeons, or even driving instructors and their pupils and so on, which have become ubiquitous on TV in Britain. The list of people and situations covered seems never ending, as we become more intrigued or voyeuristic in relation to the mundane lives of others. Rather differently, it seems that 'ethnographic filming' is being applied by advertising and consumer research to record daily consumption habits. At the widest, the diary is more than a chronological list of events but a reflection and ordering of experience (Clandinin and Connelly 1994: 421). There is also a sense that in writing or otherwise recording our experiences we are exploring and confirming the sense of what we are – an affirmation of our existence or being.

Within sociology, the use of diaries has not been a common feature of research. When diaries have been used sociologists have applied several types of method, e.g. asking individuals to fill a diary or give a detailed 'log' of a particular day (Plummer 1983: 17–21). Participants may also be asked to give written or tape recorded responses at particular intervals which are then analysed, or respondents may be interviewed later on their entries (Slim *et al.* 1998: 117–18). Mass-Observation in Britain used 'day surveys' and wartime monthly diaries in their research from a panel of volunteer respondents during World War II (see Jennings and Madge [1937]1987; Calder and Sheridan 1984; Sheridan 1985). Of course, diaries are commonly 'pre-existing' rather than requested by the researcher. Finally, diaries, letters and interviews at the time (e.g. from archives such as Mass-Observation, see Sheridan 2000), and recollections obtained recently, especially of major events in the past, may be brought together by social historians, local history groups, museums, commercial or other organizations and aimed at a broad 'popular audience'. For example, Inglis (1990) used a wide range of (old and new) oral and other sources in her study of the evacuation of children from British cities in World War II (see also Townsend and Townsend 1990). Many local bookshops and newsagents in Britain sell numerous histories on the local town in wartime or other topics containing photographs, commentaries and reminiscences.

Allport, in his evaluation – *The Use of Personal Documents in Psychological Science* (1942), regarded the private diary as providing a significant view of the life since the individual records significant personal feelings and events without the limitations of 'task-attitudes' which very often shape the letter or autobiographical writing and interviews (Denzin 1970: 228). The

---

Box 4.7

Townsend, C. and Townsend, E. (1990) *War Wives: A Second World War Anthology.* London: Grafton.

This is a collection of moving wartime experiences drawing on letters, diaries and memories of British and German women from very different backgrounds and war situations. The editors introduce the short extracts with some added concluding comments on the individuals' postwar lives.

Box 4.8

Inglis, R. (1990) *The Children's War: Evacuation 1939–45.* London: Fontana.

This social history of the evacuation of children in Britain during World War II uses a variety of library and archive material, including a range of documents from Mass-Observation (e.g. questions to children at the time on what they thought of the war), previously published personal accounts, and interviews with evacuees. The material is woven into a detailed commentary on the development of the evacuation and its social effects. The author seeks to give the personal experience of the evacuee children – she too experienced evacuation, from China back to the USA.

---

diary, for Allport, can be an intimate journal, a memoir or a log. Denzin says the intimate journal may be confessional in nature, the memoir may be similar to an autobiography but more an 'accounting' of the life and rather less about the more 'personal' aspects, and the log is a list of events or trips and is usually 'depersonalized' (Denzin 1970: 228–31). Feminist researchers helped to reinvigorate the examination of personal documents, including letters and diaries, to enable an understanding of women's experience and conditions beyond published sources, and connections between 'public' and 'private spheres' (see Anderson 1997). While recognizing certain methodological drawbacks (e.g. that such documents may be from women of a particular background), nevertheless they are important sources on women's lives to be compared with more public documents (see Reinharz 1992: 156–9). Within historical study, diaries (and letters and autobiographies) have figured prominently and questions of authenticity, authorship, credibility, sincerity and 'record', as Scott outlines, have been subject to scrutiny (Scott 1990: Ch. 8). He argues that authenticity and authorship are fundamental, particularly where someone else may have edited or censored parts of a document or the originator may be in doubt.

Credibility is not simply about factual accuracy but also (sometimes more importantly) the sincerity of reported views of feelings. The motivation to write a document (to justify, rationalize, or leave a 'record') and its importance as an activity for the self can be issues. Finally, interesting similarities and differences in how (e.g. the conventions used) and what (e.g. parts of life) is related can be found between memoirs, diaries and interviews gained from the same people (Thompson 1988: 244–5).

Again, a variety of other personal documents or artefacts in addition to letters and diaries, including, for example, web pages, lonely hearts advertisements, wills, CVs or even the way we 'personalize' spaces such as the office, may be considered autobiographical. Included here can be a whole range of individual or family 'memorabilia' – watches, photographs, rings, presentational items and heirlooms of all kinds can have tremendous significance for people, evoking many memories and often forming part of family myths and traditions (see Plummer 1983; Donnachie 1994). One source that is still underused in research, although often utilized in television histories, is the home video that can provide much visual and verbal information. These various personal documents may all be described as part of 'autobiographical' expression and be used to stimulate 'stories', thoughts and feelings. Photographs and other visual sources should be considered like other texts as having associated meanings (see Scott 1990: Ch. 8). It has become more common for old family photographs to be 'rescued' and placed in prominent positions in households, and so become a source of conversation. These can be taken as expressions of individual and family identity and can be a significant aspect of biographical investigation. Finally, a distinction may be made between 'documents' and 'records' (which may echo a distinction between speech and writing), with the former closer to speech and more 'personal' while the latter are more 'formal' and possibly 'restricted by laws regarding privacy, confidentiality, and anonymity' (Hodder [1994]2000: 704). However, in practice this distinction may be difficult to sustain in many cases where access to 'more personal' records may face similar restrictions.

Autobiographies have at least an initial difference from letters and diaries – the latter are contemporaneous (written within the day or soon after) with events and experience and are thus seen as having an advantage as a 'record' (Golby 1994: 105). It is worth remembering that individuals usually hope to give a positive view of themselves in public; even letters and diaries which are written as private may have some possible future audience in mind.

Case study
Ackroyd, P. (1991) *Dickens*. London: Minerva.

There are a wide variety of ways of producing a biography of an individual. As Smith describes, using the example of the life of Darwin, there are various sources from the author, which may be referred to by a biographer – autobiographical pieces, letters, diaries and the research and published work of the subject (cf. Darwin [1839]1997; Desmond and Moore 1991; Browne 1995; Slater 1996; Hibbert 2000). Dickens, a favourite for critical assessment of his novels and for biographies, can be taken as a case study to assess the use of autobiography and biography within biographical research. Dickens, in fact, wrote an autobiographical account of his life and was the subject of a biography by his friend Forster (1874) which has been followed by numerous other life studies and voluminous assessments of his literary work. There have also been collections of his journalism and exhaustive 'encyclopaedias' of his life, including summaries of his works, his London settings in life and novels, his connections with people and organizations, his 'hidden' life, his travels and reputation and so on (see Hardwick and Hardwick 1990; Tomalin 1991; Schlicke 1999).

The 'taken-for-granted' view of the biography is that it gives a 'picture' of the individual; usually the person described is famous in politics, sport or entertainment. Commonly, there is a chronology in approach, from early to subsequent career with details of main events and relationships. In examining an autobiography the assumption is that the told life will uncover the individual personality or feelings and intentions not usually relayed even perhaps to those close to the giver. Within the autobiography something may be given of the inner life alongside accounts of current and previous relationships with others.

Ackroyd's (1991) widely acclaimed and massive account of the life of Dickens gives perhaps the fullest 'portrait' of his life – including detail on his differing moods, his behaviour as others saw him, and his clothing and general appearance. It is an attempt, by utilizing as much information as possible, to provide the reader with an account that gives at least the impression of 'knowing' him. As Ackroyd says, he tried to bring in every source on Dickens's life – even the small details which may be reflected in the elements of his novels, in an attempt to give the incidentals of his life and his surrounding world. Here, the difficult task is to find, in the routine daily events, expressions of character and behaviour, the novels and other writings of Dickens, the origins of his creative endeavour and also to place him as part of his wider society (Ackroyd 1991: xvi). A further connected feature of Ackroyd's biography is a chapter where Dickens has a 'true conversation between imagined selves' including Wilde and others; a 'meeting' with Dickens; and a self-interview where he reveals his biographical method. This approach consciously blurs the fact–fiction divide in an imaginative attempt to uncover and report the life. At the furthest, this kind of work by biographers in postmodern guise may stand accused of using a mix of a cavalier use of facts and too much interpretive imagination (Roos 1994: 6). A postmodernist reply to this view would be that it is the nature of literature which is being challenged and the assumptions of a holism and chronology in subjective experiences coupled with an underlying notion of the 'centred self' (Hutcheon 1989: 23). Of additional interest is Ackroyd's view that his biographical treatment of Dickens may be historically specific. It may be seen as mistaken in several decades' time to emphasize how Dickens perceived reality – his own life and understanding of others – through his fiction (Ackroyd 1991: 944). Finally, Ackroyd also sees the writing of biographies and novels as having points of comparison; for instance, both must have an understandable narrative to provide an ordering of the world (Ackroyd 1991: 945–6).

Given Dickens's hectic daily round of letter writing, editing, writing serial parts for his novels and other activities it is not surprising that his 'imaginative' works of fiction and other parts of his everyday life were closely interrelated. At one point he compared life to a dream – as though he imaginatively moved between the different forms of consciousness, one influencing the other. Roberts (1996) argues that Dickens in *Bleak House* ([1853]1971) provides a 'moral statement' – a working out or thinking through, primarily through the character of Jarndyce, the guardian to the wards Clara and Richard, of his own life dilemmas (Roberts 1996: 81).

Dickens, in his novels, demonstrates a morality similar to some other Victorians whose public face was reflected at an inner psychological level. It was an opposition to forms of selfishness – wishing to find ways of effective social intervention but avoid self-obsession and indifference (see Newcomb 1989: 72–3; Collini 1993; Roberts 1996). Through Jarndyce, the resident of Bleak House, Dickens was able to examine his deep personal dilemmas in the social world through the imaginative form of the novel: 'For instance, he "fictionalised" real individuals in his novels, letters and other accounts and also "factualised" his fictional characters (by giving them a perceived reality in his various writings and performances)' (Roberts 1996: 87; see Ingham 1992: 133–44).

Of particular interest here for biographical method is Frank's idea that Dickens was exploring a 'romantic view' of the self in his later, increasingly dark and deeper fiction (Frank 1984). Using psychoanalysis, phenomenology and other philosophical and literary perspectives Frank argues that there is an emerging 'vision of the narrative self' and personal change:

> The autobiographical process, the one in which Dickens's David Copperfield will participate, becomes an act of self-creation. It repeatedly draws attention to the fictive status of the self, especially through its appropriation of other narrative conventions.
>
> (Frank 1984: 8–9)

The life and work of Dickens demonstrates the complex interrelation between his fiction and his daily life, between fictionalization of his life and the lives of others, and the processes of creation and recreation of his past, his present concerns and the attempt to find a future moral path. Novels for much of the social sciences would not figure as a research source, being regarded as mere 'fiction'. Within cultural and literary studies, however, they have long been taken as part of the genres of cultural production, reflecting wider historical cultural formation (cf. Williams 1958, 1961, 1977). For biographical study novels do provide insights into the interrelations between the author's inner and outer life. In the case of Dickens, this is more than the common recognition that *David Copperfield* (in particular) had an autobiographical cast or the simplest view that novel writing is 'autobiographical' since it is written by an author – at the extreme, a comment that could be made of any document, as a 'human document'. Dickens's novel writing was part of his busy daily activities – his other writing (letters, journalism), family and other personal relationships, professional activities, speeches and performances – and it was 'blurred' with them. Where the 'factual' ('real') life ends (of himself and others) and the imaginative world of his novels begins is not easily distinguished – the two coalesce. Rowland has combined the surviving parts of Dickens's autobiography with autobiographical 'fragments' from his letters, novels, essays, stories, travel writing and speeches to compile an early life in his own words (Rowland 1997). The life and the text interconnect as the author not only invests imagination or creativity in the novel but lives through fiction, just as fiction is lived. Biographical writing in this vein, as attempted in recent work, has tried to give the fullest portrayal of the 'life' – dress, voice, mannerisms, health, moods, and personal responses by others – along with the interweaving of chronology, summarized works and biographical experiment, including the deliberate use of genres, e.g. fictionalized speech. It is through the novel that the author may reveal the interior life and pressing concerns that are held secret or indecipherable in other contexts but are the impulses informing the range of daily biographical activities. In this way, the novel may be more revelatory of the self than other forms of writing.

Fiction and non-fiction

The questioning of the fact–fiction dichotomy erodes the stated differences between autobiography and other forms of writing – for instance, again the novel may be revelatory of the author's self and his or her relations with others. A comment by the English novelist Alan Sillitoe is apposite here on connections between his personal life and his novels. While he says his novel *Saturday Night and Sunday Morning* is not autobiographical, within it he declares he found his 'true voice' (Hawthorn 1987: 81). Hawthorn comments that this is not the voice of Sillitoe in the 'everyday' but neither is it purely 'invented' because it is described as my 'true voice'. For Hawthorn, it appears we have a number of voices upon which we, or writers in particular, can draw (Hawthorn 1987: 81). In addition, the view of the autobiography, within all its forms of expression (life story, memorandum, interview responses, the novel and other writings), as showing an inner truth, has been open to some scepticism. What is revelatory and what is 'fictive' in the presentation of a life to an audience even where the audience is the individual's own self? However, as Chamberlain and Thompson observe, the debate on the differences between fiction and non-fiction is 'increasingly arid' as the novel has also been perceived as containing a combination of 'experience, observation and imagination' and with auto-biography and other historical writing part of the genre of narrative (Chamberlain and Thompson 1998a: 3). More widely, it is claimed that novels may not only be used to reveal the inner life of the author but also as a source for wider cultural features relating to the family, gender, class, crime and health and all manner of popular discourses (Hammersley and Atkinson 1989: 131).

The exploration of 'factuality' within the novel and the 'fictionality' of research writing has produced a greater hybridity or meshing of forms of writing than is usually perceived, at least as relating to traditional genre distinctions (see Atkinson 1990). So, novel writing may share similarities with biography and ethnography and other methods in that there are stories related and types of description, dialogue, characterization that are present but not explicitly recognized and developed (Hammersley and Atkinson 1989: 131). Differences may remain since it can be argued that in autobiographical story writing or telling while there may be a striving for coherence and summary of the life (and lives still remain incomplete) the narrative has its inconsistencies – whereas in the novel the narrative usually has its logic and completeness (Roos 1994: 10). However, even here the distinction may not be so clear; for example, the novel may be authored so as to be fragmentary, inconsistent and moving backwards and forwards in time. The work of the novelist and essayist A.S. Byatt is of interest here. She has recently commented on the renewal of the historical novel in Britain – spurred by an 'impulse' to write histories of the marginalized. At the same time, she says recent historians (such as Schama) have attempted to bring back narrative to history (see Hobsbawm 1997). Thus, a new sense of storytelling in the novel (after a period of fragmented, non-linear and experimental forms) finds a counterpart in historical writing – the notion of 'history is fiction' has produced a new concern with fiction as history (Byatt 2000b: 11, 38). In a recent novel, *The Biographer's Tale*, Byatt explores current critical thought and the complexities involved in the construction of biography (Byatt, 2000a). It is the story of a critic's attempt to write a biography of a great biographer: to fit the bits and pieces of a life together, to solve puzzles – including those of his own life – and to discover what is fact and what is fiction. Ultimately, for communication to be possible in novels (and in autobiography and biography), there has to be what Bakhtin calls a 'dialogic relationship' – 'that artistic form and meaning

Box 4.9

Hoggart, R. (1958) *The Uses of Literacy*. Harmondsworth: Penguin.

Richard Hoggart, along with E. P. Thompson and Raymond Williams, laid the foundations for British cultural studies. In his classic study, *The Uses of Literacy* (1958), Hoggart analyses working-class home and communal life, including entertainment and reading, over a thirty-year or so period in the early twentieth century. The growth of literacy and values such as educational improvement are examined and contrasted with the spread and effect of newer forms of mass culture on working-class life. Hoggart draws upon his own personal experience as a working-class school boy in Leeds – while also taking working-class culture as a site for serious cultural analysis. He describes the 'scholarship boy' who becomes separated from family, peers and background, anxious and uprooted, and ill at ease with the middle classes (see also Hoggart 1968; see Roberts 1998). The study is a complex interpretation of his own personal mobility, working-class cultural change and shifts in popular cultural forms and values.

emerge between *people*' (Dentith 1995: 13). An audience has expectations according to pre-existing conventions and social context.

As a final point, the novels and 'popular' life stories that researchers read may also play a part in the forms of writing they employ. For example, the links between the social realism of the early American novel (and ordinary lives presented in magazines) and 'city' journalism and the work of Park (a former journalist) and his colleagues at the University of Chicago during the 1920s and 1930s have been commonly noted, and parallels between literary writing forms and ethnographic writing have recently been made (Atkinson 1990: 28–34; see Agar 1995). Of course, the life story in the life history document and the novel both contain a human story and our responses, as readers, include recognition and feeling.

Conclusion

Autobiographical and biographical writing are complex practices, which appear to defy simple generic classification. Life writing or 'personal documents' can take a wide range of forms and the 'autobiographical' can include numerous artefacts, including photographs and seemingly trivial materials, but may be invested with a great deal of significant meaning for the individual or group. In terms of published work, in addition to letters and diaries (private but published later or written for publication), the novel and other writing by an author for the 'public' can be adjudged to be 'auto-biographical'. Thus, for biographical research a very wide span of source material can be addressed, to enable an understanding of individuals and their responses to social circumstances. The challenge to 'authorship' has been a focus of contemporary literary criticism studies in relation to the construction of 'texts'. This issue has widened the question of the interpretation of texts – whether the attention should be the author, the text or the audience or, more fundamentally, whether the focus should move from authorship to the ambiguities or multiple voices of the text and the expectations and 'reading' of the audience. For biographical research, discussion of biography and autobiography shows the interrelated nature of forms of writing and the broad array of materials, which can be defined as 'autobiographical'.

Recommended reading

Anderson, L. (2001) *Autobiography*. London: Routledge. (A concise and informative review of the historical tradition of autobiographical writing and an examination of psychoanalytic, feminist and poststructuralist criticism with attention to subjectivity, representation and narrative.)

Biography (USA). (A journal which takes an interdisciplinary approach to the study of biography and biographical writing.)

Evans, M. (1999) *Missing Persons: The Impossibility of Auto/biography*. London: Routledge. (Evans considers a range of auto/biographical writing including men in the twentieth century and work on the Royal Family. In noting the popularity of auto/biography she argues that the intent to reveal the individual life presumes it is possible to know the individual; auto/biography is founded on fictions).

Marcus, L. (1994) *Auto/biographical Discourses: Theory, Criticism, Practice*. Manchester: Manchester University Press. (This is an examination of the complexity or 'hybridity' of the genre of autobiography in relation to such traditional distinctions as subject–object, public–private and fact–fiction.)

Sim, S. (ed.) (1998) *Postmodern Thought*. Cambridge: Icon Books. (A comprehensive review of the origins of postmodernist thought and its cultural context. It outlines postmodernist developments in philosophy, cultural theory, popular culture, cinema, music and other fields and includes a detailed dictionary of names and terms, and descriptions of the work of Derrida, De Man, Barthes and other leading writers.)

Swindells, J. (ed.) (1995) *The Uses of Autobiography*. London: Taylor and Francis. (This text examines a wide variety of writing on autobiography from a number of disciplines. It outlines the use of autobiography in historical contexts and across a range of countries, and in various practices such as 'performance art' and education. The book places the writing of autobiography within its social context and how it may be used to understand prevailing socio-political circumstances.)

5) Auto/biography and sociology

Auto/biography – definitions and relations

In 1993, *Sociology*, the journal of the British Sociological Association, produced a Special Issue on Biography and Autobiography in Sociology. This
issue marked a recognition of the revival of interest in the use of autobiography and biography within the discipline (*Sociology* 1993). These
areas of biographical research had lain semi-dormant within the discipline
since the late 1930s (see Chapter 3). An issue of *Current Sociology* in 1995
on biography consolidated the new position of the study of lives within the
discipline (*Current Sociology* 1995).

The express purpose of the Special Issue was to note the 'popular fascination' with autobiography and biography as reflected in awareness of the
critical and analytical discussion given to the genres across a range of disciplines (history, literary theory, anthropology, women's studies and cultural
studies) (Stanley and Morgan 1993: 1). It was a response within sociology
to the rising interest in the 'life', which built upon the earlier well-known
works by Bertaux (1981), Plummer (1983) and Denzin (1989) in the
previous decade. Sociology had seemed to lag behind the more complex
treatment of epistemological and other questions in the study of lives found
elsewhere. The notion of autobiographies as representing the conditions of
the lives of those involved rather than as being conceptualized as 'the textual
(graphing) construction of a self (auto) that actually does not exist in life

(bio) in the unitary and coherent form invoked through the conventions of the genre' was being scrutinized (Stanley and Morgan 1993: 1). Forms of biographical work, for Stanley and Morgan, had been present in socio-logical research through life histories, in types of interview and ethnographic practice. Additionally, work in various sociological sub-disciplines was not unconnected to biographical analyses, such as life course, work career, deviancy and the related areas of self and identity formation. As Stanley and Morgan point out, the production and analysis of lives through oral or life histories had been used in the study of events or process by interviews, as in ethnographic research, but now a more 'explicit' examination was challeng-ing 'modernist assumptions' concerning the subject and self (Stanley and Morgan 1993: 2).

The term 'auto/biography' as defined by Stanley reflects number of con-cerns:

Auto/biography . . . displaces the referential and foundational claims of writers and researchers by focusing on the *writing/speaking* of lives and the complexities of *reading/hearing* them. It also thereby unsettles notions of 'science', problematises the referential claims of social research, questions the power issues most researchers either silence or disclaim.

(Stanley 1994b: 89)

Stanley argues that these are not merely the concerns of auto/biography but also found in oral history and other fields. A textual concern does not imply that auto/biography is uninterested in everyday social lives or research as a type of practice (Stanley 1994b: 89). These various concerns have not been confined to British sociological work on biography; in var-ious ways they have also been very apparent within research groups in the European Sociological Association and the International Sociological Association. The rise of auto/biography is also part of a broader renewal of interest in the study of the life-course and biography. This growth is wit-nessed in the proliferation of books, specialist journals, research groups, courses and conferences. As Erben describes, these developments have been part of a trend which has a common thread that recognizes that indi-vidual motivations and social influences are not easily distinguishable (Erben 1998b: 4). This view purposefully attempts to show the interpene-tration of the individual and social structure as part of the narrative for-mation of identity.

The individual-society relation is seen rather 'less as a methodological hin-drance than a way of observing in the explanation of the *narrative* features of human identity, how the structural and interactional are intertwined'. In this way, biographical and autobiographical work can be conceived as a means of examining the 'the significance of selves' in connection with broader social values (Erben 1998c: 1).

Box 5.1

Stanley, L. (1992) *The Auto/Biography I: The Theory and Practice of Feminist Auto/Biography*. Manchester: Manchester University Press.

Within *The Auto/Biography I*, Stanley gives a very broad exegesis on the practices of autobiography and biography and the construction of a feminist auto/biography while also placing her own life and work. She is concerned with the interconnection between the individual and social structure, and the construction, presentation and reception of biographies and autobiographies. The ground covered moves between discussions of her family history, the photograph, the modern novel, feminist biographies, Victorian women's lives and serial killers. Her approach is shown in detail in her complex editing of the extraordinary diaries of a domestic servant, Hannah Cullwick, who was secretly married to Arthur Munby, her employer (see Stanley 1984). Stanley takes the reader through stages and changing interpretations as she undertook her reading/editing and challenges the 'microscope' (more information will give a closeness to the 'truth') approach of conventional biography.

Individual experiences and auto/biographical writing

A useful comparison can be made between auto/biography and oral history to highlight the auto/biographical 'programme'. For Bornat, there appears common ground in that both are concerned with how knowledge of lives is constructed and the nature of remembering the past – or how accounts are formed. Each then has an interest in reflexivity and 'both acknowledge the possibilities of a merging of categories: the individual and the social, the past and the present, fact and fiction, writing and reading' (Bornat 1994b: 18–19). Even so, Bornat argues that there are also substantial differences – the 'tasks' of both are different: for auto/biography theorizing seems to be a goal rather than, as in oral history, a means. In terms of method, while they share a concern with relations between self and society, in oral history these are 'interrogated' rather than 'imposed' on (oral, written or visual) texts. Finally, she says, there is a political difference with auto/biography 'challenging orthodoxies' in academic discourse whereas oral history is more directly political in its practice and concern for implications (Bornat 1994b: 19). Within auto/biography some would say that epistemological issues and questions of power in the construction of accounts are shared with oral history, but that auto/biography does have a wider methodological intent. For instance, Liz Stanley, who has done much to 'popularize' the idea of 'auto/biography', says there are common epistemological concerns arising in the exploration of connections between the current and the past, e.g. questions of memory. But she adds that there is attention to 'textual *politics*' – although it would be a mistake to say that auto/biography is merely dealing with the 'text'; the remit is the broader relations of power between the producers of the text and how the audience (readers/listeners) receives it. Thus, there is an interest in analyzing accounts in which connections are made with wider societal structures and processes (Stanley 1994b: 89). It is not merely a focus on the set of research relations between writer–researcher–audience but also the enveloping social frameworks that auto/biography explores. It is 'epistemologically oriented' with political issues arising from the changing distinctions between past–present, fact–fiction, and self–other. Within this work there is an analytic attention to both biographies and auto-biographies as revealed in written, oral, and visual texts while there is a conception of the active author engaged in 'textual political production' (Stanley 1994b: 89). Finally, auto/biography takes as a starting point the intent to shift across boundaries between different fields of study, genres and disciplines and while sociology provides its basis, it sees itself as actively interdisciplinary (Stanley 1994b: 89).

Whereas the starting point of oral history is with the oral testimony – usually 'translated' into the written account by the researcher – auto/biography attempts an initial inclusiveness to engage with a wider range of biographical and autobiographical accounts and forms (letters, diaries, novels, CVs, the pictorial). The 'text' is more central and the nature of auto/biographical representation, including in the formation of identity, is a usual starting point. For auto/biography it is the fuller representational and interpretative process from individual–researcher–audience in their contexts which is at issue; the 'text' is more broadly conceived than 'the oral' (or its written-down form) and interpretation more than the 'historical'. This is not to suggest that oral history has ignored different forms of materials (oral, written, filmic) and interpretation. In auto/biography there has been a strong influence from literary studies and critiques in relation to biographical representation, for example surrounding the issue of whether the autobiographical and biographical refer to the 'actual' life of the individual and also, centrally, the life of the writer/researcher. Certainly, oral historians have not been unaware of such issues and do consider them but in auto/biography they are more central themes. Epistemological and theoretical concerns have been so to the forefront in auto/biography that some critics might suggest that analysis loses sight of what is being sought – knowledge and understanding of 'real lives'.

Running through much of the debate in auto/biography on lives and representation has been a postmodern or deconstructionist influence; the implication that 'the self is *constructed* in auto/biographical writing, rather than being fully-formed, and then *represented* (either partially or in total) by the auto/biographer' (Aldridge 1993: 56). Aldridge says that questions surrounding the selectivity of memory, seeing the past through present time, the interlinkings between the writer's life and what is written, the postmodern challenge to the idea of a knowing stable self, and the active reader, all challenge the notion of the text being simply referential to the life (Aldridge 1993: 56–7). In part, this challenge has drawn auto/biography away from a given method of data collection towards a wide number of sources or 'texts' (and intertextuality), including letters, diaries and novels, due to the influence of literary studies. But, for writers such as Erben (1998b) and Stanley (1994b) in auto/biography, the individual does not disappear into a text construction; the text is actively produced as part of daily life. The proponents of auto/biography attempt to retain the connections with 'real lives' by analysing how lives are written and communicated and read by an audience. According to Stanley, auto/biographical work, the researcher as a producer and not simply a recipient of 'knowledge', leads to a deep questioning of ideas of 'science' and the referential assumptions within research practice (Stanley 1994b: 89).

Feminism and auto/biography

Feminism has had a considerable influence on auto/biographical research, for instance in an emphasis on relating individual experience and the cross-disciplinary approach to ideas and practice. At a general level, in auto/biographical research, there is the attempt to transcend established academic boundaries – to see the points of connection and interrogate traditional demarcations. In order to avoid the separation of the 'personal' from the 'socio-political' and uncover the hidden lives of women, a guiding principle from feminist research is the use of an historical perspective in which to place the research activity and the previous influences on the researched (Reinharz 1992: 250). Feminist perspectives have given auto/biography the notion of the 'personal is political' which, in feminist research, begins research from the standpoint of women's experiences.

It can be argued that the interest in biography and auto/biography has increased due to the focus on the personal or intimate in the social sciences, including here the uncovering of the lives of women but also the attempt to rectify the neglect of various minority groups. In part, for Evans, this shift has been due to a return to the 'smaller scale' because of a recognition of the limits of the 'grand narrative' (M. Evans 1993: 5). A 'new pluralism' is developing which allows for 'liberating possibilities', especially for women and sexual minorities – and a new emphasis on those who are not male, white and celebrities (M. Evans 1993: 6). Reinharz argues that feminist researchers seem especially attracted to writing across disciplinary boundaries and broadening methodological conventions, for instance as in Liz

Stanley's injunction to consider the historical in order to understand the present (Reinharz 1992: 250; see also Stanley 1984; Olesen 2000). The eclectic outlook of feminist research, and its similarity with auto/biographical work, is demonstrated in Reinharz's 'meta-induction' or 'inductive definition' of feminist methodology which includes multiple research methods, guidance by feminist theory, the researcher as a person, and the 'special' relationship between researcher and researched, and audience (Reinharz 1992: 240; see Eichler 1997: 12–13).

In short, feminist analysis lays emphasis on the reflexive aspects of practice – the self-monitoring but interrogative nature of research in which the individual and social action are consciously placed within the wider sociopolitical context; while later feminist work has recognized 'emergent complexities' including the differentiation of women's experiences and issues surrounding the researcher's own life and characteristics (Stanley 1993: 44; Olesen 2000). The questions of voice and power in the interview relationship are major areas in feminist writing in that women should be empowered to give their voice – to speak for themselves. The difficulty here is how much the researcher should 'mediate' and whether some mediation is unavoidable (Reinharz 1992: 137). There are differing views on how much the researcher's interpretation is to overlay the voices of women. Reinharz points out that even when the researcher is not speaking it does not mean that interpretation has not taken place. Involvement brings interpretation, and feminist researchers should give the audience an analysis, which indicates the approach being applied (Reinharz 1992: 137–8). Finally, Stanley and Wise add that feminist theory should not place the academic as the 'expert' but practise a 'grounded' approach which avoids simplistic inductivism. In their definition, feminist theory is drawn from experience subject to the analytic awareness of 'enquiring feminists' which is reflexive and self-reflexive and widely accessible; it should not be held 'sacrosanct and enshrined' in texts which are continually scrutinized (Stanley and Wise 1990: 24). An openness of intent and a reflexive monitoring are taken within auto/biographical research as important aspects of its practice.

Intertextuality – written and oral texts

The issue of 'intertextuality' raises questions surrounding 'representation'. The idea of intertextuality derives from a poststructuralist view of texts as composed of references to other texts or transforming other texts and, from a postmodern perspective, a view that meanings relate to other meanings in some endless signification. Dentith points out that the term, deriving from Kristeva's particular appropriation of Bakhtin during the 1960s, means two things. First, that particular writing uses other forms of writing and draws on and 'reinflects' or 'redirects' the discourses present in society. Second, there is a radical review of subjectivity – involving the erosion of subjectivity in relation to aesthetic work or, more profoundly, the loss of any subjectivity as subjects are seen as sites where multiple texts are interrelated (Dentith 1995: 95–6).

In auto/biography, the intent is more limited or, rather, 'grounded': various types of texts include or refer to others in a kind of conversation of discourses but, importantly, intertextuality is reformulated within a sociological context rather than as a limitless 'play of meaning' found in an extreme postmodernism (Sim 1998: 284–5). It also seeks to avoid the 'real problems of epistemological ambivalence, political ambiguity and occasionally unconstrained pluralism within postmodernism' (Boyne and Rattansi 1990: 39). A concern for intertextuality, for auto/biography, should not be left to the deconstructionists:

> *Intertextuality:* Representations of reality and reality itself cannot be prised apart. We understand the social world through the lens of prior representation, because whenever something is invoked which happened somewhere else, or in some other time, or to someone else, then representation is being utilised. A concern with representation is not the prerogative of deconstructionists, but is fundamental to any sociological understanding of social interaction.
>
> (Stanley and Morgan 1993: 3; see Hutcheon 1989: 54)

While not following the extremes of trends in intertextuality and representation, a key notion in auto/biography is that a variety of texts should be investigated without giving an advantage to one but rather to establish the interrelation between written, oral and other mediums (Temple 1994: 31). For instance, Temple discusses the interpretation and representation debate in the context of the differences and similarities between written and oral texts and the assumption that the latter are sometimes claimed to be more authentic. Rather than applying some given idea of 'validity', she prefers to stimulate a discussion around how types of accounts are produced (Temple 1994: 32). Oral historians, she argues, have assumed oral accounts to be more interactive in contrast to the more static, 'given', written account. Instead, she says, types of texts should be seen as 'social moments'; using her own research on British Poles and her associated personal experience she argues that both written and oral texts can be interrogated although in a different manner. In both, meaning is mutually constructed or negotiated by writer/teller and researcher; texts 'cross-reference' each other – there is not a 'hidden truth'. She concludes that, since the spoken may also be rehearsed while the written can be relatively spontaneous, one type should not necessarily be privileged over another (Temple 1994: 37–40).

Hermeneutics, phenomenology and narrative texts

Within auto/biography the stress on everyday action and meanings, derived from phenomenological sociology, Meadian interactionism and the *verstehen* tradition of Dilthey and Weber, has been brought within a broadly hermeneutical stance on biographical investigation. For Erben:

Biographical method, the study of life history and life courses, as we may call it, is concerned with the hermeneutical investigation of the narrative accounts of lives and selves. Hermeneutics is, quite simply, the theory or science of interpretation, and hermeneutical investigation is a method of analysis applicable to all forms of cultural life. For hermeneutical research, cultural life is regarded as a composition of cultural texts. Texts are areas of signification having cohering and recognizable cultural identities, e.g. a hockey match, *Hamlet*, a hospital ward, the class system, Mrs Thatcher, an unemployed school leaver. In the case of a biography, a life or self is regarded as a text.

(Erben 1996: 160)

Erben says the auto/biographical method connects with the notion of the 'hermeneutic circle' – including the accumulation of interpretations as texts are considered and a recognition of consciousness of the interpreter (Erben 1996; see Brown 1978). He makes a plea for a bridge 'between hermeneutics (where the emphasis is on the exegetical interpretation of the data) and phenomenology (where the emphasis is on the establishment of subjects' meanings)' by indicating a mix of types of hermeneutics (for example, from Gadamer and Ricoeur) and the 'sociological phenomenology' or '*verstehen* method' (cf. Weber). By a '*verstehen hermeneutics*' subjects' meanings can be placed within a hermeneutic understanding (Erben 1998b: 7). The aim is to broaden a phenomenological approach since, as Scott explains, a 'purely phenomenological perspective' assumes that individuals have a complete understanding of their perspectives operative in their ordinary actions. There are limits to individuals' knowledge of the contextual structuring of their lives and they may not be fully aware of the unconscious basis and unintended consequences of their own actions (Scott 1998: 33). For writers such as Erben, rather than a forlorn attempt to reflect an individual life fully, attention should rest on the ambiguity and incompleteness of lives.

According to Erben, in terms of procedure, verstehen hermeneutics can exercise 'good faith' and a clear methodology as 'safeguards'. In particular, in biographical research 'authenticity' can be achieved by 'analytical coherence', 'referential adequacy' and an 'instrumental pertinence' (Erben 1998b: 8). Erben sees parallels with literary analysis and, as elsewhere in auto/biographical writing, he cites C. W. Mills's notion of 'imagination' and applies this to qualitative research, particularly as part of interpretation, to identify important aspects and relations in the data and the whole life of the individual studied (Erben 1998b: 9–10). Here is recognition of the time spent in interpretation and also the role of 'imaginative constructions' in research (see Morgan 1998) or, from a more phenomenological perspective, an increased 'awareness and openness' to 'human realities' (Bruyn 1966: 272). Some comparison can be made here with 'objective hermeneutics' as developed by German sociology, which has attempted to find qualitative alternatives to traditional scientific principles while extending beyond the phenomenological account, and has variously drawn upon narrative interviewing, grounded theory and micro-analysis of texts (Denzin 1989: 55; Miller 2000: 130–6; Thompson 2000: 284–6; see Alheit 1994). (Other writers have also sought such links, see Addison 1999.) Miller writes of objective hermeneutics:

'Objective' since the analysis proceeds on a step-by-step basis, with each supposition or proto-hypothesis being immediately evaluated against interview transcript material. 'Hermeneutic' since the researcher is aware that any material being produced by the interviewee has been generated with regard to both the interviewee's subjective perception of his/her situation and history and the interviewee's perception of the researcher and the relationship between the two of them. Finally, the researcher himself/herself will filter the material selectively through the mesh of their own perceptions at the stage of analysis; hence, 'objective hermeneutics'.

(Miller 2000: 131–2)

Rosenthal gives a particular use of hermeneutical procedure; she advocates a 'hermeneutical case reconstruction' in her studies of family and life stories:

In analyzing the interviews, particular attention is paid to the structural differences between what is experienced and what is narrated: between experienced life and narrated life, i.e. life history and life story. On the one hand, we tried to reconstruct what the biographer actually experienced during this sequence of their life and, on the other hand, how they present their life in a present-day interview.

(Fischer-Rosenthal and Rosenthal 1997: 9; see also Rosenthal 1993, 1998)

Fischer-Rosenthal and Rosenthal add:

Reconstruction and sequentiality are the key principles in this method. The texts are not subsumed under specified categories, but rather are analyzed for meaning in the context of the entire text (= interview). The sequential compilation of the text of the life story and the chronology of biographical experiences in the life history play an essential role.

(Fischer-Rosenthal and Rosenthal 1997: 9)

They say that in the analysis of the narration certain 'thematic fields' become apparent which are interlinked. Thus, the life story is not a collection of random events; instead the latter are selected and within a 'context of meaning'. The life history or life story is 'socially constituted'; they argue that their work, like the work of other German sociologists such as Alheit, Kohli, Schütze and others, examines the interrelation between the individual and society within the study of biography (Fischer-Rosenthal and Rosenthal 1997: 10).

Time perspectives – Mead, Schutz and Ricoeur

Auto/biography has placed considerable emphasis on the place of time within biographical research and utilized the writings of Mead, Ricoeur and Schutz (see Erben 1993; Roberts 1999a). In its interest in time, auto/biography is reflecting the growth of discussion on the importance of time in social theory (cf. Adam, 1990, 1995). For instance, Mead's emphasis on the importance of time and change – including the possibilities of 'novelty' – has been one source of influence:

> Mead's theory of time conceived of the past and the future as expansions out of the present, rather than the common conception of a sequence proceeding from the past, to the present, to the future. The reconstruction of the past and the anticipation of the future arise from the same foundation, the reality of the present. The past, therefore, is not a fixed condition of a structured time period, but will vary in accordance with any particular present.
> (Petras 1968: 12–13; see Mead 1932, 1964: 328–41)

So even if we had all the relevant materials from a person's life in helping to produce our portrait, the 'truth' would still reside in the present, and a later present would again reconstruct it according to its 'emergent nature' (Petras 1968: 13). As Adam observes:

> . . . reality to Mead exists in the present. The present implies a past and a future, but they are denied existence. Any reality that transcends the present, he argues, must exhibit itself in the present.
> (Adam 1990: 38; see also Zeitlin 1973: 232–3)

Schutz's phenomenology has been another influence on the question of time in biographical study. Time is implicated in his discussion of meaning, social consciousness and interpersonal relations (Adam 1990: 35). As Schutz says on the 'reflective attitude':

> What alone I can grasp is rather my performed act (my past acting) or, if my acting still continues while I turn back, the performed initial phases (my present acting). While I lived in my acting in progress it was

an element of my vivid present. Now this present has turned into past, and the vivid experience of my acting in progress has given place to my recollection of having acted or to the retention of having been acting.

(Schutz 1971: 214)

Box 5.2

Roberts, B. (1999) Some thoughts on time perspectives and auto/biography, *Auto/Biography*, VII, (1/2): 21–5.

Roberts outlines a number of 'time perspectives' that are given by individuals in describing their lives, for instance, the past as past or the past in the future, or the present in the past, and so on. Time 'orientations' are seen as general moods or outlook (e.g. nostalgia, prediction, and reminiscence) which are given in statements, summaries or metaphors. Drawing on the work of Mead and Schutz, he offers a model that may aid future research to map the movement between time perspectives in accounts and provides an alternative to the simple chronological assumptions that have informed the study of lives. This model was stimulated by a realization of the complexity of how individuals and groups connect past–present–future through the biographies he collected as part of a study of social change in a former mining valley in south Wales (Roberts 1999b, 1999c). Major industrial and environmental change had made the 'past' an important topic:

... had the 'past' and all its social traditions and resonances finally 'gone'? Would it return? Did it remain but would die? ...
A single individual could announce that the past was lost forever, while in the same commentary also maintain that there was still the traditional 'communality' of valley life; or state that things had changed but could or would return to a familiar older pattern ...
We can say that there was a movement between 'time perspectives' in the individuals and groups in the community as understandings of the past and future were located in the ongoing present.

(Roberts 1999a: 22)

Finally, the more recent work of Ricoeur on 'narrative time' has been an important source for a number of auto/biographical researchers. Ricoeur addresses the 'illusion of sequence' or chronology/chronological time; he calls for a more 'authentic' examination of narrative time which may also challenge the 'recourse to a-chronological models, such as nomological laws in history or paradigmatic codes of literary criticism' (Ricoeur 1981: 165). He argues that both chronological sequence and a-chronological models can be avoided by showing the 'deeper experience of time'. He argues that narrativity and temporality are intimately connected. Narrative structures can be studied according to the temporal dimensions of 'plot' – 'the intelligible whole that governs a succession of events in any story' (Ricoeur 1981: 167; see White 1987: 173). He says that 'anti-narrativists' in the study of history and structuralists in literary criticism have taken a chronological, linear model of time in their theories of history and fictional narratives and have emphasized 'nomological models and paradigmatic codes'. Thus, most historians have become distanced from storytelling due to a 'poor concept of "event"' and of narrative, while literary critics have either concentrated on a 'labyrinthine chronology' or on a-chronological models (Ricoeur 1981: 167). The rejection of narrative has neglected what a '. . . theory of narrative could offer to a phenomenology of time experience. To put it bluntly, this contribution has been almost null because *time* has disappeared from the horizon of the theories of history and of narrative' (Ricoeur 1981: 168).

The discussion of narrative and time has significant implications for the study of biography; for instance, Usher points to the relevance of time in biography in connection with the self (Usher 1998). He argues that just as post-structuralist writers gained acceptance for a 'decentred self' so we must deploy a 'decentring of time' in analysis. The common view of time as according to succession or flow based on the powerful model of clock time (as objective and measurable) also makes an understanding of 'lived time' difficult. Usher, therefore, questions both the notions of centred time and centred self within the development or succession model of the self (Usher 1998: 19, 22). For Stanley, lives have to be seen as 'in time' but also according to 'purpose' and audience interpretation: '. . . a purpose connected with audience as well as with that reflective engagement with the lives of self and others invoked by the term "auto/biography"' (Stanley 1994a: ii).

The question of time is therefore important in auto/biography as seen, for example, in using 'time perspectives' (Schutz 1971: 214; see Roberts 1999a) or how individuals move between past, present and future in a complex way – the past as gone or still here or to return. Individuals select, summarize or resequence events and their meaning – thus a biographical narrative is not simply linear, a chronology, but a complex interlinking of perceptions of the past and future within the experience of the present and its shifting contexts (Temple 1995, 1996; Roberts 1999a).

The researcher as an auto/biographer

The expansion of biographical research in sociology has paralleled an interest in the life of the sociologist. During the 1970s Horowitz asked leading sociologists to report on their type of sociology, its influences and effects, but more particularly he was interested in the usually hidden 'subjective side' of

---

Box 5.3

Temple, B. (1996) Time travels: time, oral histories and British–Polish identities, *Time and Society*, 5(1): 85–96.

Temple examines the relationship between time, researchers and subjects based on her in-depth interviews in eight households in northern England. She argues that research involves researchers in dealing with the past, present and possible futures – their own as well as those of the subjects of their investigations. Researchers are biographers who obtain material about individuals' lives and select and interpret what is said: 'They cannot gather or present information about every facet of people's lives, so they select what is of interest to them and interpret it from their point of view. In this sense they are also autobiographers' (Temple 1996: 85). For Temple, research on identity and ethnicity over time must recognize that an interpersonal, time-related, context-laden and changing phenomenon is being considered.

---

methodology (Horowitz 1970b; see Riley 1988). He was concerned with the 'subjective processes' underneath the seeming rationality of the sociological product and how the path of becoming a sociologist connected to the 'sociologist becoming a person' (Horowitz 1970a: 12). The later agenda set by auto/biography, while recognizing its influences from elsewhere and that its programme is not unique, is to take this attention to the life of the researcher further. It does so by questioning the assumed boundaries between biography–autobiography, self–other, and public–private. Also, as we have seen, it challenges notions of development and linearity in auto/biographical accounts and emphasizes the relations between narrative and time, and reflexivity in research. So, the researcher is also a narrator and an active producer of 'knowledge' in research. 'Auto/Biography' is not:

> . . . simply a shorthand representation of autobiography and/or biography but also [a] recognition of the inter-dependence of the two enterprises . . . In writing another's life we also write or rewrite our own lives; in writing about ourselves we also construct ourselves as somebody different from the person who routinely and unproblematically inhabits and moves through social space and time.
>
> (Morgan 1998: 655)

Thus, the researcher is also involved in writing his or her life, reflecting on experiences both within and outside the research context – both are also related. Here, there is the 'intellectual biography' of the researcher who not only 'translates' the experience of others but also writes and interprets their

---

Box 5.4

Roberts, B. (1998) An auto/biographical account of educational experience, in M. Erben (ed.) *Biography and Education*. London: The Falmer Press.

Here, Roberts reflects on his working-class upbringing and education from the mid-1950s and explores how he was able to obtain educational success. He relates the 'mystery' of his schooling to the crossing of social boundaries and the feelings of loss and anxiety the changes produced: 'I wanted to learn and do well but the experiences of streaming and selection produced an anxiety and protectiveness towards family and social background.' He connects this experience to wider changes in educational opportunities and accounts of others who have recounted a similar process. Roberts concludes that his academic interest in identity and biography, he now realizes more than previously, has been intertwined with his auto/biographical concerns.

---

own life (Stanley 1993; see Temple 1997: 608–9). Finally, identity is 'narrational' and 'lives' are formed by the narratives through which time is experienced which also has consequences for how the researcher sees him/herself (Erben 1998b: 13). The practice of the researcher in the auto/biographical approach is given a central position – summarized by 'research as auto/biography' or Stanley's 'auto/biographical I' (Temple 1994: 32–3). Temple argues that the importance of 'the autobiographical I' is due to its ability to allow others (an audience) to relate to a text – so the researcher has to make

---

Box 5.5

Stanley, L. (1994) Sisters under the skin? Oral histories and auto/biographies, *Oral History*, Autumn, 22(2): 88–9.

Stanley relates her own family background and academic interests and career to the practices of oral history and auto/biography. She says: '"Oral histories" . . . seal the circle between now, the present, and then, the past: stories "telling the tale" of past people and events, which are used to shape the present by proscribing and prescribing the acceptable possibilities. Oral history conceived thus is also a metaphor for the family life I grew up in' (Stanley 1994b: 88).

---

assumptions apparent: 'The connections between the autobiography of the researcher and the biography of the subject are described by "auto/biography" and the "I" denotes a process of knowledge construction in which the researcher is active' (Temple 1994: 33).

The researcher and the researched subject

The traditional conception of the researcher has been of someone who maintains a personal distance from those researched and the context studied. The ruling notion was of an objective researcher who collects data and who, it is assumed, provides a superior account of the cultural situation of the group. More latterly, the role of the researcher's life in the research process is increasingly part of methodological discussion – the inequalities of power in the relationship, the differing definitions and collaboration, the 'voices' in the text and the construction of the research text in drawing on varied disciplines and genres.

Stanley employs the idea of 'auto/biographical I' to indicate and explore the interrelations between the researcher's own life – autobiography – and the biography of the researched subject. This means that we do not merely recognize that we include others as colleagues and researched in writing about our lives. As researchers we should clarify and reflect on how our life experience before and during the research affects our activities, assumptions, interpretations and so on. Implicated here is the complexity of experience, how the researcher and the researched influence each other and collaborate in biographical exchange (Temple 1994: 33; see Stanley 1992). Stanley and Wise argue forcefully that in traditional research, feelings and emotions are not seen as acceptable and should be prevented whereas, they say, this is a simplified and inaccurate view of research practice. Instead, research includes an interactive relationship – the researcher is a 'person' present in research – a fact which should be seized upon rather than extinguished (Stanley and Wise 1993: 161). In addition, in writing the research report, as auto/biographical and other researchers have made clear, reflexive researchers should examine how writing takes many forms and monitor their own auto/biographical presence.

Despite greater openness and collaboration the questions of power in the research relation remain, such as the different rewards arising for those involved, the researcher's responsibility towards the researched and the finished document, and so on (Cotterill and Letherby 1993: 72).

In summary, questions regarding the degree of collaboration, the extent and nature of the researcher's voice and biographical experience in structuring research, while not unique to auto/biographical research, are key issues in its practice. At the same time, there is importance attached to the reception or reading of accounts; despite genre conventions and other factors, the text cannot fully define how an audience will give meaning to its content.

Individual lives and social lives

A prominent feature of auto/biography is not only the aim to understand individual lives but also their production within the 'social'; it claims that biography can show the personal feelings and beliefs as they arise in the interplay of 'individual' and 'social' elements. Auto/biographical work, it is argued, deals not merely with individual but also social definitions – individuals as acting, experiencing, but within social contexts or structures. Thus, the dichotomy between individual and society, and action and structure, should be challenged and the individual seen as a 'social being' (see M. Evans 1993: 12).

'Autobiographical experience' is to be set within the group and not conceived solely as individual. During its telling, the autobiographical account can relate the biography of others (Stanley and Morgan 1993: 2). In the auto/biographical approach individual narratives are taken from a wide variety of sources not usually referred to within sociological enquiry (Erben 1996; Morgan 1998). Auto/biography tackles the individual–society connection in two ways: first, in situating the writing of autobiography within its socio-historical context and, second, relatedly, auto/biography reflexively examines its forms of practice. On the latter, for example, auto/biography has taken the argument found elsewhere that the lives given by minority or oppressed groups challenge the 'universality' of the developmental, linear narrative in autobiography which historically represents a dominant, male, white model (Usher 1998: 26). Those in subordinate positions may have alternative understandings and narrative forms; they can demonstrate a multiple or 'decentred subjectivity' (Usher 1998: 26–9). On the former individual–society connection, it is argued that auto/biography has to be reflexive regarding its own socio-historical position. It has placed itself as part of the 'biographical turn' or the rise of the 'personal' in the social and human sciences. Evans comments that in the social sciences the questioning of 'grand narratives' by postmodern theory has not merely allowed space for an interest in the 'small scale' she further suggests that the notion of the disappearance of the 'future' or, further the postmodern sense of a variety of 'existant futures' gives a 'new vitality' to 'the past' (M. Evans 1993: 6–7).

Case study
Auto/biography and education

Auto/biographical research has examined a very wide range of areas across disciplines; some studies have practical social policy implications, while others are more concerned with important methodological questions. In the latter, issues addressed have included the use of letter writing, diaries and other unusual (for sociology) sources and interview relationships, writing one's own autobiography, and the researcher's relationship with those studied. Substantive areas have included the body, death and illness, nationalism, sexual identities, intellectual influences on researchers, the CV, historical biographical records and past personal relationships, lives of famous writers or those prominent in other fields of public life and community studies (see Sparkes 1993, 1997a, 1997c; Erben 1998a; *Auto/Biography* (UK journal)). Within these varied sources and interests at least three areas are prominent – methodological discussion, an interest in literary sources (novels, diaries) and figures, and educational experience (e.g. in schooling, college, and special needs). In fact, the concern with education has been quite pronounced – perhaps auto/biographical writers are drawn to the area due to their own position and reflection on their own (usually long) educational experience. But, it may also be due to the questions of transition, change in identity and circumstance that biography in education reveals (Scott and Usher 1996; Erben 1998a).

Chris Mann in her study of how adolescent girls make choices in their lives provides an example of auto/biographical work in education (Mann 1994, 1998a, 1998b). She worked in a number of educational establishments and applied a range of qualitative methods to 'investigate the ways family dynamics contribute to the educational success of young women'; she collected about sixty quite short narratives from girls coming to the end of schooling. Group discussion had enabled some complex or hidden factors to arise; she asked them to write an 'educational autobiography' within which, if they wanted, to explore these private elements. Mann allowed the girls to reflect on their stories; she asked her respondents to attempt both to remember and explain through the narrative (Mann 1994: 61–2). She describes these stories as written in the 'flood of experience' giving hopes, fears, joy and pain. One example, Sally's Story, relates:

> 'Weirdo', 'a stupid snob' and 'Concorde nose' – these are some of the names people called me at my primary school which I guess shows the shallowness and ignorance of their lives. It all started when I was about 8 or 9 years old I suppose. We hadn't moved house very long, and were strangers to the area, which I suppose in a rather rural area such as this was rather unusual.
>
> (Mann 1994: 62)

Sally adds:

> When I left primary school to go to secondary school everything changed. I made new friends who respected me, and I enjoyed the work and the atmosphere of the place too . . . Mum encouraged me a lot with

my work at school and that gave me the motivation I needed. I think the stability of my home life helped as well . . .

(Mann 1994: 62–3)

Mann comments that Sally presents herself as intelligent; in early schooling she was seen as a threat due to her different and single parent family background. She interestingly describes her reactions to Sally's story – her relationships in the group, her choice of a conversational and humorous style, and her personal response to her 'voice'. Mann identified with this story because as a child she had been brought up in a council flat but had been 'grudgingly' received into a 'rather smart middle-class primary school in a "nice area" ': 'In that sense I was a stranger . . . all my early school memories are of being the outsider . . .' (Mann 1994: 65)

Drawing on 'feminist autobiography' she emphasizes her initial research stance as founded on women's experiences. She based her work on a view of past and current everyday experience in biography as part of wider relationships that shape individuals (Mann 1994: 60). More particularly she is influenced by feminists (e.g. Steedman; Walkerdine) who have given the 'contextual aspects of educational experience' and 'use an autobiographical approach to describe their experiences as working class achieving girls negotiating class, gender, home and education' (Mann 1994: 60). Mann contrasts her work with the male autobiography which often gives a 'vision of masculinity that projects a unified transcendent self'; but for women to write an autobiography they have to address 'those earlier selves, and the contemporary selves "still in hiding" ' (Mann 1994: 60–1).

The focus is on relationships and a recognition that these are shaped within 'the similarities and differences of the people involved, and will depend on issues of class, age, race and gender', and that the manner and type of stories related are grounded in power relations and various audiences. She advocates a textual analysis – processes of 'listening' – to understand the lives of the girls studied which pays attention to the narrative direction of the story, 'emotional and intellectual presentation of the "I" ', the researched–researcher relation and the wider socio-cultural context (Mann 1994: 61). Elsewhere, Mann gives the following benefits of educational life histories in understanding how girls understand educational choices:

These educational life histories suggest that the negotiations girls are involved in, and the strategies they adopt as they make choices about education are all part of the process of defining identity . . . The life histories suggest that while identity may be conceptualized within large collective social identities such as class, race and gender, these elements work together in unexpected and subtle ways. In addition, as girls negotiate interactions between the triangle of school, home, and friends, perhaps personal relationships give a psychological undertow to the struggle to find an educational identity. Educational life histories offer a means of exploring such complexities. They also offer a methodological approach that may map changes in social meanings.

(Mann 1998b: 57)

Auto/biographical work on education has included reflections on the researcher's own social origins and educational experience (cf. Roberts 1998), as well as the 'auto/biographies of learning' (Parker 1998: 118), stories of individuals with learning difficulties, and teachers' lives. On the latter, Sparkes explores the emerging relation between a researcher and a teacher according to gender and sexual orientation and shows the ethical dilemmas surrounding trust, friendship involved, and the possibilities for the initiation of change (Sparkes 1994a, 1994b). He argues that rather than merely giving a voice in the construction of life histories, there is a need to see the potential for solidarity and for possibilities of initiating change. Sparkes describes the 'emerging' personal relationship with the young teacher and the self-scrutiny of his own feelings and the issues of 'voice' and 'representation' in this type of research. A parallel study of a teacher is Scott's interpretation of the life of a woman raised in Ireland in the 1950s and 1960s and her subsequent teaching in London (Scott 1998). She reports her autobiography and shows the themes of nationality and class background, educational reforms and her view of her own (and others') past professional practice. Scott shows his own relation to the subject and the usefulness of the auto/biographical approach in the 'interweaving of the two different agendas of the person and biographer', how the present discourses and narratives are the way into the past, and that the 'public and private' are inseparable. He argues that the individual interacts with wider social structures so that private actions are also public acts; and that the autobiography is always

fragmentary, comprising parts as opposed to wholes, narratives that never quite come to fruition, disconnected traces, sudden endings and new beginnings. What gives it its meaning is the act of methodological closure agreed between the person and her biographer.

(Scott 1998: 43)

The subject of education in auto/biographical research is an area in which auto/biographical researchers can readily examine their own schooling within the educational biographies of others and thus interrogate the boundaries made between researcher and researched, situations and structures, selves and others, and texts and lives.

Conclusion

Auto/biography argues that texts are formed in a social process – as 'social moments' – and challenges the view that 'works' can be distinguished from lives. Auto/biographical work is a 'multi-sided' practice and includes the collaboration between all participants (Morgan 1998: 655–6). It has attempted to bring together, within sociology, influences from postmodern and feminist thought and other sources (e.g. hermeneutics) alongside 'sociological' contributions to biographical research (e.g. Merton, Mills). In its 'eclectic approach' auto/biography has offered a number of areas for exploration – this eclecticism, for some critics, might imply a vagueness in its approach and intent. Other critics might cite an over-concentration on the researcher's role or the construction of 'texts' to the detriment of the 'true' purpose of biographical research – the understanding of the 'real' lives of others. But, on the issue of 'real lives' and representation, auto/biography challenges the view that biographies simply reflect lives as lived while also contesting that 'all is mere representation' in accounts. There is an aim to explore how individuals use experience, including the construction of biographical 'texts' as part of lived experience. Another important area is the connection made between time and biography: here auto/biography posits the complexity of the social construction of time in accounts, the 'time/narrativized' nature of life experience, and a questioning of the conventional assumption of chronological sequence and developmentalism in analysis (see Stanley and Morgan 1993: 3). More profoundly, at least for some researchers in auto/biography the challenge to conventional positions on biography is part of an intended 'epistemological revolution' in the social sciences (Stanley, 1994a: i).

Recommended reading

Auto/Biography. (This is the journal of the Auto/Biography Study Group, which is part of the British Sociological Association. It is both sociological and cross-disciplinary with much discussion of literary and other texts. It includes work on a very wide range of contexts (health, historical topics, national identities, and the body) and theoretical and epistemological issues. Work of the group appeared in *Sociology* (1993). Special Issue: 'Biography and Autobiography in Sociology', 27(1), February.)

Erben, M. (ed.) (1998) *Biography and Education: A Reader*. London: Falmer Press. (This reader has contributions from leading figures in auto/biography. Major theoretical and methodological issues are considered such as the interrelation between biography and autobiography, and the individual and social structure, with reference to the field of education. Empirical areas are addressed, including college dropouts, learning difficulties, school teaching and historical analyses of education.)

Stanley, L. (1992) *The Auto/Biographical I: The Theory and Practice of Feminist Auto/biography*. Manchester: Manchester University Press. (This book explores in detail the complexities implicit in the term 'auto/biography' through a theoretical discussion and a number of research examples.)

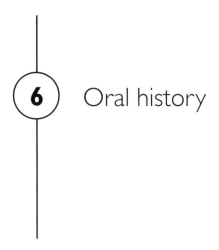

6 Oral history

Oral history – definitions

Oral history has had a startling expansion in its work in the past twenty years or so and has developed across the world (see *Bios* 1990; Grele 1998). This growth in the collection of first-hand accounts has implications for how the 'past' is constructed and the practice of history (Perks and Thomson 1998a: ix).

The secondary status of oral history within the general social sciences and a traditional neglect in methodological texts is being overcome (Reinharz 1992: 132). One particular problem in its expansion has been the confusing use of terms to describe its data and method, for instance not only oral history itself, but life stories, memoirs, personal stories, and in-depth interviewing have been used. According to Yow, oral historians have probably given more time and effort to questions of definition and usage than other disciplines (Yow 1994: 3). Oral history researchers have noted that other research may be using similar methods in their studies under different names within a variety of disciplines or by wider community groups (Reinharz 1992: 129). Even so, oral history, unlike some other practices, has the benefits (and problems) of direct personal contact with the researched (Reinharz 1992: 132). For Ritchie, taking a pragmatic approach to oral history practice:

Simply put, oral history collects spoken memories and personal commentaries of historical significance through recorded interviews . . .

Tapes of the interview are transcribed, summarized, or indexed and then placed in a library or archives. These interviews may be used for research or excerpted in a publication, radio or video documentary, museum exhibition, dramatization, or other form of public presentation.

(Ritchie 1995: 1)

Yow also takes such a stance and sees what is important is 'there is someone else involved who inspires the narrator to begin the act of remembering, jogs memory, and records and presents the narrator's words' (Yow 1994: 4).

Some differences in the preferred use of terms to describe participants are also apparent due to the implications different terms carry:

Some oral historians dislike 'interviewee' for its passive sound and have searched for a more active designation, like 'informant,' 'respondent,' 'oral author,' and 'narrator,' the last term often being used by folklorists and social scientists.

(Ritchie 1995: 10)

Other terms used include subjects, researched, respondents, interpreters, and tellers, among others.

Oral historians, commenting on the researcher's role, have argued that the oral history interview is more than simply an attempt to obtain a 'complete interview', on tape/transcript. Even if the researcher only nods a response there is a relationship – a 'conversational narrative' (Grele 1998: 44).

More broadly oral history has been described as a 'genre' or a 'cluster of genres' (Portelli 1998: 23; see Chamberlain and Thompson 1998a). Portelli notes that the term 'oral history' indicates a type of discourse which is both a 'narrative of the past' and a 'medium of expression'. He draws attention to its 'linguistic and narrative dimensions' including the 'speech and performance' of the individual; here the use of genre in oral history brings the influence of the novel, folklore, and mass media as well as issues relating to the oral and written nature of narrative (Portelli 1998: 23). Oral historians have had a growing awareness of its practice as a 'dialogic discourse' (cf. Bakhtin) which involves not merely the utterances of the narrator but, in addition, the relation with the researcher in the interview and his/her subsequent finished study (Portelli 1998: 23). Portelli concludes:

Oral history is therefore a composite genre, which calls for a stratified critical approach: in addition to the uses of genre in the collected discourse of the narrator(s), we need also to recognize genre in the public discourse of the historian, and genre in the space between them.

(Portelli 1998: 23)

There is increasing sophistication in the way that oral historians see their practice, for instance the connections with social context and discourses, how the historian is placed within historical and other theorization, the psychological processes of memory, and how oral history practices and presentation are seen as connecting with wider genres. In moving from the notion of 'objective' interviewer to one who is a more involved participant, oral history has benefited from feminist discussions of the interview and research relation within a number of fields. In relation to theoretical developments, Ritchie advises those now entering the field:

> Beginning oral historians should not be discouraged by the complexity of hermeneutics (the principles of interpretation), discourse analysis (language in use), or deconstruction (hidden and unspoken information in a narrative).
>
> (Ritchie 1995: 9)

Uses and types of oral history

Writers in oral history have commonly identified various forms of research in the collection of individual accounts. For example, Gluck identifies three traditional types of oral history gained from tape-recorded interviews – the 'topical interview' (e.g. on a specific occasion), the 'biographical oral history' (an experience of a particular individual) and the 'autobiographical interview' (based on the course of the individual life) (Gluck 1996: 217–18). As she recognizes there is considerable overlap between these types. But they do reflect a common recognition that oral histories are collected for different purposes: perhaps for experiences of particular events or processes (e.g. migration), shared life-course, occupational, communal or generational experiences of a group, or for a concentration on the particularity of lives. The various kinds of accounts of individual lives in oral history can either be presented at length or edited and interpreted by the researcher, or be group or communal histories based on localities, organizations or institutions, or be different sets of interviews used for comparison (Thompson 1988: 237–8; Reinharz 1992: 128).

Reinharz (1992) gives examples of different (feminist) oral history products, which indicate the diversity of the research undertaken. She says pre-existing oral histories may be reanalysed by utilizing the 'techniques of literary criticism and ethnography', or 'paired histories' can be examined for individuals' views of each other. She adds that oral histories can also be used to discover empirical regularities and a quantitative analysis can be carried out on groups of oral histories. Finally, oral history projects can be found in public exhibitions (in museums and historical interpretation centres at historical sites) alongside written materials, photographs and other artefacts. Oral history projects may cover a wide range of settings – each concerning particular issues and purposes. Yow gives a wide variety of such oral history projects: in community studies or public history which may have a group, a town, or an organization as their focus; also biography, and family research with different issues being raised according to type (Yow 1994: 143, Chs. 7, 8). Similarly, Dunaway and Baum present oral history as applied to local, family, women's, and ethnic history (Dunaway and Baum 1996: Part 3). They also describe the 'interdisciplinarity' of oral history – the collection and analysis of oral data in anthropology, education/teaching, ethnic studies, folklore, gerontology, legal studies, literary history, media studies and media production, sociology and community studies, and women and gender studies (Dunaway 1996: 10–17).

An oral account may be presented with written material from other sources – official records, family details, letters, photographs, and so on. These documents have been used to illustrate or confirm a life story, or as a starting point to stimulate memories (as in reminiscence practice and research), or to register memories. An associated issue here is the relative merits of oral and written accounts by individuals of their historical experiences of the 'past'. A traditional criticism of oral histories is that they are not as reliable as written contemporary accounts. Oral historians can reply that this not only fails to recognize the increasing utility that history finds in oral history but that written accounts are also fallible and subject to bias. They can also argue that oral and written documents have different bases and are subject to different kinds of evaluation. Finnegan observes on this issue that oral forms, because they are transmitted by word of mouth each time of recounting, are affected by new influences whereas the written document, once recorded, is permanent (Finnegan 1996a: 132).

An oral account in its telling and retelling is open to various kinds of influences – not only other oral accounts, but also written sources (books, newspapers) and the media – which may directly relate to the individual's past experiences. Finnegan adds that oral forms are very affected by types of audiences of the specific time – the 'performance' is interconnected with the social context (Finnegan 1996a: 132). Again, the interviewed–interviewer relation (or the expected audience) is important for the account produced. For Gluck, the 'autobiographical oral history' is a 'strange hybrid' – it is a collaborative production between the interviewer and interviewee, and so is 'unique' in encompassing both voices (Gluck 1996: 218–19). Even so, we can say that a story orally delivered may also be rehearsed and may have been told many times before although in rather different circumstances prior to the researcher's intervention. Similarly, a written account may have been told previously but, in being requested by a researcher, be 'collaborative' in some degree. This involvement may be intended to be part of empowerment or advocacy, for example in giving a 'voice' to groups such as refugees, or to older people through reminiscence work, or those who have suffered discrimination or violence (see Perks and Thomson 1998b: Part III). For Gluck, a 'new literature' is achieved for those whose experiences do not usually reach the public arena (except in folk culture) (Gluck 1996: 219). From this, oral history has claimed a broader possibility as a method of enhancing 'historical consciousness' and an 'opportunity to democratize the nature of history' (Grele 1991: xvi).

Origins

Oral accounts have been used by historians for many hundreds of years from the Greeks or even earlier in military accounts and later through to the work of social reformers and others in the nineteenth century (Thompson 1988: Ch. 2; Ritchie 1995: 1–5; Grele 1996, 1998; Nevins 1996). The emergence of a definable field of oral history perhaps lies in the interwar period with the work of Allan Nevins in the USA. Gradually, oral history evolved and became established by the early 1970s as the publication of articles and books increased and working groups of researchers and conference series became established (Grele 1990; Dunaway 1996; Starr 1996). With the growth in publications and research projects came the exploration of research questions concerning the nature of oral and written materials, the reliability of oral evidence and the implications of oral history for historical practice. An important feature of the development of oral history was the holding of international meetings in Europe in the late 1970s in Italy and England. These connections between European and American scholars expanded very quickly in subsequent years with joint meetings, further conferences and in publications such as the *International Journal of Oral History* in 1980 (see Thompson 1988; Perks and Thomson 1998b). Dunaway describes these events as part of a sequence of several generations of oral history work from 'pioneering figures' in America such as Allan Nevins and Louis Starr, to writers in the 1960s who used oral history to 'describe and empower', and to those in the 1980s who had grown up with the new technologies (see Dunaway 1996; Thompson 2000: 65–6). In Britain a generation of younger writers (academic historians, librarians and museum personnel) were inspired by George Ewart Evans's research on the experience of rural life and Tony Parker's work in the 1960s onwards, and joined together to form the journal *Oral History* (Bornat 1994b: 19–20; see G. E. Evans 1993; Howkins 1994; Thompson, 1994). British oral history may also be set within a 'broad tradition' investigating and reporting on 'ordinary lives' including the documentary film movement, 1930s studies by academics, journalists and campaigners on the effects of the Depression and later sociological community studies, autobiographies and novels by working-class writers in the interwar period (e.g. the miner B. L. Coombes, see Jones and Williams 1999a, 1999b), the rise of labour and social history, and the work of archives and media programmes on war experiences (Thompson 2000: 72–4).

Box 6.1

Evans, G. E. (1993) *The Crooked Scythe: An Anthology of Oral History*. London: Faber and Faber.

This is a collection of pieces from Evans's interviews (mainly from Suffolk) with farmworkers, craftworkers, domestic servants, fishermen and others from *Ask the Fellows Who Cut the Hay* (1956), *The Pattern under the Plough* (1966) and other work. The anthology shows how Evans was able to inter-weave knowledgeable commentaries on rural conditions and events (e.g. harvest), skills, and traditions with voices of rural people revealing their everyday concerns and outlook. For instance, after noting the old rural custom of 'telling the bees' he gives the following typical description from a Suffolk man:

> If there was a death in the family our custom was to take a bit of crepe out to the bee-skeps after sunset and pin it on them . . . If you didn't do this, they reckoned the bees wouldn't stay, they'd leave the hives – or else they'd pine away and die.
>
> (Evans 1993: 44)

Within the 1980s Dunaway identifies a third generation as including Paul Thompson, Alessandro Portelli and Ronald Grele and others who began to have a more sophisticated conception of the oral history interview and the construction of memory, e.g. how 'histories' are formed in the interview by the communication between narrator and the researched (Portelli 1981; Grele 1985; Thompson 1988). Issues such as the types of interview, indi-vidual subjectivity, myth and silence within the oral history process were beginning to be discussed: 'Now a debate emerged in the profession over the purpose of oral history: was it intended to be (1) a set of primary source documents or (2) a process for constructing history from oral sources?' (Dunaway 1996: 8–9).

Thus, by the 1980s a critique of assumptions about the practice of oral history interviews and presentation was coming to the fore. A reinterpreta-tion of the nature of the interviewer's role and the conduct and analysis of the interview was taking place. Instead of the detached oral historian merely collecting the 'facts' and then allowing historical interpretation to proceed, a new view was emerging. The position of the oral historian came to be seen as rather more problematic – more than just empathy but a subtle involve-ment was apparent, which implicated his or her own identity. Oral history was now being seen as more than merely filling the gaps left by conventional historical approaches, but as a realization and a formulation of the field of the oral historian as a self-conscious practice which should be made more explicit in the modes of representation. By the late 1980s, the 'oral history' movement was truly international. Parallel developments were also beginning to take place across Europe, central and south America, Australia and many other countries (*Bios* 1990; Dunaway and Baum 1996: Part 5; *Words and Silences* 1998; Thompson 2000: Ch. 2).

Development and purpose

The 'history of oral history' demonstrates a shift towards a critical re-examination of its purpose. Grele describes the emergence of a 'community of interest' along with a number of key turning points (Grele 1991: xvi–xvii). First, the publication of Paul Thompson's review of the origins, scope and methodological practice gave oral history a degree of status and respectability as an academic pursuit (Thompson 1988). International conferences and journals, and compilations of international research papers (see Thompson and Burchardt 1982) provided a further stimulus to oral history practice. Grele argues an examination of oral history shows that it is necessary: '. . . to move beyond simply documenting the past to an understanding of how oral history can change the manner in which we study the past, and how those we interview relate to history and social change' (Grele 1991: xviii).

Oral history has retained its stated commitment to broaden its scope by including in addition to the traditional oral accounts of those with high status or power, interviews from the 'unheard' to enable them to give their historical perspective. The daily work, community and family experience of women, working-class and marginalized groups are to be recovered. But this initial approach has undergone a re-evaluation. Reflecting on the early growth of oral history, Thompson stated:

> Our early somewhat naïve methodological debates and enthusiasm for testimonies of 'how it really was' have matured into a shared understanding of the basic technical and human issues of our craft, and equally important, a much more subtle appreciation of how every life story inextricably intertwines both objective and subjective evidence – of different, but equal value.
>
> (Thompson, cited in Thomson *et al*. 1994: 34)

This development required a new communicative and interpretive sensitivity to the interview process – to the verbal and interactive elements of the relation between the participants. The work of Frisch, Grele, Portelli, Passerini, and others (see later) brought a new sophistication: for example the narrator is now recognized not merely as a 'source' but as an active part in the historical interpretation – and again, the interview is seen as part of a negotiated, collaborative relation (Perks and Thomson 1998b: ix). The

---

Box 6.2

Parker, T. (1988) *Red Hill: A Mining Community*. London: Coronet.

Parker was a pioneer of oral history in Britain in the 1960s. He entered oral history interviewing from radio work and has reported the lives of various types of offenders and those who in various ways were at society's margins, in a series of books (e.g. Parker 1971, 1985; Thompson 1994). In *Red Hill*, Parker gives the voices of miners, local women, Coal Board officials, the police, and many others in a community affected by the bitter 1984–5 British miners' strike. As in other work, information on methodological procedure is sparse and the introduction to each interview is limited. When the latter runs to several sentences it often describes the individual's appearance and manner, the room of the interview, the house and immediate area. One of the longer introductions is for miner 'Bernard Wilkinson' who was against the union leadership and its decision to strike. He is described as a very large, burly man, with bright blue eyes; he had a comfortable bungalow some ten miles from the village: 'He wore a sleeveless roll-necked canary yellow pullover, a check shirt, check trousers, and light grey leather shoes' (Parker 1988: 81).

Parker headed Wilkinson's account as 'My long and happy retirement':

> I'm retiring early next year when I'm fifty . . . We've got this nice house, our daughter's going to college, and what's to come now is what I've worked for twenty years for, my long and happy retirement, thank you very much. I'm going to enjoy every single bloody minute of it.
>
> (Parker 1988: 81–2)

---

further influences from postmodernism and other sources, according to Dunaway, have 'prompted a more process-oriented reading of history and culture. As a consequence, oral history has experienced a surge of interest in subjectivity and in nontraditional sources' (Dunaway 1996: 7).

Areas of sociology and psychology have been found to be instructive for a more sophisticated debate on methodological and theoretical issues, and to have enabled a move from a positivist orientation to a more reflective and interpretive practice (Bornat 1994b: 19). Bornat notes two influences on the shift to more concern with interpretation. First, the work of the 'Italian school' – Alessandro Portelli's study of steelworkers in Terni, and Luisa Passerini's study of Fascism have been very influential (Bornat 1994b: 20; see Passerini 1979, 1992a; Portelli 1991). Here mental representations, subjectivity and myths, and connections with wider social and ideological representation, are interrogated rather than an oral account simply assumed to reflect 'what happened'. Such work fitted with the realization that questions of memory and 'false testimony' required further attention (Thompson 1995). The second major influence was the work of Michael Frisch (1990). He argued against oral history as merely a means of gaining information on neglected areas or a direct communication of the past 'bypassing' historical interpretation. These positions Frisch famously

---

Box 6.3

Passerini, L. (1979) Work ideology and consensus under Italian fascism. *History Workshop*, 8, Autumn, 82–108.

Passerini draws upon her collected life stories of workers from two generations born before and immediately after 1910 to explore working-class subjectivity, ideology and work experience. In a sophisticated analysis of working-class consciousness under fascism she explores the contradictions between the forms of dissent and consensus. She questions the traditional conception of fascism; a wider notion is required beyond political activity which recognizes that acceptance and consensus within daily subjectivity can contain more potential political dissent. It is a 'speculative' analysis which depends upon insights from oral accounts which are connected with methodological and theoretical issues such as the significance of irrelevancies, inconsistencies or discrepancies in replies and the nature of work ideology and working-class consciousness in daily life.

Box 6.4

Portelli, A. (1991) *The Death of Luigi Trastulli and Other Stories: Form and Meaning in Oral History*. Albany, NY: SUNY.

This influential book is a collection of essays which includes research in Terni, Italy and Harlan, USA. Brought up in Terni, Portelli was initially attracted to the songs produced in the two areas that mixed working-class awareness and traditional folk expression. Much of the book details his investigations into industrial culture – industrial conflict, class relations, politics and non-work activities. Beginning with the story of Luigi Trastulli the chapters have a strong methodological thread, including oral history as a form, the researcher and interpersonal relations, historical 'truth', time, space and memory.

Box 6.5

Frisch, M. (1990) *A Shared Authority: Essays on the Craft and Meaning of Oral and Public History.* Albany, NY: SUNY.

Frisch presents a collection of his essays that show the width of oral and public history. Concerns surrounding how oral materials become represented in public, the structures of collective memory, audience reception, and the nature of the interviewer–narrator relationship are examined. Cases studied include audience reception and critical evaluation of television documentaries on China and Vietnam raising issues of presentation, interpretation and power, the historical knowledge of students, urban public history, and the presentation of urban history in museums.

---

characterizes as 'more history' or 'no history'. Instead, Frisch seeks to go beyond these polarities to investigate what the interview actually represents: in doing so, individual, generational and other dimensions of memory and its relation to experience and history become key areas of oral history, not simply the 'method' (Frisch 1998: 33).

The issues here relate to the connections between individual experience and collective memory as social changes take place; oral history's prime role is seen as analysing the individual's account within a general socio-cultural context. In short, Frisch's intent is to place historical memory at the heart of oral history to discover how individuals understand the past and relate it to the present social situation. The complex issue of memory – both individual and public – has certainly become more important in subsequent life history work.

The 'more history' and 'no history' views underplay the degree of interpretation by researched and researcher in the construction of the oral history document (Grele 1991: xvi). These stances are seen as misguided since they fail to see the interactive nature of the oral history relation – interpretation, selectivity, and editing through to the final report. While an interactive practice, nevertheless oral history is said to have the benefits of adding to our understanding of the past and the legacy today. Here, for Grele, many of the principles of historical analysis and criteria for interviewing can be accepted by oral historians but, he says, there is a need for a much more conscious history in which the ordinary members of the public are part of the production of their 'own histories' (Grele 1991: xvi). This is a challenge to the role of the historians – coupled with a questioning of social history and history more generally as the distinctions between history, anthropology and myth have been reassessed. An emergent view is that we live our narratives and we carry them historically. In short, oral history claims it has questioned and altered traditional historical practice (Dunaway 1996: 9). Thompson declares: 'Oral history gives history back to the people in their own words' (Thompson 1988: 265).

Oral history practice is increasingly concerned with multimedia and multi-forms in terms of sources and presentation. Oral history interviews may feature in television history documentaries on topics such as past work experiences, family relations and generational change, wartime activity, political events and other topics. Already, there are numerous web-sites by oral history organizations and journals, media companies (e.g. the BBC ONLINE oral history sites) and access to a wide variety of research bodies, museum archives and local and national libraries (see Perks 1999). The Internet is bringing new possibilities for the dissemination of oral history work and is already extending discussion of ethical and other issues surrounding the publication of life stories.

Box 6.6

Millennium Memory Bank, National Sound Archive, British Library.

Based at the National Sound Archive, the Millennium Memory Bank is reputed to be the largest oral history collection in Europe with around 6000 interviews, amassed in conjunction with BBC Local Radio during 1998–9. People of all ages and backgrounds were asked to describe changes during their lives. Sixteen themes guided the interviews on areas such as beliefs and fears, where we live, crime and law, leisure activities, growing up and getting older and what next (the future), providing radio programmes under the heading 'The Century Speaks'. The National Sound Archive also has some 300 oral history collections and a great range of other recorded materials (tapes, videos and disks). Details of the Memory Bank are on the Web and the NSA has a catalogue of its oral history and other collections online (Perks 2000).

Developments in recording hardware and software are making sophisticated and better quality recording possible and giving new means of storage of oral histories. Internet web pages and discussion groups are bringing new ways of presenting material in text, picture and sound and a diversity of 'interactivity', as well as new possibilities in communicating with 'subjects' and co-workers (Read 1998). There are a number of major CD-ROM publications from large research programmes containing oral histories, a range of qualitative data analysis packages, and popular family tree-making guides which allow indexing and searches (see Smith 1998; Blatchford 2001). The 'technical' training of oral historians will no doubt greatly increase to meet these developments and transcription companies, and publishers may take on a wider role in the field.

Ethics

The recollection of past events is inextricably connected with people's current life and its place in the group and wider surroundings. The oral historian's intervention can raise difficulties for the interviewee and ethical dilemmas for the researcher:

> Interviews which explore the ways in which a person has remembered his or her past can be rewarding for the interviewer but may be disturbing or even damaging for the interviewee. Unlike the therapist, oral historians may not be around to put together the pieces of memories that have deconstructed and are no longer safe.
>
> (Thomson *et al.* 1994: 34)

Oral history practitioners realize they may recover memories that are painful and unpleasant or later question accounts given by individuals. Thomson points to a dilemma between constructing histories which may be critical of the memories given (and the researcher may feel that a trust has been broken) and the 'duty to society and history' to challenge powerful myths which dominate lives (Thomson *et al.* 1994: 35). This is not merely a 'professional' issue but has a personal dimension for the researcher. As Yow points out, the researcher may have gained a liking for a person and be reticent in breaking a 'trust'; on the other hand, they may find it hard to resist a contrary view (Yow 1994: 178–80). Grele adds that because individuals give a great deal to the researcher there is an obligation to give a careful consideration of what is told and why it is given (Grele 1991: xx). The researcher has further obligations in collecting interview material. Oral historians have paid considerable attention to important ethical and legal issues surrounding informed consent, confidentiality and access to archive research. These complex areas are commonly raised in practical research texts, archive guidance and by professional bodies and journals.

Feminist historians, in particular, have highlighted a number of ethical dilemmas surrounding the inequalities of the oral history interview relation, the hierarchical nature of interpretation, and possibilities for 'exploitation', for instance when the participants are from radically different backgrounds and parts of the world (see Gluck and Patai 1991b; Sangster 1998: 92).

Evidence, truth and the researcher

The strengths of oral history have been claimed to lie in giving a view of ordinary lives in work and community settings, providing oral accounts where written sources are lacking, and in enabling individuals (and groups) to have a voice and an interpretation of their lives. While proponents of oral history may see their material as a corrective to the bias of existing historical sources, a range of issues concerning evidence, comparability and cross-checking with other materials – in short, questions concerning reliability, validity and representativeness in relation to the use of oral accounts – have been raised (Burgess 1982: 133). One response to some criticism has been to recommend a comparison of oral data with other sources and checking the internal consistency of the life story account. Oral history has been very much concerned with establishing the value of its materials and approach and meeting standard methodological concerns (see Ritchie 1995; Dunaway and Baum 1996). Nevertheless, there has also been a trend to substitute or find some distancing from such criteria. For Bornat, oral history has shifted from an 'obsessive concern' with validity to a more 'relaxed attitude' which has allowed a focus on interpretation by researched and researcher (Bornat 1994b: 20).

Questions of bias, credibility and truthfulness still feature strongly in oral history textbooks, for example whether interviewees give deliberately false or misleading information, forget and reorder events and experiences, or deceive themselves and the interviewer (Yow 1994: 177). However, Portelli, among others in the late 1970s and early 1980s, began to argue for changes in methodological criteria, for example on credibility:

> The credibility of oral sources is a *different* credibility . . . the import-ance of oral testimony may often lie not in its adherence to facts but rather in its divergence from them, where imagination, symbolism, desire break in. Therefore there are no 'false' oral sources. Once we have checked their factual credibility with all the established criteria of historical philological criticism that apply to every document, the diver-sity of oral history consists in the fact that 'untrue' statements are still psychologically 'true', and that these previous 'errors' sometimes reveal more than factually accurate accounts.
>
> (Portelli 1981: 100)

Critics have commonly raised the questions of validity and reliability of oral historical materials with reference to the inconsistencies of memory (see Hoffman 1996: 89). Diaries and letters are seen as having an advan-tage by being contemporaneous records. However, Hoffman argues that checks can be made to oral accounts, and oral history has the benefit of pre-serving the experiences of those that lack literary skills and time to write down their lives (Hoffman 1996: 92). His conclusion is that oral history is one primary resource among others: written documents in an archive or elsewhere can also be self-serving although considered as a 'record' of experience and events (Hoffman 1996: 92; see also Ritchie 1995: 7). While autobiographers cannot be expected to have the same interests as the researcher, the interviewer can prompt respondents to discuss areas they might not have considered (Ritchie 1995: 9). Finally, against the charge that oral history interviews are often conducted years after the event, when memories have grown imprecise, it is argued that the trained oral history interviewer can raise further questions where answers are factually doubtful. A rather different reply, as by Portelli above, is that oral history is not merely interested in 'facts' but in the respondent's perception of what is 'true'.

The role of the interviewer in oral history has also been questioned by the view that oral history interviewing does not have the same 'checks' as other interview forms. Yow argues that oral historians should make apparent their own motivations and interests and make clear their own social background and experiences so as to make their own strategies and biases visible (Yow 1994: 177). The self-accounting by the researcher and how she/he may influence the oral history interview by personality, attitudes and social position of class, age, gender, ethnic group are important – the interview situation, the types of question and response require monitoring (Yow 1994: 180). For Grele (in an early influential article) the question of interviewing and the standards of research preparation are subject to the usual assessment of interview procedure. As in other historical research, sources can be checked and evidence can be evaluated but he adds that questions of method have to be taken further: for instance, interviewees are selected because they represent historical processes rather than some statistical criterion (Grele 1998: 41).

The Popular Memory Group, commenting on oral history writing during the early 1980s, declared that '*the study of popular memory can begin only where empiricist and positivist norms break down*' (Popular Memory Group 1982: 226, original italics). In particular, they argued there had been a 'richness' of material collected but a 'failure to deal with cultural forms':

> . . . there is a kind of guilty pull between the desire to present popular memory directly (with its own unacknowledged interpretative framing) and the desire not to abandon the overarching interpretive responsibility of 'the historian'.
>
> (Popular Memory Group 1982: 234)

This has an echo of Grele's early comment on oral history as having a lack of theoretical analysis and the criticism that it had continued to be a 'movement without aim' rather than an important means for the analysis of culture (Grele 1998: 42). To understand oral history as a 'joint activity' or 'conversational narrative' certain sets of relations have be examined. Grele called for a wider notion of 'historical cognition' to place the information and the elements of the interview – linguistic, performatory, and cognitive. This process will integrate these structures and allow an understanding of what is narrated and why. Interviewees, he argues, must be seen as having a perspective on the past and as carrying a culture which is related to dominant or oppositional forms of ideology – or some mix of these; as researchers we also have a view of the past which we bring to the interview. Thus, the oral historian identifies the ideological outlook and cultural context of the interviewee and, thereby, the story, Grele argues, becomes a cultural narrative (Grele 1998: 48). The question may still be posed here of how an individual can be said to represent an historical process. A number of means have been deployed in oral history (and elsewhere) to meet this issue: for instance, Passerini's (1979) exploration of day-to-day subjectivity and wider work and class consciousness; the placing of 'popular memory' within hegemonic relationships (Popular Memory Group, 1982); relating the particular oral account to broader social types (Thomas and Znaniecki [1918–20]1958); identifying how individual myths reflect and draw upon wider mythical structures (Samuel and Thompson 1990b); or by placing a story (as a whole or in part) within a collection of others as part of wider historical interpretation of a group, a community or around a topic (Thompson 2000: 270).

Political standpoint

As the 1970s closed oral history began to examine more carefully the idea that working-class or disadvantaged groups more generally can simply be given a voice through a collaborative–democratic assumption of practice. Not only was the role of the interviewer being seen as more problematic but the voice of the interviewee may itself be influenced by the wider 'social production of memory' (Popular Memory Group 1982). An attempt to resolve the question of power was made by Frisch (1990) who advocated a 'shared authority' to overcome the differences between perspectives. By involving people in how memories are given it provides them with an alternative to being only objects with 'information'.

The notion of 'shared authority' can have its limits in giving individuals their own experience and perspective in the interview and text while allowing for the researcher's own interpretation. One answer is to broaden the idea of the oral history interview. Taking a feminist stance, Gluck says women's oral history is a 'feminist encounter':

> even if the interviewee is not herself a feminist. It is the creation of a new type of material on women; it is the validation of women's experiences; it is the communication among women of different generations; it is the discovery of our own roots and the development of a continuity which has been denied us in traditional historical accounts.
>
> (Gluck 1996: 217)

Thus, by studying other women a feminist researcher also gains a greater understanding of her life (Gluck 1996: 217). This perspective raises many

---

Box 6.7

Stuart, M. (1993) 'And how was it for you, Mary?' Self, identity and meaning for oral historians, *Oral History*, 21 (2): 80–3.

Mary Stuart, in her assessment of Frisch's (1990) notion of 'a shared authority', argues that to question others is also to hold oneself to examination. In giving the opportunity to express what happens to that voice, what right have we to critique? Stuart relates the self-examination – a reopening of an area of experience that had been closed for many years – prompted by undertaking several interviews and participant observations in her own research on women who had lived most of their lives in a convent. She argued there is the creation of our own selves in research and we should examine our own meanings (Stuart 1993: 81). After asking one interviewee what she felt about being interviewed she was jolted by the comment 'And how was it for you, Mary?'

---

questions regarding the relation with the interviewee, including the view that biographical experience and identity of both participants are implicated, political commitment, and the issue of a participatory, collective, democratic research practice (Benmayor 1991). The impact on the researcher of other people's stories reveals the research process as a complex insider–outsider relation (Olesen 2000: 227). In the interview, and in later reflection in or outside the process of writing, it can be argued that questions of power and possible differences in interest will still intrude. At base, the issue is the degree to which the voices of the researched will continue to be 'mediated' (edited, interpreted, contextualized) by the researcher. What if you disagree with, or even detest, the values and perspective of the respondents? (Yow 1994: 64). The purpose of the research is another factor; even if empowerment or advocacy are stated goals, and academic interests are restrained, the shaping of voices will remain an issue. Another potential concern, ironically, is that the more researchers contemplate their own life and position in research the criticism may be that they have become more interested with their own preoccupations than with the voices of others.

Again, a major challenge to the assumptions and practice of oral history came from the Popular Memory Group (1982) who were developing the debate on the oral history 'movement' and the possibilities of a socialist local history found within the *History Workshop Journal* (see White 1981; Worpole 1981). It not only gave a critique of lingering empiricism but also of the 'democratic' assumption, and the unequal nature of the interview relation (Popular Memory Group 1982). Its assessment of oral history and other historical work drew upon various types of cultural analyses, including feminist work. The Group gave detailed assessments of oral history writing and community oral history within an analysis of more general 'history making' such as in the representation of history on TV and in heritage institutions. The Group asked why the work on 'popular memory' and its construction, despite its rise in oral history, communal history projects and popular autobiography and an intention to have a democratic and radical practice, had produced 'meagre' political results. In its view: 'history-writing . . . involves becoming "historians of the present too" . . . We define popular memory first as an *object of study*, but, second, as a *dimension of political practice*' (Popular Memory Group 1982: 205, original emphases).

Oral history practice, in the Popular Memory Group's analysis, is set within its wider academic and other historical practices such as popular autobiography, community projects and in a political and historical context (Popular Memory Group 1982: 211). While there is a recognition of the radical credentials and possibilities of oral history, and its connection with community oral history projects, women's history and forms of political engagement, it has failed to press through its own self-critique, including an awareness of the fuller relations of the interview, and the limitations of its political engagement. The Group saw a need to situate memory and the study of the 'past' within the context of the ideological and hegemonic present – and also within the interlinkings between private and public histories. In short, a fuller 'social production of memory' is advocated. This view of oral history was very influential on debates on practice in the 1980s, even though some regarded it as a 'relatively crude alternative' (Thomson *et al.* 1994: 34).

Methodological and ethical dilemmas continue in oral history practice, for example between the theoretical challenges of postmodern, sociological, feminist and hermeneutic understandings and the mission to report the historical experience as given by the respondent. Further, tension exists between the standards set by empiricist, 'scientific' standards to ensure reliability and validity of the 'facts' of the account and the attempt to interpret the construction of the interview – the making of 'history' by the respondent and researcher. Other problems surround the differences between professional interests and community or institutional objectives; between the professional and the amateur; and between writing for an academic audience and giving history back to the people – ensuring individuals' experiences are reported and are given a legitimacy. Controversies, for example, can arise in presenting 'public histories' (in museums and at historical sites, or more broadly in TV films, videos or on the Web) of major events which question generally accepted views (see Ritchie 2001). Finally, there is the issue of the difference between the respondent's interpretation of historical experience and that provided by the researcher – how the respondent's historical understandings are to be related to their wider and shifting ideological context.

Box 6.8

Humphries, S. and Hopwood, B. (2000) *Green and Pleasant Land*. London: Channel 4 Books.

Steve Humphries has written a variety of television series, with accompanying books, on topics such as changes in work and family life drawing on oral history interviews (cf. Humphries and Gordon 1993). In *Green and Pleasant Land* (2000) and the television series the 'untold story' of the harsher reality beneath the imagery of the British countryside is related. Some one and half thousand stories were collected, mainly from people born between 1920 and 1940. Around fifty were interviewed in depth and filmed, selected because of their broad and vivid experiences. The stories of aristocrats and servants, labourers, farmers, gamekeepers and poachers are presented. Each chapter has an historical introduction, which provides a setting for the testimonies on childhood, the semi-feudal estates, sexual behaviour, the agricultural depression, wartime experiences and changes since World War II.

Oral history's commitment to 'giving voice' has developed and expanded as work has been undertaken across many countries. Oral histories of the dispossessed, those who have experienced traumatic incidents of war and persecution and those in struggle and political repression have been recorded. Important also here is the complex role of oral history in the processes of 'truth and reconciliation' between communities – the difficulties of 'coming to terms' with the legacies of the past where, for instance, there are competing claims (for land and resources) and past crimes need to be recognized.

Case study
Bertaux, D. and Thompson, P. (eds) (1993) *Between Generations: Family Models, Myths and Memories*. Oxford: Oxford University Press.

Oral history subject matter covers an enormous range but in recent years, certainly at international level, a number of important themes can be identified: migration in various continents, the memories of World War II, trauma and memory, and the reshaping of memories of the pre-1989 upheavals in eastern Europe (cf. Benmayor and Skotnes 1994; Rogers *et al.* 1999). Common threads within much of this work have been intergenerational transmission through the family and related issues of changes in identity, social mobility, and the processes of memory. For example, Daniel Bertaux and Paul Thompson have made substantial contributions to the study of family processes by the use of 'life stories' (Bertaux and Bertaux-Wiame 1981; Bertaux 1983; Bertaux and Thompson 1993a, 1997; Bertaux and Delcroix 2000; Miller 2000). Bertaux argues that life histories 'lead inevitably to family histories' and offers the idea of 'social trajectory' rather than social mobility to denote the 'time dimension of mobility processes'. He adds that the term can be applied beyond individuals to the study of families and professional groups (Bertaux 1991: 84–5). Commenting on French research he points to the usefulness of the concepts of transmission and transmissibility to identify what is passed from generation to generation. He calls for the study of family histories to show how the social trajectory of members is constructed, and the relations between family members and the 'blank spaces' between families that indicate the operation of class relations. Studies in the sociology of the family, he argues, have tended not to be over time, and even the use of the family life cycle has not uncovered the 'internal dynamics of real families' (Bertaux 1991: 87–88). Bertaux and Thompson in their edited volume *Between Generations* (1993a) argue that the family:

> . . . remains the main channel for the transmission of language, names, land and housing, local social standing, and religion; and beyond that also of social values and aspirations, fears, world views, domestic skills, taken-for-granted ways of behaving, attitudes to the body, models of parenting and marriage – resulting in the condensation of experiences characterizing particular class groups . . .
>
> (Bertaux and Thompson 1993b: 1–2)

These areas are not the exclusive provinces of the family; for instance the 'encroachments' of formal education and also social mobility research show that a change towards 'meritocratic' selection rather than 'ascription' (following family occupations) has intruded (Bertaux and Thompson 1993b: 3). In understanding family transmission, Bertaux and Thompson recommend a 'family systems' approach found in therapeutic settings of the 'contractual' relationships and rules that govern 'boundaries and differentiation between generations' (Bertaux and Thompson 1993b: 8). The book *Between Generations* more generally draws on research from a wide range of countries to examine how societal shifts affecting the family can disrupt existing forms of family transmission, how family histories (of holocaust survivors) may be constructed to provide a continuity while avoiding disturbing aspects of the past, and the part family memories, myths or secrets play in current transformations in Eastern Europe and elsewhere. Reporting on an Anglo-French research project linking the fields of family and social mobility studies (using a mix of qualitative and quantitative methods), Thompson argues:

Telling one's own life story requires not only recounting directly remembered experience, but also drawing on information and stories transmitted across the generations, both about the years too early in childhood to remember, and also further back in time beyond one's own birth. Life stories are thus, in themselves, a form of transmission; but at the same time they often indicate in a broader sense what is passed down in families.

(Thompson 1993: 13)

Thompson gives interpretations of life story excerpts from a number of subjects (drawn from a hundred families) – for instance, an ex-miner, a steel-worker, a lecturer, a businessman and a university student – who tell their own story and in doing so a family history of previous generations. He points to the fact that although mobility studies have emphasized the influence of parents and other family elements the focus has been on occupational mobility of individuals. Statistical approaches that have been applied via survey questionnaires have been work-centred and commonly based on male careers. A family orientation and in-depth interviews produce new insights on social mobility, according to Thompson, including the very different patterns of mobility for men and women (with the latter peaking early) and (in Britain) the effects of long-distance migration. He also found that the interviews revealed a longer pattern (beyond the immediate family context) – individual mobility is often a result of a 'dynamic' across two or three generations and a smaller family size. There was an interconnection between socio-economic and familial factors in tracing geographical mobility. One Welshman, who had moved as a teenager to the South East and whose many male older relatives had been injured or rendered sick through pit work, said: 'one of the reasons why me father moved up here was because he didn't want his children working in the pit'. Such decisions were not merely individual but family decisions (Thompson 1993: 17).

A number of approaches are brought together in Thompson's analysis: the means and content of the transmission of 'family material and cultural capital', the importance of occupational models (for both males and females), transmission through social networks and a notion of the family as 'an inter-generational system of interlocking social and emotional relationships' (Thompson 1993: 20, 27). He gives the example of a three-generational family of teachers who equated familial control with teaching; the grand-father said 'we both took the attitude that preaching at them and using the heavy hand was a bit stupid – that would be counterproductive'; instead the grandmother would 'explain to them why she thought it and that was it: they would listen to her' (Thompson 1993: 21). Thompson concludes that family stories are the 'symbolic coinage of exchange between the generations, of family transmission' and in the way they are retold and their content and form are 'part of the mental map of family members' (Thompson 1993: 36).

The collection of life stories within families across generations can show how 'collective memories', 'myths', 'denials and silences' are passed down and how 'models' are constructed which affect perceived opportunities and choice. What is claimed in family research in oral history is that the collection of in-depth interviews can deliver information and explanations of cross-generational changes in relationships and mobility that conflict with common conventional or sociological wisdom (Thompson 1993: 19; Miller 2000: 67).

Conclusion

Oral history is a complex practice. From its beginnings in recording the lives as told by ordinary people – agricultural labourers, union members and others – it later became increasingly aware of theoretical and methodological issues. It met opposition from more established history regarding the nature of its sources; it became concerned with issues relating to the role of the researcher and also the difficulties in its commitment to a democratic or socialistic practice. As with other qualitative methods there has been much debate about the question of whether to abide by traditional, positivistic criteria for evidence and, in addition, even whether there is an overriding radical remit to give the version of history as seen by those with less power and access to the societal channels of communication. Other questions became apparent such as the relative merits of oral and written texts and the degree to which oral history practice shares 'generic' features with 'literary–artistic' endeavours. While giving prominence, as its name indicates, to 'oral' and 'history', was the field after all a mix of genres and as much concerned with the construction of the present as recording the past? Also, there is a striking range of oral history practice – as within academic research, community projects, and commissioned research for organizations. Finally, a range of work from psychology, cultural and literary studies, and feminist work has informed oral history. But, as Thomson observes, the increasing awareness of differing interpretive schemas, the complexity of theories of memory and problems of the researched–researcher relation create a continuing 'tension' with its 'commitment to democratic and empowering practice' (Thomson *et al.* 1994: 35; see Thomson, 1994, 1998).

Recommended reading

Perks, R. and Thomson, A. (eds) (1998) *The Oral History Reader.* London: Routledge. (This text includes work from leaders in the field and considers critical developments, interviewing, advocacy and empowerment, and making histories. It includes introductions to sections and an extensive bibliography of handbooks, collections, periodicals and key publications and international contacts.)

Ritchie, D. A. (1995) *Doing Oral History*. New York, NY: Twayne. (This book gives detailed guidelines and information on researching and writing, preserving, videotaping and other practical issues. It also contains a detailed bibliography.)

Thompson, P. (2000) *The Voice of the Past*, 3rd edn. Oxford: Oxford University Press. (A revised and updated edition of the 'classic' introduction to oral history. It provides an extensive list of further reading and an interview guide.)

Yow, V. R. (1994) *Recording Oral History: A Practical Guide for Social Scientists*. London: Sage. (This is a practical guide and review of research studies. It contains an interview guide, research principles, and record keeping, as well as reviews of key texts at the end of each chapter.)

For international developments of oral history see: *Bios*: Special Issue 1990 (Germany) – this contains a review of oral history in the Americas, China, Eastern and Western Europe, and German-speaking countries; Dunaway and Baum (1996): Part 5; *Oral History* (UK) – reports news of international work, conferences and journals; The International Oral History Association holds conferences, has a website and publishes a bulletin, *Words and Silences*.

7 | The narrative analysis of lives

Narrative analysis – definitions

Much has been written about a 'narrative turn' in the human sciences as an important development in social analysis (Atkinson 1998: 74). The study of narratives has broadened from its origin in literary and related areas of study to cut across a number of disciplines (Alasuutari 1995; Berger 1997; Crossley 2000b). More specifically, the 'narrative study of lives' has become a substantial area for analyses of life experience and identity as connected to social groupings, situations and events (Lieblich *et al.* 1998: 8–9; see Josselson and Lieblich 1993). Narrative analysis, it has been argued, is an alternative to the traditional 'scientific' understanding of the individual as 'abstracted' out of his or her context rather than as part of it (Josselson 1995: 31):

> We have . . . entered a new age, the age of narrative, an interest that is sweeping a range of academic disciplines. The historians, grappling with narrative frames of reference, are wondering about the relationship between history and literature and between history and autobiography . . . And people in literature are wondering about how to distinguish what has usually been thought to be literature from autobiography. Just as within psychology, the question of how to treat people's lived experiences embarrasses our more technical understandings of intellectual conceptualizations.
>
> (Josselson 1995: 31–2)

A key moment in the development of the study of narrative was W. T. Mitchell's edited volume, *On Narrative* (1981). This book gave a higher profile to existing work in literary studies and elsewhere on narrative theory and recognized the potential of cross-disciplinary work (Hyvärinen 1998: 10). Mitchell began his volume as follows:

> The study of narrative is no longer the province of literary specialists or folklorists borrowing their terms from psychology and linguistics but has now become a positive source of insight for all the branches of human and natural science. The idea of narrative seems . . . a mode of knowledge emerging from action, a knowledge which is embedded not just in the stories we tell our children or to while away our leisure but in the orders by which we live our lives.
>
> (Mitchell 1981: ix–x)

Polkinghorne, a well-known figure in the study of narrative, says that 'narrative inquiry' is set within qualitative research and deals with the stories that are 'used to describe human action'. He adds that qualitative researchers have applied the notion of narrative in various ways, but in 'the context of narrative inquiry, *narrative* refers to a discourse form in which events and happenings are configured into a temporal unity by means of a plot' (Polkinghorne 1995: 5).

Narratives, more generally, have been defined according to a number of 'typical characteristics':

> A degree of artificial fabrication or constructedness not usually apparent in spontaneous conversation . . .
> A degree of *pre*fabrication. In other words, narratives often seem to have bits we have seen or heard, or think we have seen or heard . . .
> Narratives typically seem to have a 'trajectory'. They usually go somewhere, and are expected to go somewhere, with some sort of development and even a resolution, or conclusion, provided . . .
> Narratives have to have a teller, and that teller, no matter how backgrounded or remote or 'invisible', is always important . . .
> Narratives are richly exploitative of that design feature of language called *displacement* (the ability of human language to be used to refer to things or events that are removed, in space or time from either speaker or addressee).
>
> (Toolan 1988: 4–5)

While the notion of 'narrative' can be applied to various forms of group or other expression in the media and popular culture (see Berger 1997), the increasing attention to individual narratives has resulted in a focus on individual meaning and experience. It is argued that since narratives can empower people by giving more intimate understandings of their lives and contexts, structuralist attention to power and rules, and 'social functions', is subverted (Manning and Cullum-Swan 1994: 465).

Narrative has been used in various ways in qualitative research, for example 'to refer to any data that are in the form of natural discourse or speech (e.g. interview protocols)' or 'to describe the form of the collected body of data they have gathered for analysis' when presenting the completed research (Polkinghorne 1995: 6). In contrast with the 'positivist scientific paradigm' which emphasizes quantification, generalizability, hypothesis testing, and validity and objectivity, Muller says the idea of narrative:

... is firmly grounded in qualitative traditions and stresses the 'lived experience' of individuals, the importance of multiple perspectives, the existence of context-bound, constructed social realities, and the impact of the researcher on the research process.

(Muller 1999: 223)

Even so, narrative researchers have given criteria by which to evaluate studies. For example, Lieblich *et al.* offer 'width', 'coherence, 'insightfulness' and 'parsimony' based on their experience as researchers (Lieblich *et al.* 1998: 173).

For biographical research, the construction of narrative can be regarded as providing the individual with a 'purposeful engagement'; narrative 'is the type of discourse composition that draws together diverse events, happenings, and actions of human lives into thematically unified goal-directed processes' (Polkinghorne 1995: 5). A more precise meaning of narrative has developed which holds that individual life experience is 'storied' (Polkinghorne 1995: 7; see also Sarbin 1986). 'Narrative' has been applied, therefore, to refer to both 'story' and a method of inquiry.

Clandinin and Connelly are careful to define 'narrative inquiry', 'story' and 'narrative'. They argue that narrative relates both to a phenomenon and a method – the former can be termed story (people tell stories of their lives), the latter narrative (researchers collect stories) (Clandinin and Connelly 1994: 415–16). Of course, researchers also have their own stories as well as writing the research narrative (Clandinin and Connelly 1994: 416). Finally, simply equating narrative and story can be a limitation. Riessman identifies a *number* of 'narrative genres' (e.g. habitual, hypothetical, and topic-centred) according to conventional elements which are chosen by tellers and 'persuade differently' (Riessman 1993: 18).

Narrative analysis

Within the human sciences there are numerous theoretical approaches to written, observational and oral data. For textual analysis, these have included discourse, semiotics, language and conversation, and hermeneutics, among others (Riessman 1993: 5). While narratologists have been influenced by these currents and there is not a single method of narrative analysis, Riessman (following Bruner 1986) points to a central concern with how individuals interpret their contexts and the significance attached to human agency and imagination (Riessman 1993: 5). Similarly, for Manning and Cullum-Swan (1994) narratives or stories take the view of the teller and have a beginning, middle and end, can take various forms, be told to different audiences and in varying contexts. They say narrative analysis 'is rather loosely formulated, almost intuitive, using terms defined by the analyst' (Manning and Cullum-Swan 1994: 465). They add that metaphors and other elements of narrative are often 'defined poetically and artistically' and are 'quite context bound', for example in organizations (Manning and Cullum-Swan 1994: 465). Bruner (1986), from within psychology, has done much to promote the narrative approach to understanding lives within their social settings, and show agency and meaning in narratives. As Josselson also describes:

> It is an effort to approach the understanding of lives in context rather than through a prefigured and narrowing lens. Meaning is not inherent in an act or experience, but is constructed through social discourse.
>
> (Josselson 1995: 32)

Often seemingly allied to the study of narrative is the idea of 'discourse' – with the terms sometimes used interchangeably. The reason may be that just as 'narrative' has various meanings, discourse also has a number of different emphases concerning the analysis of language used in written or spoken 'texts', wider meanings in events, and the adoption of a political stance (see Widdicombe and Wooffitt 1995; Van Dijk 1997). For example, Potter and Wetherell say there are at least four uses – as in conversational exchanges in social settings such as classrooms; the effects of discourse structures, for instance on understanding and recollection; how scientific texts and talk are constructed to demonstrate rational and 'warrantable' action; and lastly, those writers (cf. Henriques *et al.* 1984) drawing on semiology, poststructuralism and other influences (e.g. Foucault) within sociology, psychology and cultural studies. The latter 'have tried to show how institutions, practices and even the individual human subject itself can be understood as produced through the workings of a set of discourses' (Potter and Wetherell 1994: 47). Thus, various discourses may inform, for example, particular decisions in sexual behaviour. Potter and Wetherell say that there are three features of discourse analysis which are relevant for social research. First, the form and content of talk and texts as social practices. Second, the concern with 'action, construction and variability' or the different actions that are performed in discourse by drawing upon an existing 'range of styles, linguistic resources and rhetorical devices'. Third, the manner in which alternative discursive ideas are countered by the 'rhetorical or argumentative organization of talk and texts' (Potter and Wetherell 1994: 48). An area of some possible commonality between a use of discourse and the application of narrative is perhaps where the latter focuses on the working of organizations, power and control (see Mumby 1993; Bloom and Munro 1995).

However, the idea of narrative, certainly in the study of biographical research, is resistant to incorporation into discourse or discourse analysis since the emphasis is not only on plot and story (and the consideration of time) but also on individuality and the interplay between the individual and the social. Individuals, while using wider modes of thought and expression (e.g. myths, symbols, beliefs), construct their own narratives according to their interpretation of experience in socio-cultural contexts. The term 'discourse' also carries conceptual, methodological and other assumptions. As Widdicombe and Wooffitt point out, when commenting on Parker's work (Parker 1992), where discourse analysis draws on Foucault, Derrida and Barthes, there is an underlying socio-political theory concerning the conditions and nature of power relations and even a political goal (Widdicombe and Wooffitt 1995: 60–1).

Second, there is the encompassing use of 'texts' – speech, writing, non-verbal communication and all manner of phenomena that have meaning and can be analysed according to discourse. Such a procedure lacks analytic discrimination since all seem to be at the same interpretive level, and further, for Widdicombe and Wooffitt, a relevant discourse appears to be given to text (usually speech) without fully revealing the basis for the analysis (i.e. in the specific observation of part of the text) and the interactional context. Despite a commitment to giving the powerless a voice, unfortunately the focus on specific instances of language use as reflecting discourse can lessen what individuals are actually saying and doing with their utterances in action in social contexts (Widdicombe and Wooffitt 1995: 62–5). The focus on the given 'text' fences off a conception of an acting, social individual. Even where the text is a diary or autobiography such self-accounting self-reflection remains referential within the text. While some discourse or deconstructionists may begin to realize the need for a subjective, reflexive, biographical actor, strict textual analysis limits the notion of prior author, the performance of writing/speaking, the interactional context and anticipated audience (Crossley 2000a,b).

Psychologists who have developed the narrative examination of lives have sought to broaden their work across disciplinary boundaries. Josselson and Lieblich argue:

> Narrative approaches to understanding bring the researcher more closely into the investigative process than do quantitative and statistical methods. Through narrative, we come in contact with our participants as people engaged in the process of interpreting themselves. We work then with what is said and what is not said, within the context in which life is lived and the context of the interview in which words are spoken to represent that life. We then must decode, recognize, recontextualize,

or abstract that life in the interest of reaching a new interpretation of the raw data of experience before us.

(Josselson and Lieblich 1995: ix)

Josselson is concerned with how narrative understandings are gained and asks how we enter the experience of another and how we decide what to highlight for investigation (Josselson 1995).

Narrative models of knowing are models of process *in process*. When we record people's narratives over time, we can observe the evolution of the life story rather than see it as a text in a fixed and temporal state. As a novel leads inevitably to its end, personal narrative describes the road to the present and points the way to the future. But the as-yet-unwritten future cannot be identical with the emerging plot and so the narrative is revised.

(Josselson 1995: 35)

Box 7.1

Josselson, R. and Lieblich, A. (eds) (1999) *The Narrative Study of Lives, Making Meaning of Narratives*, 6. London: Sage.

This yearly publication draws on contributions in narrative research from psychology and a range of disciplines. In this issue a chapter reviews qualitative research texts, which is meant to alert academics and students in narrative research to wider methodological discussions. Two chapters (Eakin, Nielsen) illustrate 'meaning-making' in narrative research through different reanalyses of Gullestad's (1996) work on autobiographies in Norway. Other chapters include a detailed analysis of interviews and case studies of children which show various ways of interpreting what is not said or 'unsayable' (Rogers *et al.*); an investigation through family interviews, gender, generation and values to demonstrate that powerful unconscious transmission takes place (Hollway and Jefferson); and life histories and institutional settings (Mizrachi, Abma) revealing women's orientation to achievement and the transformative power of life stories. Further chapters include one on girls' diaries which analyses these as performances related to developing experiences (Crowther) and another which looks at how writing biographical fiction connects with the author's own formation of identity (Dien). Finally, a chapter using autobiographies alongside survey data examines the meanings of love: 'What does love mean to people?' 'What are their love experiences?', and explores differences and similarities according to age, gender and generation (Haavio-Mannila and Roos).

Josselson (drawing on Bakhtin) argues that 'an empathically grounded narrative psychology take as its aim the explication of the architectonics of the self – the ways in which parts are held in dynamic relation to one another and maintain themselves in unending dialogue' (Josselson 1995: 42–3).

It is possible to identify a number of forms of narrative analysis relevant for biographical research. Some analyses have a more formal procedure. Rosenthal, for example, outlines several steps – gathering biographical material (chronology, factual material), giving the individual's own interpretations (including silences, emphases) and, then, the reconstruction of the life alongside its interpretation (Rosenthal 1991, 1993; see Chamberlayne *et al.* 2000; Miller 2000: 128–36; Wengraf 2001). During analysis it becomes apparent that parts of the general narration are thematically connected. Thus, aspects of the narrative are not random but selected and are related themes within the overall meaning of the biographer's interpretation of life. This thematic field analysis approach involves a rigorous attention to hypothesis construction by careful reading of texts and an attempt to generate patterns (e.g within a group). Riessman (1993) and Cortazzi (1993) (following Labov) consider the structure of narrative. By a close attention to the content of interview stories the specific narrative elements are identified and comparisons with others in a group can be made.

Box 7.2

Miller, R. L. (2000) *Researching Life Stories and Family Histories*. London: Sage.

Miller outlines in detail three approaches to biographical and family history research – realist, neo-positivist and narrative. These are considered in detail with reference to the collection and analysis of life histories. He argues that each indicate different types of interviewing. The approaches are contrasted through the consideration of interview material from 'William', a middle-aged, married professional from Northern Ireland. For Miller there has been much development in the means of data collection in recent years but less agreement on procedures of analysis. In short, the realist is concerned with factual reliability and with concept generation through induction and grounded theory procedures, the neo-positivist concentrates on the validation of prior theory via empirical material and deduction, and the narrativist is interested in the overall outlook of the individual and the structuring of the account within its social setting (including the research situation). Miller explores the possibility of a general biographical perspective that transcends the boundaries of past/present/future and self/society – giving time and structure in the biographical account.

Box 7.3

Riessman, C. K. (1993) *Narrative Analysis*. London: Sage.

Riessman provides an introduction to narrative analysis from the telling to the transcribing. She begins by providing a personal narrative of her growing interest in the field. While sympathetic to the feminist intent to 'give voice' she argues that decisions in representing lives by the researcher take place at various points during research. She gives detailed comparisons of three models of narrative study from her own research on divorce narratives and other research on women's health and activism. She found that men and women construct the voicing of emotion differently. The other studies are interesting explorations of how public activism occurs and its relation with the personal story. In her interpretation of Cindy's narrative, Riessman found it had a coherence and sequence – a poetic interpretation seemed applicable according to parts, rules and stanzas. Cindy used a metaphor (walking as if under a cloud) that linked the beginning and end of her narrative. This approach to narrative differed from the comparison of plots or stories, or the identification of core narratives.

As Thompson points out, narrative approaches may focus on genre, for example how interviews contain other genres or various types of story, anecdote, or jokes (Chamberlain and Thompson 1998b; see Finnegan 1998; Portelli, 1998). Polkinghorne, using Bruner's distinction between paradigmatic and narrative cognition, makes an interesting separation between the '*analysis of narratives*' (applying paradigmatic reasoning) in qualitative research which uses inductive analyses (for example, Glaser and Strauss's grounded theory) and seeks the refinement of conceptual categories and '*narrative analysis*' where the result is an 'emplotted narrative' – 'a story, or a storied episode of a person's life' (Polkinghorne, 1995: 13, 15). The difference is between the construction of taxonomies across the material and narrative procedures used to produce 'explanatory stories'. Rather differently, Lieblich *et al.* (1998) have provided an examination of life stories (and other narratives) along two dimensions: holistic vs. categorical approaches – depending on whether a part or the whole narrative is the focus, and content vs. form of a story – according to the details, the meanings, motives, images or the structure/form, coherence, style, voices and timing in the story. Thus, four types of narrative study are possible (Lieblich *et al.* 1998: 12–14). While differing approaches often allude to what may be 'hidden' or not fully apparent, for some others there is a more central focus on both conscious and unconscious dimensions of narrative (see Hollway and Jefferson 2000).

Box 7.4

Hollway, W. and Jefferson, T. (2000) *Doing Qualitative Research Differently.* London: Sage.

Hollway and Jefferson (2000) argue for a 'free-association narrative inter-view method' to gain a more humane, complex view of the human subject. In a study of the fear of crime, risk and anxiety on housing estates such questions as 'Can you tell me about how crime has impacted on your life since you've been living here?' were asked and analysis of portions of inter-view transcripts are presented. Included also is a long 'psychosocial case study' of 'Ron' – who responded to the interviewer's question on the impact of crime on him that crime had given him most of what he had! They adapt the approaches of Schütze (1992) (see Jovchelovitch and Bauer 2000) and Rosenthal (1993) to gain individuals' 'meaning systems' by these principles: 'use open questions, elicit stories, avoid "why" questions and follow respondents' ordering and phrasing' – and see similarities here between the Gestalt approach (the whole is more than the parts) and their own psychoanalytic method of free association. For Hollway and Jefferson, free association gains entry into concerns (anxieties and the efforts to defend against them) not apparent in traditional interview procedures and thus, revealing inconsistencies and avoidances undermines narrative con-ventions (Hollway and Jefferson 2000: 34–7). Elsewhere they describe the reproduction of gender, generation and anxiety and emphasize the unpre-dictability of cultural reproduction, pointing to the strength of unconscious meanings due to the emotions they invoke. The interviews they report were obtained by knocking on doors and following up family leads on an estate (Hollway and Jefferson 1999).

Time and narrative

The functioning of 'plot' in stories is related to the use of time. The elements of the story are selected, ordered and rendered meaningful within the com-pleted account according to time:

> Lives have to be understood, as Erben (1998b) argues, as lived within time and time is experienced according to narrative. Narratives – of past, present or future – are the means by which biographical experi-ence is given an understandable shape.
>
> (Roberts 1999a: 21)

It is through 'plot' that events are 'timed' and made meaningful and assem-bled into a 'story' (see Rosenwald and Ochberg 1992; Polkinghorne 1995:

6–8). Within 'plot', for Ricoeur (1981) the variety of events is rendered into an 'intelligible whole'. Individuals, from a narrative viewpoint, move between different 'time perspectives' as they reflect on the past, contemplate the present and rehearse the future (see Schutz 1971; Bellaby 1991; Roberts 1999a). Clandinin and Connelly connect time with other features of narrative study – 'time and place', 'plot and scene' operate in conjunction to form narrative experience (Clandinin and Connelly 1994: 416).

For Toolan, a distinction can be made between narrative and forms such as description and commentary, and he relates this to the recall of events that are spatially and temporally distant from the giver and recipients (Toolan 1988: 5). The general attempt by the individual is to unify the interpretation of experience, to summarize in a phrase or metaphor. Gergen and Gergen argue that the successful narrative is one that orders events as they relate to the attainment of a particular 'goal state'. They say there are three prototypical or primitive narrative forms – stable, progressive and regressive evaluations in relation to the overall goal which can combine to give tragic, happy-ending or other more complex versions (Gergen and Gergen 1984; see Gergen 1999: 70–2). Nevertheless, it can be argued that the 'plot' of a story cannot be complete – ambiguities exist and, of course, our lives continue while the ending is unknown. As Polkinghorne points out, a tale, such as autobiography, is only partly composed into a 'single plot line' (Polkinghorne 1995: 8).

Various criticisms can be made of the use of 'narrative' and the wider 'narrative turn' – 'realists' can respond that, in such analyses, all becomes fiction, that a relativism intrudes, or that lives become studied for their form rather than relationships with others or 'real events'. Further, is there a pre-narrative experience informing 'narrative processing' taking place in daily interaction, which may be grasped by some psychological and other analyses (Hyvärinen 1998: 166)? A feminist or radical response may also include a word of caution – that narratives may appear to provide a forum for empowerment and self-definition through a recovery of 'voice' and alternative perspectives but they often reflect dominant conventions and hide ideologies, such as patriarchy. Thereby, they can restrict new possibilities of expression and alternative actions (Popular Memory Group 1982; Bloom and Munro 1995: 111).

Myth and narrative

The study of myth in the accounts of individuals and groups has come to play an increasing role in narrative, life story and other analyses (Samuel and Thompson 1990b; Finnegan, 1998). Of course, the analysis of myth stems from history and anthropology (and Barthes's semiology has also been influential). For example, in the structuralism of Lévi-Strauss myths (like music and dreaming) are 'machines for the suppression of time': the study of 'rep-etitions' and 'thematic variations' enables an identification of the uncon-scious structures of the mind (Leach 1970: 112).

Tonkin argues that historical study has dismissed myth, whereas in fact the two have much in common; academic history and myth are both narra-tions of the past (Tonkin 1990, 1995). White, exploring the 'historical imagination', has extensively (and famously) written of the 'past' as com-posed by the narratives of historians (White 1973, 1987; see Martins 1974: 269–70). Oral and social historians have recently paid much attention to the power of myths – not merely in the 'public sphere' (as in ceremonial):

> . . . the most powerful myths are those which influence what people think and do: which are internalized, in their ways of thinking, and which they pass on consciously or subconsciously to their children and kin, their neighbours, workmates, and colleagues as part of the per-sonal stories which are the currency of such relationships. What each of us selects and absorbs from publicly offered myth is crucially influenced through this continual mutual exchange of individual experience.
> (Samuel and Thompson 1990a: 14–15)

For Samuel and Thompson oral historians 'have an exceptional chance to examine this vital connection between myth in personal narrative and in public tradition . . . The mythical elements in memory, in short, need to be seen both as evidence of the past, and as a continuing historical force in the present' (Samuel and Thompson 1990a: 15, 20). Of particular importance, they argue, is to examine the 'continual exchange' between private and public myths. For instance, the myth of the 'self-made individual' is both a powerful ideological construction while finding expression in private accounts of life experience (Samuel and Thompson 1990a: 9; see Hankiss 1981; Peneff 1990). An influential exploration of the relations between myth and history (from within oral history) is provided by Luisa Passerini. She argues, in a discussion of 'mythbiography', that a number of meanings can be applied to the connection rather than merely as at opposite symbolic and analytic poles – with oral history moving between each end (Passerini 1990: 49). For example, applying Barthes's use of myth as an 'expression of alienation' she examines myth as a compensation in working-class life to help reshape identity where job skill and political role are reduced (Passerini 1990: 51–2).

The focus on myth in narratives or life stories again raises the question of time – in the formation of experiences, both mundane and dramatic, into a story or account through spontaneous or more 'considered' recollection. Here, there has been a challenge to the chronological or linear or develop-mental conception of the 'life' as in Ricoeur's and other work (see Ricoeur 1981, 1984, 1985, 1988; Bruner 1986). For instance, Hyvärinen says that Ricoeur's general attempt was to understand narrative and time from the different approaches of history, literature, and the phenomenology of time and by seeing narrative as not a repetition or reflection of the experience of time but as an active emplotting (Hyvärinen 1998: 165–6).

Within personal narratives we can often discern 'personal myths' (see Olney 1972: 89–150; Hankiss 1981; McAdams 1997). Clausen, commenting on the 'life review', argues that in looking back we can only take account of a part of our lives; but myths will have been formed which are elements of our self-conception (Clausen 1998: 212). Thus, the formation of narrative has been implicated in the 'construction' of the self. As Gergen and Gergen argue, the view of the self at a particular moment may not make sense without some connection with a notion of the past (Gergen and Gergen 1984: 173). They add:

> . . . in our experience of self and others we seem to encounter not a series of discrete movements, endlessly juxtaposed, but coherent sequences, cross-time patterns, and overall directionality.
>
> (Gergen and Gergen 1984: 173)

Gergen and Gergen argue that 'self-narratives' give an understanding of the 'temporal character' of human action by providing connections, coherence, movement and direction (Gergen and Gergen 1984: 174–5). By the establishment of a 'goal condition' previous events are chosen and ordered which make the goal probable. However, they regard narratives as not simply individual but a result of social interchange; our story is not merely one's own but a social phenomenon (Gergen and Gergen 1984: 174). Peneff (1990)

Box 7.5

Murray, K. (1989) The construction of identity in the narratives of romance and comedy, in J. Shotter and K. J. Gergen (eds) *Texts of Identity*. London: Sage.

Murray makes links between narrative and the formation of both personal and social identity. In a study of how individuals decide to undertake travel and marathon running he outlines how individuals create an individual distinctiveness and a place in the social order. He found a number of narrative structures – romance, comedy, irony and tragedy. Murray sees types of narrative as 'sedimented' forms that have a history and tradition: the narratives uncovered were reflected in Western traditions of storytelling. Thus individual narratives are provided by the social order while a distinctiveness in the narrative account is possible for the individual – the narrative 'mediates' between the individual life and the narratives present in the social order.

makes a similar link with broader social narratives or 'mythical frame-works'. Myths provide images of the individual and the society, for example the common myths of 'unhappy childhood' and 'self-made man' through which people revise and relate their lives in a social context (Peneff 1990: 45; see Finnegan 1998: 23).

In short, mythological elements or 'rhetorical forms', following Barthes, can be said to play an important part in social ideologies as justifying and confirming existing social patterns by giving descriptions and interpretations of social situations (Sontag 1983: 139–45).

In considering the formation of narrative the issue of memory is raised. Freeman attempts to link narrative and memory by using the term 'rewrit-ing the self': 'the process by which one's past and indeed oneself is figured anew through interpretation' (Freeman 1993: 3). It is part of the construction of selfhood:

> this very process, in addition to being an interpretive one through and through, is also a *recollective* one, in which we survey and explore our own histories, toward the end of making and remaking sense of who and what we are . . . this means . . . doing significantly more . . . than inquiring into a discrete phenomenon that happens to be interesting in a 'mindful of life' way and potentially instructive for addressing certain fundamental concepts and problems in hermeneutics. We will in fact be inquiring into some of the very conditions of self-understanding – and indeed selfhood – that are woven into the fabric of contemporary life itself.
>
> (Freeman 1993: 6)

The question of self leads to a further issue – the 'unity' of narrative. According to some researchers narratives may not always establish a coher-ence in identity, may be unstable constructions, lack a goal or direction, be used according to context, or perhaps restrict a deeper self or social under-standing. As researchers we may be attempting to give 'unity' to lives – including our own. Griffin observes:

> When, as a feminist researcher, I 'speak for' other women (and some-times 'for' men), I cannot avoid telling *my* story about *their* lives. I can use the voices of Others from (my understanding of) their positions, but I can never speak/write *from* their positions. I cannot become them, I can only pass on selected aspects of (what they have shown me about) their lives.
>
> (Griffin, cited in Sparkes 1997b: 34)

As researchers and writers, our own practices can be considered as involv-ing the construction of narrative. Richardson argues: 'narrative is quintes-sential to the understanding and communication of the sociological . . . The issue is not whether sociology should use the narrative, but which narratives will be provided to the reader' (Richardson 1995: 199). There can be a sense that individuals are the stories they tell – as we relate our origins, or our present actions or future intentions, or we give narratives of our education, employment and family life, we are creating and recreating both for our- selves and the audience whom we are. Identity formation within the oral accounts can be seen in statements that say whom we are, where we are from and what our next social movements will be. For some writers, 'The story *is* one's identity, a story created, told, revised, and retold throughout life. We know or discover ourselves, and reveal ourselves to others, by the stories we tell' (Lieblich *et al.* 1998: 7; see also McAdams 1997; Day Sclater 1998).

Case study
Finnegan, R. (1998) *Tales of the City: A Study of Narrative and Urban Life.* Cambridge: Cambridge University Press.

Narrative research has been applied in psychology, anthropology, sociology, medical research and education in the study of particular issues, for example, in relation to life change (illness, ageing, divorce, work career/retirement, migration) (see Riessman 1993; Hatch and Wisniewski 1995b; Lieblich *et al.* 1998). It can also be used to explore the cultural iden- tity of groups and communities. In *Tales of the City* (1998) Ruth Finnegan draws on the 'stories' she collected from 35 individuals from one estate in Milton Keynes – a new city just north west of London planned in the late 1960s which contained around 150,000 people by the mid-1990s. Six stories are presented while another 29 are introduced in support. She describes in detail the collection, interpretation and editing of the interviews, including issues concerning the performance, conventions and writing. The book demonstrates a broad use of narratives – not merely individual stories but academic theories, planners' work and other conceptions (e.g. pro- fessional) of the city. Of her examples, she says:

> In one sense the Milton Keynes examples resemble other story-telling in their potential for being used for almost anything that the teller and the listener(s) choose. They can be told to comfort, amuse, attack, com- plain, show off, protest, overbear, scandalise, woo, bore, satisfy an interviewer – and a thousand other things. There can be no definitive list of uses any more than of individual people or their situations.
>
> (Finnegan 1998: 80)

Thus, the analysis draws on a broad range of narrative theories as well as anthropology and other disciplines. Her intention is to examine the many 'tales' of the city – the 'myths' and the everyday stories of life within the community – how the stories attempt to interpret and shape experience. In an earlier article on the research she began by the questions: 'What makes personal narratives not *just* the narratives of individuals? And can we learn anything from exploring how they interact with our more theoretical stories about social life?' She is intent to explore 'interactions between personal narratives and the images put forward by planners, the media, and academic theorists, thus bringing together recent approaches to personal narrative with work on urban theory' (Finnegan 1996b: 13). Finnegan admits that not all writers would include performance rather than mere text. She attends mainly to verbal stories rather than visual media and applies story to cover story and plot.

She points to the traditions of the study of literary narrative including individual creativity and conventions of style and, to some extent, dispersal and audience. This tradition has also been part of work within anthropology and related fields on oral stories, including the influence of myth on individual and cultural life (Finnegan 1998: 4). She argues that while the literary model of narrative has been widespread in the study of individual lives it has also widened in application to study accounts of groups and organizations. Thus, the notion of 'story' is now widely used to understand virtually everything involving individual experiences, group relations and major institutional practices. Even academic accounts can be seen as constructed like stories with a 'telling' and the use of genre conventions (Finnegan 1998: 5). Thus, she looks at academic theories, the ideas and plans of planners and the accounts of local people. Finnegan attempts to avoid the relativism of the 'postmodern turn' where at the extreme any distinctions between accounts are eroded. While utilizing recent approaches her aim is to locate 'features of story' and apply these to a 'cluster of accounts' – 'tales of the city' or 'multiple narratives' through which the experiences of urban cultural life are shaped. Thus, she attends to how accounts can be regarded as types of 'story'; through narrative the character and role of these accounts can be more fully understood (Finnegan 1998: 8). Implicated here are the dimensions of myth, plot, performance and 'art-ful communication' within narratives from a number of disciplines (sociology, folklore, anthropology and literary studies) (Finnegan 1998: 8). Urban theories, ideas of planners including on the garden city and of Milton Keynes itself, local publications (books, pamphlets), and the work of local groups and societies are seen as sources which local people can use for their own 'tales' (Finnegan 1998: 54). She argues:

> There is something about the concept of a 'new city' which seems to attract the extreme versions of the tales (especially the pessimistic ones) and for some tellers Milton Keynes has been quintessentially cast in that role. Perhaps Milton Keynes' significance thus lies not just in its concrete reality but also in its symbolic role as the current focus for the creative retelling of some deep myths of our culture.
>
> (Finnegan 1998: 55)

Finnegan makes a contrast between 'correspondence' and 'coherence' models of analysis. She takes a pragmatic view, a broad 'coherence' notion of 'truth' in analysing stories, but she also remains attached to the idea that the researcher should retain 'evidential criteria' for interpretations offered and be able to distinguish between forms of storytelling. The givers of stories relate their accounts as describing reality and, thereby, are subject to an evaluation of their truth (Finnegan 1998: 168).

The interesting feature of Finnegan's study of Milton Keynes is the analysis of the variety of narratives of the city and their differences and cultural position – the humanistic self-narrations of local people contrasted with the pessimistic academic and other accounts of urban life. She is aware that narratives are formed by 'accepted conventions' but she recognizes that the individual narratives she collected may have been given differently on previous occasions. Interestingly, she found that the respondents in giving their accounts felt a satisfaction and some control in their lives by being able to provide narratives of their experience. A significance of the study is that it offers the possibility of relating numerous personal and public narratives over time.

Other 'models' of life study

While narrative analysis has enhanced the study of lives, rather different 'models' of study of 'the life' have been prominent within the social sciences and have also undergone recent development. Whereas narrative commonly uses the notion of 'story', these depend upon differing ideas or interpretive or theoretical 'models' to describe analyses of the individual's long-term experience by life history (a natural history metaphor), life span (to bridge, or cover), life plan (an outline to follow), life cycle (again a natural history metaphor), life review (to look back and assess), and life time (subjective coherence and continuity) (see Elder 1981; Salmon 1985; Bryman *et al.* 1987; Cohen 1987; Dex 1991b; Coupland and Nussbaum 1993; Alheit 1994; Giele and Elder 1998b). Giele and Elder outline the life course perspective as composed of a number of principles – the examination of social change according to the shifting pace of transition and life events of groups and individuals. It is an interrelation between how social change influences individuals and groups and, in turn, how groups influence social change:

> *Life course* refers to a sequence of socially defined events and roles that the individual enacts over time. It differs from the concept of the life cycle in allowing for many diverse events and roles that do not necessarily proceed in a given sequence but that constitute the sum total of the person's actual experience over time . . . The life course concept also allows for the encoding of historical events and social interaction

outside the person as well as the age-related biological and psychological states of the organism.

(Giele and Elder 1998a: 22–3)

Shirley Dex seeks to bring together life and work histories to show the interrelation of lives and structures: 'They are a recognition of the importance of
the overlap in the chronology between individuals' lives and social and institutional structures as well as between related individuals' (Dex 1991a: 1–2).
The term 'life review' has been variously used. Robert Butler, in his well-
known early paper 'The Life Review', considered reminiscence as a normal
and beneficial aspect of life which is important in the evaluation of past difficulties and the formation of self-identity (see Thompson 1988: 160; Bornat
1998: 192–3). A little differently, Chivers connects the life review and the life
plan:

> I think that Schutz's . . . concept of life-plan helps us to interpret the
> situation. The idea of the life-plan is of the dominant influences in our
> lives that seem to achieve their way across a range of experience, even
> though we may follow different courses of action and promote a vari-
> ety of projects. Reflection can help us to perceive this life-plan and that,
> I believe, marks a crucial step in the study of life review.
>
> (Chivers 1997: 84)

The process of the life review 'involves the acceptance of one's past life
without regrets . . . as a way of reaching such an attitude of mind by sifting
through memories and putting right what still can be corrected' (Coleman
1991: 129). However, the notion of the life review as being unavoidable has
been questioned especially where older people may be under stress or where
reminiscence without 'review' may be more comforting (Coleman 1991:
129–30). Clausen makes a distinction between 'spontaneous' and 'written
life reviews' and comments:

> Life reviews tend to be fragmentary. Except as a person endeavors to
> describe chronologically the story of his or her life in an autobiography,
> it is doubtful that anyone attempts a full life review . . . It seems impos-
> ible to trace a continuous developmental thread through the intervening
> shadows unless one has maintained a diary or log of the life journey. By
> 'life review', I refer to a person's efforts to reenvision episodes or long
> sequences from the past.
>
> (Clausen 1998: 192)

A further notion is that of the 'script' as a schema in psychology (Cohen
1989: 110–17) or the 'social script' which, like some versions of the idea of
myth, can refer to the stock of explanations and meanings that are present
within more general societal modes of thought (see Thompson 1993: 35).
Also, pioneering advances have been made in terms of 'age cohort' and

historical change as in the work of Riley and Elder in for example, the latter's work on experiences of the Depression showing how the life stage can be linked to historical events which have consequences for subsequent lives (see Elder 1981; Giele and Elder 1998a; O'Rand 1998; Riley 1998; Miller 2000: 24–37).

Mandelbaum draws a useful distinction in anthropology (also found in sociology and psychology) between 'life passage' studies (or life cycle) and life history studies – the former relates to how groups socialize their off-spring into societal members while the latter entails the single individual's experiences and relations to society (Mandelbaum 1982: 146). Life passage studies, he says, have shown us the 'constants' of life experience but rather less of its 'dynamic and adaptive' dimensions; life histories illuminate the shifts between life stages and how choices can affect social change (Mandelbaum 1982: 146).

These various models of biographical study – life as a plan, course, script, cycle, passage and so on – exhibit a diversity of assumption and focus in the collection and analysis of the individual life in terms of transitions, stages or direction. The idea of 'narrative' also has its particular features relevant to analysis – the application of plot and story carry notions, for example, of related structural parts, dramatic form, and an ending. A narrative model, as in the case of the other models, carries its limitations – while individuals attempt to make sense of experiences their lives are not entirely expressed in a consistent, non-contradictory fashion that fits a narrative or story mode. The significance for some of the other models of life for narrative analysis is in the emphasis on group transitions, age cohorts and contexts of social change within socio-historical structures. Across the various types of analysis there is the issue of longitudinal study – whether narrated lives are prospective or retrospective (is our current outlook set according to a previous experience or a current reformulation?) and the possibilities of collecting lives over time as 'stages' in life and wider social changes are experienced.

Conclusion

The prime focus of the chapter has been on narrative analysis in biographical research – how stories are constructed and interpreted. Narrative analysis is a mode of research, which has spread across a broad span of disciplines, and it has claimed distinctive epistemological and methodological foundations. Writers have further argued that the analysis of lives marks a significant 'turning point' in the human and social sciences – a decisive break with positivist analyses towards a meaningful, interpretive, humanistic procedure in the understanding of lives. While different approaches to narrative interviewing and analysis are possible the central feature is the careful listening and reading of the words and stories of the teller.

Questions remain, however, not only about the significance of narrative analysis in general for the future of various disciplines but more particularly for the biographical understanding of individuals: Are we our own stories (our selves 'storied')? In the telling of the story (to an audience and our selves) do we reaffirm and reconstruct the self? Are there aspects of the self that are unspoken – the embodied or unconscious elements which influence narrative formation? What part does time play within these constructions? How are we to study the relation between narrative and time? Are narratives intrinsically 'timed'? How might narratives be evaluated? It is argued that the individual narrative, while not immune from dominant modes of expression (types, symbols, metaphors, explanations), does allow an insight into how we compose our lives. Even so, does the term 'narrative' impose its own limits as a metaphor of story in analysis?

Recommended reading

Crossley, M. (2000) *Introducing Narrative Psychology: Self, Trauma and the Construction of Meaning*. Buckingham: Open University Press. (This text provides an introduction to theories of the self and identity, narrative psychological approaches and the application of narrative analysis to particular contexts.)

Giele, J. Z. and Elder, G. H. Jr (eds) (1998) *Methods of Life Course Research: Qualitative and Quantitative Approaches*. London: Sage. (An extensive introduction to research and issues in life course and life cohort study by leading writers.)

Hatch, J. A. and Wisniewski, R. (eds) (1995) *Life History and Narrative*. London: Falmer Press. (This book examines a wide range of issues within life history and narrative analysis including criteria for narrative analysis and the question of representation with general reference to educational research.)

Hollway, W. and Jefferson, T. (2000) *Doing Qualitative Research Differently: Free Association, Narrative and the Interview Method*. London: Sage. (This text is both a practical guide and an introduction to methodological issues in qualitative research. In particular, it examines the construction of narrative with reference to free association.)

Lieblich, A., Tuval-Mashiach, R., and Zilber, T. (1998) *Narrative Research*. London: Sage. (A guide to models of narrative research with examples and commentary on reading, analysis and interpretation.)

The Narrative Study of Lives (1993–). London: Sage. (A yearly publication which is concerned with narratives, life history and psychobiography with writing from psychology and sociology (and other disciplines).)

Riessman, C. K. (1993) *Narrative Analysis*. London: Sage. (A short introduction to narrative analysis which indicates its use, including a wide range of references, across numerous disciplines, raises methodological and theoretical issues and provides 'practical models' of analysis using examples.)

8 Memory and autobiography

Types of memory

An important feature of the growing interest in biographical research is the degree of interdisciplinary connection as researchers recognize shared interests, common issues and the advantages of cooperative work. Thus, researchers in one area may be made aware of elements in their own practice that they had not fully considered or the benefits of theoretical, interpretive, or other developments in an approach taken elsewhere. The question of the nature of memory is one important area where disciplinary interconnections are being made.

'Memory' is a complex term, which has been subject to a variety of definitions and approaches (see for example in psychology, Morris and Gruneberg 1994). It is also commonly used alongside terms such as recall, recollection, reminiscence, retrospection and review, and often associated with various descriptions of memories, including nostalgia. Attempts have been made to distinguish between some of these terms. For example, Hastrup says:

> Memories . . . are placed in the time they are remembered, narrated, reinterpreted, sometimes rejected and often forgotten. Recollections are immediately experienced. Memory makes a critical difference to these: in being remembered an experience becomes a memory.
> (Hastrup, cited in Coffey 1999: 127)

Memory has been subject to the construction of various types of models and different views of its content and activities – including questions regarding whether it should refer to an overall process, its role in self or personality formation, and its connection with wider social influences. Memory, in one general view, appears as a range of interconnected systems for the sorting of the massive range and types of audio, visual and other information received and a process of extraction of these given the correct cue. It is through 'memory' we can 'recollect' the past and current understanding is made possible (see Baddeley 1999: 19). But it can also be said there is a 'prospective memory' – remembering to do something in the future.

Within cognitive psychology certain well-known distinctions have been made. Much discussion has taken place on how memories of events and experience are 'stored' and 'retrieved', how things are remembered or forgotten and the application of stimuli for recollection. The initial distinction usually made is between sensory, short-term and long-term memory. Sensory memory is mostly discussed in relation to the audio and visual senses and perhaps can be seen as more concerned with the initial processing of information. As its name implies, short-term memory involves those experiences that may be part of more mundane, everyday interactions. Obviously, long-term memory concerns items which stay for lengthy periods, and refers to more permanent organization. From these traditional separations a number of other distinctions have been made, for instance, the multi-storage model posits differences between the saving of visual, audio and other data in repositories for information before they are passed onto long-term memory. Attention has also been given to the idea of rehearsal in the construction of long-term memory and the coding of memories (see Eysenck 1993; Baddeley 1994, 1999). Baddeley has offered the notion of 'working memory' as a more satisfactory conception of short-term memory (Baddeley 1999: 304). Research and discussion of long-term memory has responded to the identification of types of memory and storage by making further distinctions: first between practical or procedural memory – to know how to perform a particular task, e.g. the skill of swimming, driving, and so on – and declarative memory or the knowledge of certain things (events and facts). Within declarative memory – separations are made between factual or semantic memory – what a particular item is (e.g. a banana) rather than details about how that knowledge came about – and episodic memory, concerning personal events (changing jobs, holidays). A problem arises in that it can be difficult to maintain these kinds of distinctions and models (see Morris 1978). For instance, the common idea of memory involving storage containers for a variety of different types of information has been challenged. Instead, more processual or hierarchical views of memory have been offered which stress how memories are processed or are semantically related in networks or levels (see Robinson 1986; Eysenck 1993: 85; Baddeley 1999: 19–20). The long-term remembering of events, according to Hunter (1964), in the distortions and omissions which arise, has an analogy with rumours and folk tales. He concludes that recall can be more an 'imaginative construction' of elements into a 'coherent whole' than a 'literal reproduction'. While usually 'unaware of this constructive characteristic', sometimes in retelling rumours and folktales the individual may consciously add to the drama of the story to engage the audience (Hunter 1964: 183).

A particular type, flashbulb memory or memories, has been posited where a dramatic event is said to deliver a good recall of the details due to its personal effect. People remember, it is held, especially well where they were and how they heard of the event. Some have held that there are certain distinctive features of such memory which enables the remembering of the when, where, how – and what reaction they had to the dramatic happening (e.g. the shooting of President Kennedy). For other writers, flashbulb memory has no special features but holds elements in common with other 'narrative forms' of storytelling and is no different from other clear memories (Cohen 1989: 128–31). Neisser suggests that:

> . . . we remember the details of a flashbulb occasion because those details are the links between our own histories and 'History'. We are aware of this link at the time and aware that others are forging similar links. We discuss 'how we heard the news' with our friends and listen eagerly to how *they* heard. We rehearse the occasion often in our minds and our conversations, seeking some meaning in it.
>
> (Neisser 1982: 48)

He adds that the more we search the more 'compelling our memory of the moment becomes'. The rehearsal may or may not produce 'accuracy' but (he says) the 'existence' is important (rather than the content). Neisser prefers the term 'benchmark' to 'flashbulb':

> . . . such memories are not so much momentary snapshots as enduring benchmarks. They are the places where we line up our own lives with the course of history itself and say, 'I was there.'
>
> (Neisser 1982: 48)

The area of 'autobiographical memory' has been developed in recent years as an attempt to provide a more dynamic conception of memory (Brewer 1986; Rubin 1986a; Conway 1990; Conway *et al.* 1992). Autobiographical memory has been concerned with how events are placed within time by individuals, perhaps according to a period (e.g. the time in a certain job), specific dates (e.g. birthdays, religious festivals) or a major event (public tragedy) (see Brown *et al.* 1986). It can further be said to have taken a significant change in direction away from being 'almost exclusively psychoanalytic or clinical in orientation and diagnostic or therapeutic in aim' (Cohen 1989: 117). In particular, writers have attempted an account that includes many aspects of the psychology of the individual while allowing for the individual's active participation within the social environment (Rubin 1986a; Conway *et al.* 1992). Conway, in his attempt to give a 'structural model', seeks to include a dynamic conception:

> . . . autobiographical memories are not *prestored* in memory in the form of more or less discrete units but rather . . . memories are *dynamically constructed* on the basis of knowledge drawn from different memory structures.
>
> (Conway 1992: 169)

Conway distinguishes between the 'phenomenological' record of specific events and thematic knowledge which 'indexes' it:

> When a person has the experience of remembering a past event then knowledge drawn from the phenomenological record, thematic knowledge, and the self all contribute to the construction of a dynamic representation which constitutes that memory.
>
> (Conway 1992: 169)

Here the 'reconstruction' of memory is of special importance:

> . . . memory is much more often a reconstruction than a reproduction [and so] questions . . . arise about the constructive abilities of our memories that are independent of those memories' relations to past events . . . If memory creates as well as distorts, the principles of that creation need to be understood, and this does not always require knowledge of a particular stimulus presentation.
>
> (Rubin 1986b: 4)

Rubin adds that there are two criteria for judging autobiographical memories – according to the occurrence of past events and how 'real' the individual regards them (Rubin 1986b: 4). The study of autobiographical memory has not sought to discard connections with other areas of psychology, such as personality study, cognitive psychology and social psychology. It utilizes both experimental psychology and more 'real world' research (e.g. diary writing, prospective memory research). Thus, there are questions concerning how more exactly it relates to other areas of psychology. In addition, it has sought to include influences from the humanities and social sciences (Rubin 1986b: 7–8). A common thread in the study of autobiographical memories is the strong connection to the self as both the 'experiencer and the product of the experiences' (Cohen 1989: 118) – its role in the construction of the self and the self's construction of memory. Cohen identifies a number of issues in the study of autobiographical memory concerning: its determinants, distribution over the life span (e.g. older people recalling recent events and those in their early adulthood), dating and accuracy, and whether it refers to content or a processing system (Cohen 1989: 118–20). In terms of content, its different elements – images, schemes, events, and so on – need some clarification (see Brewer 1986). In positing a more dynamic conception of memory, a number of ideas have been offered. For example, Conway gives the idea of memories being 'on-line' and puts forward a 'generative retrieval process' which selects from the structures of long-term memory (Conway 1992). Again, a key feature of autobiographical memory is the attempt to link memory with the formation of the self – a phenomenological connection – as well as place the process of remembering as part of a social context.

Box 8.1

Brown, N. R. et al. (1986) Public memories and their personal context, in D. C. Rubin (ed.) *Autobiographical Memory*. Cambridge: Cambridge University Press.

Brown et al. investigate the knowledge people have of recent history – public memories, and the connection with the knowledge they have of their own lives – personal or autobiographical memories. After reviewing a range of approaches and studies of recall (e.g. flashbulb memories) they report on their own experimental research work on how individuals carry out the dating of political and non-political events (e.g. the fall of the Shah of Iran, the Three Mile Island accident). They found that facts were stored according to the event, an event's relation with others, and the individual's personal situation. The connection between personal and public memories is complex. The authors report that political events tended to be more causally related, indicating that they are part of identifiable narratives. Non-political occurrences were dated more according to autobiographical facts. They suggest that the way individuals date events by inductive judgements give an insight into the organization of long-term memory.

The narrative view of memory has a rather different orientation from most psychological accounts; there are possible areas of overlap with auto-biographical memory. Here, instead of a notion of 'rehearsal' found in some views of memory are ideas of construction, or 'rewriting' (Freeman 1993), and some evaluation or attempt to provide coherence for the construction of the self may be offered (see Gergen and Gergen 1984). There are a number of different emphases in the narrative approach – one common view is that meaning is formed via participation in a social process. Taking this view, Josselson argues:

> Narrative is the representation of process, of a self in conversation with itself and with its world over time. Narratives are not records of facts, of how things actually were, but of a meaning-making system that

makes sense out of the chaotic mass of perceptions and experiences of a life.

(Josselson 1995: 33)

Thus, any notion of 'memory' would have to be situated within the reshaping of the story as plots are developed or even replaced to meet the current position in life of the teller. Here is a stress upon process and time: those elements of experience that are selected are placed within a narrative that attempts to provide a continuity and coherence – but the narrative remains open to alteration as the future is uncertain (Josselson 1995: 35) (see Chapter 7).

Box 8.2

Freeman, M. (1993) *Rewriting the Self: History, Memory, Narrative.* London: Routledge.

Freeman explores deconstructionist and constructionist views by considering selfhood, recollection and the 'fictionalisation of the past'. His method is to raise key questions such as whether there are 'truths beneath the fictions' or 'no true past'? These are explored through case study chapters on well-known texts by St Augustine, Sartre, Keller and others. He asks:

> . . . if in fact the concept of development is bound up with the narratives people tell about the trajectory of the past, and if these narratives are essentially fictional in nature, then development may be little more than that familiar story of progress and self-realization that many wish to tell.
>
> (Freeman 1993: 12; see Usher 1998)

For Freeman, 'life historical knowledge' is both retrospective and prospective:

> What, though, are the implications of this perspective? Is life historical knowledge essentially retrospective? Or is it more appropriately formulated 'prospectively', with what happens earlier determining, with the inexorability of fate itself, what later will be? Could it be both? It could indeed . . .
>
> (Freeman 1993: 23; see Usher 1998)

Freeman poses a number of vital issues relating to lives and stories told about them as socially constructed – for instance, how can critique be possible if we are formed by our culture? How can a different consciousness develop in narrative to shift the encircling sociocultural context?

Whether we follow some form of a social constructionist or narrative view of the perceptions of the future and the past (see Freeman 1993) or a more 'realist' grounding of accounts of past experience, the question of how individuals 'time' their biographies cannot be avoided (see Ricoeur 1981; Erben 1998b; Roberts 1999a; Chapter 7, this volume). Time and its implication in the construction of memory, it can be argued, is fundamental to an understanding of human action. In fact, the importance of an understanding of the experience and construction of time in human life has become generally more central within wider social theory and analysis. As Adam states:

> Human time is characterised by transcendence and this is expressed in many distinct ways. All human action, for example, is embedded in a continuity of past, present, and future, extends into the past and future and constitutes those horizons whilst binding them in a present. Habits and traditions, goals, wishes and intentions, values and meanings, even pragmatic action, are only possible with such temporal extensions.
>
> (Adam 1990: 127)

Individual experience is set within lived time. For biographical research an interpretation of told lives which focuses on a simple idea of the recollection of the past would fail to realize how experiences are set within temporal relations of past, present and future.

The social transmission of memories

Memories can be transmitted in numerous ways – between individuals and groups, across generations, recovered after a time lapse, or subtly or radically modified over time. The means may be according to verbal media (audiotape), or written record (diaries, letters, autobiographies, articles, memos), social practices or visual imagery (see Vansina 1973; Neisser 1982; Connerton 1992; Finnegan 1992; Radstone 2000). Texts may be remembered and presented orally (e.g. in the performance of a play) or by oral traditions (carried in poetry, song). Within oral history the issue of memory has figured increasingly as a topic for detailed consideration. The sometimes rather simple view of memory as merely reflecting reality has been challenged in a number of ways by the work of Passerini (1979, 1990, 1992a), Grele (1985), Portelli (1990, 1991) and others. These writers point to questions of subjectivity, performance and collaboration in the interview situation; memories may also be 'suppressed' as if nothing of consequence had happened in a period, or periods 'foreshortened'. Certain periods may be given changes in meaning and importance as individuals continually reinterpret or reassess their 'past' – thus, the 'timing' of narrative is not simply chronological (see Skultans 1998a, 1998b). Michael Frisch, within oral history, argues that bringing together memory, experience and history alongside a detached view gives an important means of observing how people carry their culture and history (Frisch 1998: 36).

Of course, individuals in using 'the past' are also constructing it and memories are subject to the vagaries of recollection – loss, distortion, and fiction:

> We can see how it is precisely where memory diverges most clearly from fact that 'imagination, symbolism, desire break in' . . . We can learn to spot in these accounts the typical tricks of 'dream-work': the condensations, reversals, substitutions, metaphors, and word-play through which symbolic messages are conveyed, not only in dreams, but also in social customs like rough music, in jokes, in classical traditional myth, or in contemporary personal storytelling . . . as Freud first taught us, memory is inherently revisionist, an exercise in selective amnesia.
>
> (Samuel and Thompson 1990a: 7)

Box 8.3

Skultans, V. (1998) Remembering Latvian childhood and the escape from history, *Auto/Biography*, VI(1/2): 5–13.

Skultans found that memories of childhood in Latvian narratives could not simply be understood according to chronology; the 'retrospective unfolding of narrative' led her to the idea of a 'story told backwards' due to later experiences and current perspective:

> In this way the narrative comes to order not only narrative time but also one's beliefs about real time and real events. The eternal structures of Latvian childhood remembered draw their power from the terrible events which succeeded them.
>
> (Skultans 1998a: 12; see also Skultans 1997, 1998b)

Skultans collected narratives between 1992 and 1997 following the ending of communism. Having been a child refugee, she returned in 1990 ('an irresistible yet deeply unsettling experience') and met relatives in her fieldwork, although she had some knowledge of the country from her family and story and picture books.

Grele argues that by recognizing the ideological context of the oral history interview oral historians have a way of dealing with the mass of information provided by the informant and by addressing the complex issue of historical memory can begin to reveal the deeper structures which inform what seem unconnected words or parts (Grele 1998: 48–9). The research on autobiographical memory is of interest here. Brown *et al.* in their research on the dating of different types of public events by respondents found that autobiographical experiences in personal life are often applied to date a non-political public event. In the dating of political events connection was made to broader political narrative or periods (Brown *et al.* 1986).

Luisa Passerini and Alessandro Portelli brought a sophisticated attention to how omissions and reordering of memories occur; these are of considerable importance in understanding how individuals form their conception of past events (Passerini 1979, 1990; Portelli 1990, 1991) (see Chapter 6). What is apparent in the study of memory, as emphasized within oral history, is that we are not simply dealing with individual memories but also group, generational, and more formal public accounts – these interrelate with individual memories in complex ways (see Perks and Thomson 1998b: Part IV). Passerini (1990) examines the relationship between myth and history and offers the idea of 'mythbiography'. Analysing life stories of the events of 1968 she found 'archetypes' in each but as present in different and particular forms – individuals could have taken other paths and interpreted 'a certain myth in an alternative or new way': 'Life stories can thus be seen as constructions of single mythbiographies, using a choice of resources, that include myths, combining the new and ancient in unique expressions' (Passerini 1990: 59).

Memory may take the form of myth as a 'script' – an outline of a story within which the details change but the fundamental outline or structure may vary much less. The notion of script is employed by Thompson when analysing 'family mysteries' (e.g. concerning parentage). He says, 'when the mystery is repeated in more than one generation, it can become a particularly powerful family script' (Thompson 1993: 35). The individual alters small elements or adds/subtracts as the account is given and in different contexts. There may well be previous tellings or rehearsals but the individual is not trying (usually) to provide the ultimate account; rather the individual renders variations around given themes or plot. From this perspective lives and memory are 'storied' rather than stored and within 're-collection' the importance of the 'timing' of lives is crucial to the understanding of how individuals construct their lives (Thompson 1993: 36).

Case study
Passerini, L. (ed.) (1992) *Memory and Totalitarianism*. Oxford: Oxford University Press.

In the examination of memory and narrative, psychologists, oral and social historians, sociologists and others are crossing disciplinary boundaries and seeing areas of commonality and potential development for their own work (see Thompson 1992: v). An example of the interdisciplinary approach to memory can be found in the work of Passerini and others in *Memory and Totalitarianism* (Passerini 1992b; see also Bertaux and Thompson 1993a,

Rosenthal 1998). Passerini's book includes 'The life stories of survivors of the Jewish proletariat in Amsterdam' by Selma Leydesdorff, 'The Gulag in memory' by Irina Sherbakova and articles on the past repression in Spain, the generation in the GDR who had been children during the Weimar Republic, and other articles from Germany, Hungary and the former Soviet Union (Leydesdorff 1992; Sherbakova 1992). Also included are review articles on oral history and Italian Fascism and everyday life in Vichy France. A number of the articles demonstrate the intricacies of memory and the need for a complex interpretation beyond mere reportage. For example, Lutz Niethammer's study of memories of the uprising in East Germany in June 1953 found many had placed the events in a 'niche in memory'. In answer to the question 'Where were you on 17 June?', some respondents said they had no special recollection, a relatively small number admitted taking part in demonstrations, while a third group exhibited an 'informed non-participation' or high knowledge of events but low participation. The latter appears to be a legacy of totalitarianism and provided a number of curious stories. One saw a procession but said she did not join because 'Well, 'cause I was waiting for my train', another had to hurry home through a crowd after collecting bees from a friend, 'Naturally, that's something that has to do once again with bees' (Niethammer 1992: 52–3). The articles by Stern and Leydesdorff explore the memories of Jewish survivors of World War II and contrast these with other memories and the impact that different experiences and consciousness have on our interpretations (Leydesdorff 1992; Stern 1992). Some other articles point to the context of research in the former Soviet Union – the effect of the 'fear of public remembering' and the lasting consequences for personal remembering (Khubova *et al.* 1992: 89) and the 'politics' of memory where for decades 'historical truth . . . lived on only through underground memory . . . memory itself was intrinsically a serious threat' to the system (Sherbakova 1992: 103).

In reviewing this work on memories in the aftermath of the end of the Soviet Union, Passerini says commentators have noted a possible 'new cancellation' – the attempt to eradicate aspects of the past in, for instance, the renewal of churches, new street and town names and so on. But this is to pretend that events have not taken place – it is 'the violence of the present on memory'. She argues that the past should be investigated to differentiate between aspects of heritage – values and ideas and their application, as well as the political and economic conditions (Passerini 1992a: 9). In comparing the effects of the ending of totalitarianism across eastern Europe she says that it appears that quite different experiences may be recalled in similar ways (e.g. in East Germany the confusion of names given to mass organizations under Nazism and Stalinism) while differences (e.g. between East and West Germany) are apparent in those who were considered the significant victims in World War II. Another important factor Passerini identifies in the connection between memory and totalitarianism is the length of time that the major examples lasted (Italian Fascism, Stalinism and Nazism) and, in addition, the fact that generational experience was also different. Even within a generation the kinds of 'silences' may differ about the period. For some, the silence was disrupted by 'jokes and contradictions, showing that memory has its own ways of recording and transmitting daily life and its relationship to power' (Passerini 1992a: 11). Nevertheless, 'similar mechanisms', such as 'feelings of guilt and complicity', are apparent even where there are different experiences and an 'attitude of victimization' shown in putting the 'blame on power and on their own helplessness, as if nothing could be done to resist domination' (Passerini 1992a: 11). This finding has an interesting parallel in Frisch's influential comments on Studs Terkel's *Hard Times: An Oral History of the Great Depression*, which showed how failure led to broad experiences being seen in 'personal terms' (and hid them from 'threatening historical truths') but 'survival' stimulated individuals to expand their own biographical experiences in an historical account providing 'at once a self-validating message and a culturally validating legacy' for subsequent generations (Frisch 1998: 36).

This research volume edited by Passerini on totalitarianism shows the value of the exploration of the meaning of silences, the use of justifications, the importance of different memories, how hopes and expectations for the future may shape the 'past', and the conditions under which new interpretations (and new 'absences') arise (see also Rogers *et al.* 1999). It is through memories that she believes an exploration of 'equality and cosmopolitanism' can be advanced: through sharing the diverse and plural memories of others, totalitarianism in culture and politics and its connection with memory can be challenged and a 'democratic consciousness' formed (Passerini 1992a: 18).

Family and group memories

Psychological theorization, and more particularly psychoanalysis, has been some referent for forms of biographical research (e.g. oral history) which have wanted guidance on the study of memories of individuals within family or small groups (see Chapter 6). The settings of individual and family therapy, and the exploration of the effects of past formative experiences on current relations and the operation of suppression and releasing of memories, have an initial attraction for biographical research. The notions of the unconscious, the recovery of hidden or repressed memories, seem to give some possibilities for the understanding of the workings of memory. Certainly, some form of conversation or interview is able to gather information about family and group dynamics, which may not be possible by other means (Thompson 1988: 132). However, there is a difference in setting and objectives between clinical practice and research by narrative analysis, oral history or life history interview. What has been beneficial from psycho-analysis has not been so much the practice and the range of concepts but an introduction to the questions of language and symbolism and the inner complexity of memory (Thompson 1988: 156). Types of therapy show the lesson that there is

> the need for an enhanced historical sensitivity to the power of emotion, of unconscious desire, rejection, and imitation, as an integral part of the structure of ordinary social life and of its transmission from generation to generation.
>
> (Thompson 1988: 154)

Bertaux and Thompson have pointed to the importance of intergenerational family transmission in terms of culture and language, various skills, general social outlook and the assumed patterns of behaviour of individuals (Bertaux and Thompson 1993b: 1; see Chapter 6, this volume). Thompson, in analysing life stories as a form of transmission, shows how they also indicate what is passed on through the family. Stories and images provide a 'mental map' for family members: 'Family stories are the grist of social description, the raw material for both history and social change' (Thompson 1993: 36). Another example of the study of family transmission is provided by Rosenthal who examined the impact of the lives of 'victims' and 'perpetrators' of the holocaust on subsequent generations by a detailed investigation of a number of cases (Rosenthal 1998; see also Rapaport 1997).

Public and private memories

Memories are not merely 'individual', as only based on personal experience and subsequent recall. Groups and institutions also carry representations of the past. 'Public memories' are produced in various ways by major state institutions, local government, the local and national media, businesses, theatre and tourist organizations and so on. Particular institutions are also charged with providing historical accounts, such as museums and interpretation centres at historical sites. All these institutions provide (often contrasting) representations of 'traditions', 'legacies' and commemorations in various spheres of life or the 'nation as a whole' (see Young 1993; Winter 1995; Fussell 2000). In addition, perhaps less 'public', there has been considerable growth in ethnic, local or other groups interpreting their past through oral history projects and writing and publishing historical accounts of their experiences and responses to change. So in many ways individuals come into contact – as members of public audiences or participants in communal activities – with historical imagery and interpretations of various kinds on a regular, even daily, basis (see Fortier 2000). Any individual life story that is collected is formed in relation with numerous representations of the past, what is remembered and forgotten, and often competing or changing historical discourses (Amit-Talai and Knowles 1996; Popular Memory Group 1982).

In the view of the Popular Memory Group the investigation of 'popular memory' necessitates the investigation of two sets of relations – the relation between 'dominant memory and oppositional forms' across the 'public field' and that between the operation of contemporary public discourses and the more private sense of the past in 'lived culture' (Popular Memory Group 1982: 211). This perspective and similar views by other writers challenged the more naïve approach within early oral history practice that subordinate groups were being given an authentic voice without fully questioning the interplay between dominant and other historical accounts (Perks and Thomson 1998a: 4). The theoretical and methodological problem is how this interconnection can be understood without 'losing' the 'private account' –

Box 8.4

Thomson, A. (1994) *Anzac Memories: Living with the Legend.* Oxford: Oxford University Press.

In this important study, Thomson explores the relation between individual and group memories of Australian soldiers who fought in World War I (see also Thomson 1998). In a complex analysis he contrasts the dominant meanings of nation and egalitarianism with the meanings given to their experiences by the returned troops. He utilizes contemporary journalists' writing, official histories and other sources, as well as subsequent portraits and the life stories of individuals, to explore the creation of the legend of the Anzac soldier. The official help given to the veterans often differed sharply from the conservative, public portrayal – and the painful memories of the war. Thomson found that meanings of memories could shift as years elapsed due to the intervening life experiences and public commemorations of past events. There is then a complex set of processes as new evaluations become influential on the interpretation of past events and as personal identity shifts and war memories are affected. This study not only raises important questions regarding the construction of private and public memory but also the role of the researcher. In potentially challenging the bases of these memories, political and ethical questions arise regarding the foundation of alternative accounts (see Thomson 1994, 1998; Thomson *et al.* 1994; see also Evans and Lunn 1997). Of considerable interest here would be further research which could follow groups over time and map the different historical interpretations (individual, group, public) as they change and interconnect.

the distinctive individual experience and memory – within the broader public historical representations (see Thomson 1994). The Popular Memory Group's discussion, according to some oral historians, was a 'top-down' notion of memory which neglected the variety of types of memory (Thomson *et al.* 1994: 34). Robins argues that in the Group's perspective: 'Individuals are criticized either for forgetting material they have never known, or for failing to possess a memory expansive enough to encompass social conditions the limits of which have yet to be specified' (Robins 1995: 211). Instead, he draws on a number of studies whose stress on how individuals are active in 'self-narration and self-creation' starts to show how the 'fragmented subject' of postmodernity gives a 'subjective experience of continuity as well as discontinuity' (Robins 1995: 201).

A keen area of debate has surrounded the 'construction of heritage' and national or other identities by individuals and groups (see Johnson *et al.* 1982; Hobsbawm and Ranger 1983; Lowenthal 1985; Wright 1985; Curtis 1986; Hewison 1987; Lumley 1988; Corner and Harvey 1991; Samuel 1994). A central issue has been the extent to which museums, historical 'theme' parks, forms of official commemoration and 'television history' are providing 'false' representations of the past and a 'commodified' history pushed by commercial values, dominant ideological interpretations and imagery, or a group or national desire to escape to the past at a time of rapid social change and relative industrial decline. Of interest here is the degree to which the audience is perceived as, or is in reality composed of, 'cultural dupes' or whether its members are taking part in a more subtle process of appreciation and evaluation of the 'evidence' provided. 'Memories' given in public spheres may be powerful in influence but are not necessarily uniform, and may not match the lived experience of the audience according to more 'private' memories of local groups, or reflect other social differences.

Methodological issues: recollection and selectivity

The most important point to make about memory concerns the question of definition. At the psychological and physiological 'levels' there is still very much to learn about what constitutes 'memory' – its basis, forms, content and operation. At the social 'level' there has been an increasing awareness of the complex interplay between individual and wider memories, how 'stories' are composed and retold, and the importance of a sense of the past (present and future) in establishing individual and social identity. All of these issues in memory have become subject to much academic and social debate or concern surrounding 'false memories' of forms of abuse, the coping with recurrent memories of traumatic accidents or disasters, and memory loss and the ageing processes. Important methodological questions arise regarding the reliability and validity of memory, and theoretical problems such as how the different 'levels' or 'types' work together. They also involve concerns in relation to how social intervention – therapeutic, legal, welfare – considers memory and on what basis forms of intervention are organized.

The process of memory (how memories are 'triggered', reviewed and 'sedimented') and the selectivity of memory (what is recalled, in what order, and how meanings are given and changed) provide very difficult challenges for interpretation. These challenges concern whether the focus is on individuals or groups (or both) when analysing memories, how certain aspects of the life told have been selected, and on what basis a selection from the account is made by the researcher (according to depth of meaning given by the respondent, or comparability or other purpose of the research, and so on). They also include the type of interpretive analysis adopted (theory generation or application), and theoretical perspectives (for instance, narrative theory, linguistics, phenomenology) to be employed.

There is another aspect of memory in research on individual lives. The researcher uses memory as any individual does; more specifically the researcher draws upon biographical experience from both academic practice and wider living in formulating, conducting and revising, and presenting the research product. As Coffey comments, referring to field research, ethnography 'is in itself an act of collective and individual memories' which involves our autobiographical experiences and our temporal framing as well as those of the researched (Coffey 1999: 110–13). Thompson states: 'Remembering in an interview is a mutual process, which requires understanding on both sides' (Thompson 1988: 135).

In reflecting on my own early educational experiences I found that despite having told the 'story' of my schooling innumerable times (at least in part) it seemed surprisingly difficult to write (Roberts 1998). This difficulty was in some measure due to an awareness of making a published 'record'; I found that a continuous 'editing' was taking place in the writing regarding family members and others as experiences were selected. It produced in my mind questions such as, why do we not ask of ourselves the questions we ask others? How and why do respondents in biographical research 'edit' their memories in certain ways – for themselves, for the wider audience, or for us?

Conclusion

The investigation of memory can bring dangers for interpretation unless a sophisticated (and more advantageous) approach is taken which recognizes that individuals, groups and organizations interpret their surroundings by a complex interweaving of 'fact' and 'fictionalisation' (Thompson 1988: 135). In addition, there are different memories or even competing memories of the same events: contesting dominant/subordinate memories (Popular Memory Group 1982); conflicting memories and accounts (Stern 1992; Schrager

1998); and distinctions between public/private and informal group/individual memories and so on. Different memories are not isolated but interact and have mutual influences – if only by opposition – in a complex set of processes. Memories are also delivered according to language use – employing genres and devices (description, dialogue, humour, polemic, justifications, drama, allegory, metaphor, pauses and emphasis) and so are 'performative', whether oral or written, for an audience and its intended reaction. Memories are also refined, remade, reviewed and rehearsed. Finally, there is the context of the interview (or request for a written account) – the prior expectations of the participants, the dialogical or conversational character of the interaction, and subsequent (post-interview) interaction between researcher and researched. The questions, cues, prompts, clarifications, examples, anecdotes, self-editing and reassurances and other aspects of the interaction 'frame' what is remembered, but it is not a one-way process: the researcher brings a life experience and memories which inform the relationship and may well be alluded to. The interview (or the requested, written biography) must be seen as another opportunity for individuals to tell their 'story' – one which they have given before in different circumstances and different ways (see Shrager 1998: 284–5). Memory or 'memories' are therefore not just an unchanging collection of items to be brought forward in the interview or to be written down but shift over time in content, organization and expression. What is apparent is the complexity of the processes of memory (the construction and reshaping of memory) and the broad extent to which different types can be identified. Important questions remain: why do we remember certain events? Are certain kinds of events remembered more than others?

Recommended reading

Psychology textbooks usually give some detail on memory and there are various psychological texts devoted to the subject: for example, see

Morris, P. and Gruneberg, M. (eds) (1994) *Theoretical Aspects of Memory*. London: Routledge.

The International Yearbook of Oral History and Life Stories paid considerable attention to memory with reference to migration, the family, totalitarianism and other areas:

Benmayor, R. and Skotnes, A. (eds) (1994) *Migration and Identity: International Yearbook of Oral History and Life Stories*, III. Oxford: Oxford University Press.
Bertaux, D. and Thompson, P. (eds) (1993) *Between Generations: Family, Models, Myths and Memories: International Yearbook of Oral History and Life Stories*, II. Oxford: Oxford University Press.
Leydesdorff, S., Passerini, L. and Thompson, P. (eds) (1996) *Gender and Memory: International Yearbook of Oral History and Life Stories*, IV. Oxford: Oxford University Press.

Ethnography and
biographical research

Biographical research has a place in ethnography in a number of ways. Ethnography is not merely about a group in its social context; it reveals how differing individuals interact at various moments as they move through the setting and meet the ethnographer's gaze and verbal intervention. Some individuals appear rather more than others in the ethnographic setting and the later research text as more fully rounded 'characters', others have a background or infrequent presence. Thus, there are different types of biographical presentations within ethnographic research, including those deemed 'key informants' – sought out, selected and relied upon for introductions, guidance and information. In some ethnography lives may be presented rather more than in passing but described in some detail as part of family or group relationships. Biographies also appear in another way: the ethnographer has a biographical presence as an actor who brings their personal experience and personality as an active member of the situation. Shifts in assumptions, focus and theoretical references in regard to research relations, the collection of material and the presentation of the study have affected ethnography, as in other research practices. A recent emphasis has been upon developing the 'biographical' dimension of ethnography – as in notions of bio- and auto-ethnography, researcher reflexivity and collaboration within the full research (including writing) process.

Fieldwork, ethnography and participant observation – definition and practice

The term 'fieldwork' can be used to describe investigations in anthropology and sociology, which include the use of ethnography or participant observation. 'Fieldwork', 'ethnography' and 'participant observation' are often used interchangeably, but commonly fieldwork is applied to describe a broader range of research practices. There has been a great deal of difference in guidelines and practice within these areas. Ethnography, for instance, is itself a complex practice and perhaps separable from participant observation as a general methodological approach. Participant observation is perhaps more usefully applied to the type of contact with 'subjects'. Fieldwork is a broad collection of methods (e.g. types of formal interview) (Reinharz 1992: 46; Bernard 1995).

Ethnography, in practice, is usually associated with the idea of the detached investigator of a setting who gathers disparate material by methods including participant observation for the purpose of interpreting meanings. At base, ethnography involves a closeness to others over time – by observation, interaction and also the collection of relevant material for the purpose of the study (Hammersley and Atkinson 1989: 2).

Ethnography, it is held, includes making people feel at ease, 'trusting' in relation to the researcher's intervention and the situation so that material can be gathered on their lives and circumstances. Its proponents see the uncovering of the daily events and meanings of social life as its positive contribution to social study. However, critics have argued that the method depends on the subjective observations and interpretations of the researcher, and that its procedures render the reported material open to doubt, e.g. in terms of replicability and representativeness. Its defenders respond that the subjective meanings informing action are revealed and are understandable in a manner not possible in a more restricted involvement with the social context found in less processual, quantitative survey or other research designs (Hammersley and Atkinson 1989: 2).

In short, the ethnographer seeks the everyday aspects of culture, whether it be in a different, remote location or a familiar institution such as a school, a work organization, or a housing estate (Spradley 1979: 3; Fetterman 1998: 1).

Research roles

Usually initial discussions of research roles in ethnography make a distinction between degrees of participation and observation by the researcher. Bernard gives a standard distinction in describing participant observation as ranging from more observation to more participation. Others have characterized roles at different points on the continuum between those two poles (see Denzin 1970: 189–94; Bryman 1988: 48; Bernard 1995: 138–9). But even this may be too simple since researchers may vary in degrees of expertise, previous information and so on (Atkinson and Hammersley 1994: 249). Brewer suggests an interesting contrast between 'pure participant observation' which requires a new role in an unfamiliar setting and 'pure observant participation' where an existing role is used in a familiar setting (Brewer 2000: 60–1).

What is clear is that fieldwork, ethnography and participant observation are practices containing numerous types of relations between researcher and researched – in terms of socio-historical context, forms of interaction, and biographical experiences (see Rose, 1990; Coffey, 1999).

Methodological issues

The use of ethnography (or participant observation) in fieldwork is not only commonly described in textbook discussions as having the advantage of being able to obtain materials on social life that other methods cannot or do not attempt to collect. Relatedly, the use of the method is sometimes said to give an extra means for meeting validity in a research study when added to other methods by giving a means of cross-checking data. Bernard says that there are various reasons for using participant observation in research on cultural groups since it allows the collection of particular types of data; gives a diminution of subjects' reactivity; makes possible 'understandable questions' for respondents; gives the investigator 'confidence' in the meaning of data; addresses issues of internal and external validity, and may be the most appropriate method to study an organization and community (Bernard 1995: 140–3). Thus, it has been used to criticize quantitative methods for 'reifying' social phenomena and imposing a hierarchy and control in the stance towards the subjects and setting (Atkinson and Hammersley 1994: 252). Feminists, seeking to give recognition to women's life experience and perspectives on the social world, have advocated the use of ethnography and life histories as a rejoinder against male bias, the deficiencies of quantitative methods and positivistic principles of research. In addition, it is claimed such methods open the possibilities for collecting materials applicable to change and also enable a collaborative relationship and mutual understanding between the researcher and the researched (Reinharz 1992: 46). Debate, however, has emerged on whether feminist researchers should use quantitative methods and the degree to which feminist research brings new dimensions to traditional qualitative methods (Hammersley 1992a; Reinharz 1992: 47; Oakley 1998).

Criticisms have latterly been applied to traditional ethnography itself, despite its claim to be 'closer' to the social world. A questioning of qualitative method has come from mixed sources – hermeneutics, postmodernism and constructivism – with renewed attention to the researcher's position in research and how data collection and the writing processes in the research report are informed by meanings outside the research (Atkinson and Hammersley 1994: 252). For some, even though hermeneutical and other approaches have actually aided its development, ethnography still has a fundamental difficulty – it has not shaken off the language, assumptions and debates surrounding traditional scientific procedures such as reliability, validity and representativeness (see Hammersley 1992b; Haines 1993: 346).

What appears to be the case in ethnographic research is that the critique of 'realism' within ethnography has been alongside a range of theoretical and methodological approaches (symbolic interactionism, literary theory, postmodernism, feminism) which have informed new directions and new issues. These developments have often crucially centred on the biographical experiences of researcher and researched within the sociocultural and historical setting and the questions of representation and audience. Perhaps it is more worthwhile to see older and more recent issues as a series of dilemmas (subject/object; realism/representation; past/present) to be negotiated rather than insist on a split between positivist and non-positivist camps.

Ethnography and key informants

While an orientation to the processes of interpretation and textual construction has provided a much needed recognition of the writing and reading of ethnographic texts there is the possibility of too much stress on styles of writing and intricate generic features. What may be lost or lessened are the autobiographical experiences and presence of the researcher and researched. But, the attention to the diverse and shifting meanings in ethnographic settings and the challenge to the traditional separation of the allegedly superior cultural interpretations of the researcher from the descriptions given by 'subjects' in texts brings a refocus on ethnographic fieldwork and the autobiographical processes within interpretation and writing. Here, attention is now drawn to the possibilities of a collaborative relation in research and the recognition of the 'dialogical' nature of fieldwork and interpretive writing. At its furthest, there is an attempt to see fieldwork, report writing and audience reception as a complete process of interpretation and reinterpretation between subject–researcher–audience.

Within anthropological fieldwork 'life histories' have featured in past studies but the provision of interpretive guidelines or 'rationales' was limited in early work. Kluckhohn in 1945 reported from his survey for the SSRC on life histories in anthropology (published between 1920 and 1940) that methodological issues were apparent in its application to a wide range of topics but still analysis required development (Mandelbaum 1982: 147; see Kluckhohn 1945). Even the later well-known work by Oscar Lewis has been described as rather more descriptive than analytic (Mandelbaum 1982: 148; see Lewis 1961).

Box 9.1

Lewis, O. (1961) *The Children of Sanchez: Autobiography of a Mexican family.* New York, NY: Random House.

Lewis asked a large number of questions of members of a poor Mexican family, producing detailed information on a wide range of areas which they might not have offered information or even have considered (Bryman 1988: 49). He outlines his close relationship through many hours of contact with the family, the involvement in daily problems and activities and the trust and friendship that developed. Thompson classifies Lewis's treatment in *The Children of Sanchez* (1961) under the heading of 'a collection of stories' life history type: while being less detailed than single narratives they may be used in a group for the construction of 'broader historical interpretation' (Thompson 1988: 237).

In general, while life stories are not a central feature of ethnographic research, nevertheless, as Coffey argues, 'characters are still narratively constructed, through episodes, events and the context of the setting. Lives still get constructed and told, but as exemplars of the social setting and social processes' (Coffey 1999: 128).

Perhaps the most prominent method described in discussions of fieldwork, apart from participant observation, is the 'ethnographic interview' – the most direct means of gaining 'the life' in traditional ethnography. These may vary from informal to formal, requested or unrequested with regard to the length and type of contact made, context, types of question and so on. In fact, a wider range of 'interviews' are conducted in fieldwork than often acknowledged, with some questions being formulated beforehand or in other cases arising during the contact. All the various kinds of 'interview' relation can be considered as forms of conversation – with monitoring, reflection and evaluation undertaken on the 'interview' process, during and after its completion (see Hammersley and Atkinson 1989: 113–14).

Traditionally, ethnographic texts have outlined criteria for the selection of the 'ideal' informant (see Spradley 1979; Tremblay 1982; Johnson 1990). Often, a number of characteristics of the 'key' ethnographic informant, such as willingness to participate, relevant knowledge of the culture, a particular social position, are recommended. Good communication skills and someone who is not prone to academic theorizing are other characteristics mentioned in texts. In this way the selection of informants is portrayed as different from the usual formal sampling techniques.

Box 9.2

Whyte, W. F. ([1943]1955) *Street Corner Society*, 2nd edn. Chicago, IL: University of Chicago Press.

'Doc' in Whyte's *Street Corner Society* is one of the most famous examples of a key informant. Whyte, commentating later on collaboration with key informants, said:

> The man I called 'Doc' in *Street Corner Society* (1943) was far more to me than an informant in the usual sense of the term. Beginning as my chief guide into the intricacies of Cornerville, he came to be also a collaborator in the research. We spent many hours discussing what he and I were observing. Piece by piece, he read through the first draft of the book and gave me his detailed criticisms.
>
> (Whyte 1970: 38)

Doc introduced Whyte to his friends and various social settings in the community. Whyte commented that as they got to know each other Doc ceased to be a 'passive informant'. He concluded that it was the stories of the individuals that provided a means of gaining a picture of Cornerville:

> Instead of getting a cross-sectional picture of the community at a particular point in time, I was dealing with a time sequence of interpersonal events . . . I was seeking to build a sociology based upon observed interpersonal events. That, to me, is the chief methodological and theoretical meaning of *Street Corner Society*.
>
> (Whyte 1955: 358)

Whyte has vigorously defended his field methodology and relations with those reported in the study, and his portrait of the community, against subsequent criticisms (Whyte 1992).

In ethnographic practice 'lives', it seems, are addressed through various kinds of interview with key informants and interaction and observation in different settings. Surprisingly, what have been less apparent are detailed life histories of individuals due to the intention to reveal the wider cultural meanings of the group. Nevertheless, some writers have noted the usefulness of life histories for ethnographic research. Life histories, Fetterman argues, can provide ethnographers with 'rich, detailed autobiographical descriptions'; a distinctive personal story can also deliver an informed picture of the social group (Fetterman 1998: 51).

Ethnography has also been affected by the 'biographical turn' in the human sciences. For some writers, while 'the life (hi)story approach has been popular in anthropology in the past . . . it is now informed by different assumptions, questions, concepts, formats, and writing styles' (Driessen 1998: 7). Gubrium and Holstein (1995) argue that there is 'a radical reorientation to the study of lives' in the social sciences, which offers the possibility of a 'new ethnography' which places emphasis on social construction and the active, biographical 'subject':

> We refer to this constitutive process as *biographical work* . . . Whether it is the personal past, the present, the future, a combination of them, or the life course as a whole, participants work at characterizing their lives in relation to the interpretive horizons of social settings, using available interpretive resources.
>
> (Gubrium and Holstein 1995: 46–47)

They use the ideas of 'narrative linkages', local culture and organizational embeddedness to show how 'biographical work' is provided within 'interpretive practices' as affected by different social situations. Included here are the participants' own accounts and interpretations of their own lives – elements missing from traditional perspectives. These 'reality-constituting voices' should be given as much attention by ethnographers as their own analyses (Gubrium and Holstein 1995: 56). More recently, some discussion has taken place on testimony or 'testimonio' – a 'demotic' form of life history with less intrusion by the researcher which has a sociopolitical intent to communicate marginalized experiences directly with an audience; a form of life history as 'resistance' or urgency for change which has developed largely in South America (Beverley 2000; Tierney 2000: 540).

This notion of the participants as also interpreters (or bio-ethnographers) provides a more complex view of their everyday life in organizational or other settings – not as simply 'organizational dopes' but as possessing 'the biographical basis for resistance, personal and interpersonal histories that compete with organizational categories as means of interpreting experience' (Holstein and Gubrium 1994: 268). At this point, Smith cautions against making the local voice an heroic figure against global oppression and proposes a theory of transnational urbanism and a transnational ethnography, drawing on studies of migration and social struggles, in which local cultures are not sealed nor globalism monolithic (Smith 2001).

Reflexivity and the researcher's life experience of ethnography

The 'self' of the researcher may appear in comments in field notes or in a diary (as in the well-known case of Malinowski), or may take the form of 'confessionals' or 'auto-ethnographies' (see Van Maanen 1988, 1995a; Cohen 1992; Reed-Danahay 1997). Traditionally, as described earlier, the ethnographer's work has been described as conforming to one of a number of roles with, commonly, ethnographic intervention considered along a range of 'stances'. However, a stance may change during the course of a study, for instance as the researcher becomes intimately part of the social milieu or moves from situation to situation (Reinharz 1992: 70). While the traditional description of starting the research was to begin without preconceptions, now different biographical experience and ways of seeing are not merely recognized but embraced as part of a negotiated interactive relation between researcher and researched which continues – and should be reflected upon – during the research. Also, the research context and the material collected has a legacy, not merely in terms of the notes made, but also in the memories that are held and stimulated in writing up the research text (see Coffey 1999: 127).

The discussion of research skills and relations has been transformed by debates on reflexivity, for instance as self-monitoring or self-reflection. It is important to realize that reflexivity is a part of all research and rather than a 'problem' to be avoided, the researcher–researched relation can be used to advantage in order to understand the research process (Hammersley and Atkinson 1989: 15). While, more recently, the notion of reflexivity has undergone critical scrutiny as writers have described various types, identified possible limitations and challenged its knowledge claims (Lynch 2000; Pels 2000), the ethnographer as 'biographical self' has become a central feature of research discussion (see Okely and Callaway 1992).

Where a researcher conducts a commentary or gives a general account of what took place in research, a number of common themes have usually emerged, for example on the entrance and exit (or reprise), the difficulties met and possibly overcome, and the mistakes made or avoided in research practice. Whyte ([1943]1955), for instance, gives 'reflections' on his field research and his subsequent contact with his subjects. Ethnographers may be said to give implicit or explicit narratives (or both) on the research process; more open accounts of the research 'story' began to emerge from ethnographers by the 1970s (Hale 1991: 135). For Coffey, ethnographic texts carry narrative elements found in autobiography and biography (Coffey 1999: 128). She argues that although not much detailed examination of the narrative features of ethnographic texts is made and few are completely or 'explicitly narrated', ethnographic texts do draw on elements of narrative to give a clear arrangement of actions and events. Narrative usage in following certain conventions makes connections with an intended audience (see Tonkin 1990, 1995). Mintz argues that, in fact, the researcher is in a double position – as mediating between the informant and the reader, and in enabling the reader to situate the ethnographic informants within their socio-cultural setting (Mintz 1996: 302–3).

Putting the issue of reflexivity and research relations in a simple form: the subject can be regarded as also an author, the researcher as a subject, and the

---

Box 9.3

Rose, D. (1990) *Living the Ethnographic Life*. London: Sage.

Rose investigates the history of ethnography to lay bare its 'hidden assumptions'. In doing so he gives its formative context in the corporation, market culture and the management of Empire. His sources include plays by Shakespeare, travel accounts, the East India Company's work, nineteenth-century formulations of ethnographic research, and the work of Malinowski and others. He describes his own research, for instance on 'street life' in Philadelphia, and points to other 'narrative ethnographies' in the 1980s which transformed research by a 'temporal unfolding' of narrative and placing the author within the action. In future, he says, ethnography will be a 'polyphonic', 'heteroglossic', multigenre (poetry, fiction, and pictures) construction in which the author's voice and emotions are present alongside people's lives as a discourse and narrative within the final text.

---

audience as also an interpretive subject. As subject, researcher or audience we reflect on the research process and our own experiences; by a reflexive questioning of expectations we can come to a fuller understanding of the research process (see Cohen 1992).

Marcus (1992) places the question of reflexivity into a much broader theoretical frame – the traditional practice of ethnography (its object, site and ethnographer's role) is being re-evaluated given the changing nature of local experience and collective and individual identities in the context of globalization. Culture as 'lived *local* experience' has to be understood in '*global* perspective', while investigation should explore the negotiation of individual and collective identity in both traditional and new settings. He argues that this broadening of perspective has stimulated a revival of anthropological concern with themes of 'ethnicity, race, nationality, and colonialism' (Marcus, 1992: 311–12; see *Identities: Global Studies in Culture and Power*, 1994– (US journal); *Social Identities: Journal for the Study of Race, Nation and Culture*, 1995– (UK journal)). He says that the most 'venturesome' trends in ethnography are focused on the formation of identities: the subject's identity, wider national and other identities. In this, the formation of the ethnographer's own identity (or identities) is also an issue. He calls for the 'remaking of the observed' (the ethnographic context) to account for time and space assumed in traditional ethnography and the problematization of perspective/voice as found in realist anthropology. The emphasis is on the 'oral roots' of anthropology, as transformed by power relations, modes of representation by the media and so on as the spoken voice becomes received text (Marcus 1992: 318–19). Society is to be viewed within global processes and the connection with the ethnographic setting. Marcus concludes that through the duality of voices the ethnographer's own concepts change (Marcus 1992: 320). The question of reflexivity within ethnography can lead to the charge that the researcher may become self-indulgent: that we may 'over-reveal' ourselves or the ethnography of the subjects becomes secondary to the researcher's own story.

Ethnographic texts

Numerous writers have pointed to important shifts in principles and practice of ethnography, for instance Atkinson and Coffey have noted a 'crisis in representation' in anthropological texts including 'the intellectual faith that has informed their production and reception' (Atkinson and Coffey 1995: 44; see Van Maanen 1995b). Writers have described a 'rhetorical turn' (Atkinson and Hammersley 1994: 254), a postmodern ethnography or even a postpostmodern ethnography (Tyler 1986; Marcus 1994). John Van Maanen (1995a) argues, in relation to ethnography, that there have been a number of 'phases' or 'moments' in research practice (see Denzin and Lincoln 1994c). It is a view that can be applied to other forms of research – since it crucially refers to the research relation and how it has altered due to, for example, the emphasis on reflexivity and role of the researcher. He outlines three phases or moments in ethnography: the collection of information on a particular culture, the construction of the ethnographic text according to certain kinds of practices by the ethnographer, and the reading of the text by differing audiences. These phases raise a number of specific issues. In the latest phase, a series of methodological questions have become prominent including a 'self-consciousness' involving reflexivity, and moral and political concerns. For instance, portraying fieldwork as a text has shifted attention to language and the challenge to acceptance of truth and objectivity, and new approaches have developed (Van Maanen 1995a: 9). He asks whether the focus on textual construction has moved the focus from the practice of ethnography and the collection of materials. Ultimately, he says, we can recognize both that ethnographic facts are textual and that ethnographic texts are 'factual'. But there is still an audience, which will seek from ethnography a particular requirement to be informed of localized cultures in specific historical moments (Van Maanen 1995a: 23). Thus, the consideration of research practice or the research text as a social construction does not rule out the focus on the material or embodied lives of individuals. The examination of research practice should be seen as part of all three phases of the research process and including an openness in the delineation of the researcher's role – our intentions, assumptions and expectations.

The change in the presentation of ethnography was marked by Geertz (1973, see Geertz 1988) in his well-known text, which examined the 'fictive' or literary characteristics of ethnographic writing. Further, Clifford and Marcus (1986), who drew out the literary and broader ideological influences on the construction of the text, questioned the nature of ethnographic writing. Their interrogation of the writing process has had considerable influence. The examination of styles of writing in ethnographic research has now become a more common theme in the 'reading' of empirical studies. Interestingly, Bruyn in the 1960s pointed to a range of styles in participant observation studies: romantic, realistic, poetic, factual, analytic, satiric, journalistic and existential and observed (Bruyn 1966: 245). He adds, 'Some researchers do not realize that what they discover is shaped by what they themselves are – their temperaments, perspectives, attitudes, and social and personal interests' (Bruyn 1966: 245). The ethnographic text is now seen as a complex document which contains a variety of voices – the author may take part in a conversation with him or herself as well as place his/her voice in relation to the various ones taken from interviews (Atkinson 1990: 95). Atkinson, therefore, points to multiple voices – the voice of the 'knowing sociologist' and the 'observer' and the 'social actor' which are combined to produce the finished, complex account within which the voices change and interrelate to provide an interpretive whole (Atkinson 1990: 92–4).

Descriptions of places and events carry implicit meanings and interpretations, for instance the description of urban areas may appear 'straightforward' but may contain underlying implicit sociological perspectives (Atkinson 1990: 101). Atkinson argues that at its simplest the 'story' contains the events and facts whereas a '*discours*' is often given separately as the narrator's commentary and interpretation. Also apparent may be the voice or 'I' of the participant/observer within the story or '*histoire*' and the voice or 'I' of the sociologist's *discours*. The timing of the voices can also mark the changing voices or perspectives; typically the *histoire* is given in the past tense whereas the interpretive commentary or *discours* is given in the present (Atkinson 1990: 98; see also Davis 1992; Hastrup 1992). The importance of this discussion lies in the recognition of 'voices' (the researcher's or subject's) within the text and how genres and 'timings' are interwoven to provide an account, which meets the expectations of an intended audience(s). The issues of 'voices' and 'audience' have to be addressed more fully, e.g. how the researcher's biographical 'voice' and those of others are represented and how the intended audience(s) is perceived. Atkinson describes how 'exemplars' in ethnography are taken from interviews, field notes and so on to demonstrate to the reader the familiar and mundane or the exotic and unusual according to purpose. These 'exemplars' may not be fully elaborated by the researcher's commentary but nevertheless are connected to the reader through images, meanings and expectations. It is through these and 'lesser' voices that autobiographies and biographies are present – albeit often in limited fashion – in ethnographic texts.

In summary, concentration on the text, its literary and aesthetic character, the use of devices such as metaphor, description of context, and the expectations of the audience, have been part of an emphasis on the composition of the text while challenging the author as having a superior, or privileged gaze or understanding. The 'new ethnography' has tried to problematize the notion of representation by questioning the ethnographic document as a reflection of the social world (see Atkinson and Hammersley 1994). Even so, the consideration of the researcher as a biographical actor reawakens attention to the researcher's role and *life* – as an active participant in the exchange of meanings, and as interpreter and creator of 'knowledge'.

Case study
Okely, J. and Callaway, H. (eds) (1992) *Anthropology and Autobiography.* London: Routledge.

The importance given to the place of the researcher and connections between the composition of the text and the auto/biographies of researcher and researched is now very evident in discussions and conduct of ethnography or fieldwork (see Rose 1990; Coffey 1999). The term 'autoethnography' has been used in several senses – for example, to denote research conducted by those who would formerly have been merely the 'subjects' of research as well as the researchers reflecting on their own lives and experiences (see Reed-Danahay 1997; Ellis and Bochner 2000; Tedlock 2000). Okely and Callaway's edited volume *Anthropology and Autobiography* (1992) is a detailed examination of fieldwork and self-reflection. Okely, noting the developments in autobiography as a genre in literature and other disciplines, says the volume is concerned with the past of the anthropologist in so far as it is connected to the anthropologist's practice, 'the choice of area and study, the experience of fieldwork, analysis and writing' (Okely 1992: 1). Elsewhere, Okely describes her own fieldwork experiences:

As a woman researcher, I learned also through personal experience about non-Gypsy projections. To outsiders learning of my research, I was sometimes seen as a 'Gypsy woman', with all the fantastic stereotypes . . . Thoughts came at unexpected times: on a walk, in the night, not necessarily when seated with pen and paper at a desk. After the broad schema of ideas was set down, I could look back for some exact details, incidents and statements in the chronological field notes. That is, the ideas and theories, having fermented in the subconscious, emerged by free association from unspecified experience. Only then was empirical evidence instrumentally sought as confirmation or elucidation . . . I now responded entirely to intuition and elusive memory before grounding myself in the recorded notes.

(Okely 1994: 31–2)

She concluded:

> . . . the interpretation of anthropological material is, like fieldwork, a
> continuing and creative experience. The research has combined action
> and contemplation . . . The researcher is freed from a division of labour
> which splits fieldwork from analysis. The author is not alienated from
> the experience of participant observation, but draws upon it both pre-
> cisely and amorphously for the resolution of the completed text.
>
> (Okely 1994: 32)

Okely and Callaway's volume contains a wide range of studies covering
research in very different parts of the world with reference to the autobiography of the researcher and the biographies of the 'subjects'. Articles
address issues such as racism, ageing and friendship in the field.

Box 9.4

Kenna, M. E. (1992) Changing places and altered perspectives: research on
a Greek island in the 1960s and in the 1980s, in J. Okely and H. Callaway
(eds) *Anthropology and Autobiography*. London: Routledge.

Kenna reflects on how age and gender – and also being an outsider – are
important dimensions in fieldwork following her return to a Greek island
after some twenty years since her first study as a young researcher. She had
changed as well as her personal relationships; the community had also
altered: these changes affected how she was perceived and also her outlook and research interests – the discipline of anthropology had also
shifted:

> When I first arrived in Greece, central aspects of my personal and
> academic socialisation, such as the value placed on sharing
> information and cooperating with others, were confronted by Greek
> cultural assumptions which emphasised that knowledge was power
> and hence encouraged the concealment of information . . . Changes
> in age, status and stage in the life cycle have altered my own
> perspectives and affected both fieldwork experience and analysis.
>
> (Kenna 1992: 160–1)

Of particular interest is her comment that 'Each successive backward look
offers a refocusing of its object. Autobiography, like history, is constantly
being rewritten' (Kenna 1992: 161).

Biographical experiences may be conceived as a resource rather than a
methodological impediment. For instance, in the same volume, Cohen

examines a 'self-conscious anthropology' and argues that a knowledge of the anthropologist's own self is not to be equated with research as concentrated on his or her own life. Instead, drawing on his own fieldwork and biographical experience, he says that the self can be used as a condition of anthropology – as an interpretive resource to learn about others (Cohen 1992).

Oral traditions and biography

There are a number of ways in which ethnographers have approached oral sources, including the collection of life stories. Within anthropology, Vansina, in his classic text drawing on African societies, examines 'oral traditions'. These traditions

> . . . consist of all verbal testimonies which are reported statements concerning the past . . . not all oral sources are oral traditions, but only those which are reported statements . . . Oral traditions exclusively consist of hearsay accounts, that is, testimonies that narrate an event which has not been witnessed and remembered by the informant himself, but which he has learnt about through hearsay.
>
> (Vansina 1973: 19–20)

Vansina forms a typology which includes oral traditions as passed down over generations such as titles and slogans, ritualistic oaths, forms of poetry, names, tales and commentaries (see Finnegan 1992). Oral traditions may also be found where written documents are common and where 'folk traditions' are important (Burgess 1982: 132). Here is the possibility of examining 'myth' from an interdisciplinary perspective – not as something to be avoided as unsound history (according to some historians). History and anthropology (where 'myth' is a traditional focus) may cooperate alongside other disciplines in examining myth construction at individual and social or private and public levels, and how audiences respond to myths and narratives of the past (Samuel and Thompson 1990a; Tonkin 1990, 1995; see Chapter 8, this volume). For example, applying the idea of myth to life stories, Peneff gives the 'classic' example of the self-made entrepreneur. He says: 'Such mythical frameworks are common in all societies. They are especially widespread in societies undergoing rapid development and change, where individuals tell their histories as a kind of progress or journey' (Peneff 1990: 36).

In the examination of 'myth' in life stories there is now a large body of work, across various disciplines (see Chapter 7), that have taken a 'narrative' approach and examined a range of rhetorical devices – metaphors, moral evaluations, imagery, and so on – used by tellers to describe and summarize the multitude of events and relationships in their lives (see Atkinson 1998: 68).

Box 9.5

Tonkin, E. (1995) *Narrating Our Pasts: The Social Construction of Oral History.* Cambridge: Cambridge University Press.

Based on fieldwork in Africa, Tonkin provides a case study of the narration of the past. Her intent is to examine the interrelations between memory, cognition and history. In doing so, she studies the human self as a social creation and the past as *representations* – as socially constructed and acted upon. She points to the temporal and contextual aspects of the remembering of the past – the telling in interaction with an audience, with 'memory' linking individual and social group. Included here is a discussion of the importance of convention, genres (as horizons of expectation), performance and audience in narration – a view which also has implications for academic conventions or practice based on these prior narratives.

In an earlier article, Tonkin broadened the notion of myth with reference to the practice of history (and we could add other disciplines) itself (Tonkin 1990). She claimed that many historians 'live by the myth of realism' – realism as a mode of historical writing accepted by historians (Tonkin 1990: 25). They provide 'representations of pastness' rather than 'history'. An 'horizon of expectations' is in operation, which connects the audience to the oral or written history presented. In terms of biographical material she states:

> We who use life stories need to understand, and more precisely identify how, whether mythic or realistic, poetic or phlegmatic, they always have to be structured, according to known conventions, in order to convey the desire – fearful, hortatory, or ironic – of this teller to present a self to this listener, at this particular moment.
>
> (Tonkin 1990: 34; see Tonkin 1995)

Conclusion

Ethnography or wider fieldwork has undergone a number of significant changes of emphasis from the focus on fieldwork relations to the examination of the construction of the text. Alongside these shifts has been the renewed attention to the role of the researcher – in the field as well as in the formation of the text. The biography of the ethnographer has been subject to scrutiny as someone with life experience, which informs the fieldwork relation and the presentation of the 'world' studied. In addition, while ethnography and wider fieldwork, in their various forms, have not (and could not) ignore individual lives (e.g. the key informants), 'life stories' have not been addressed as fully as they might. With the reassessment of the researcher's life and research relations an emerging reassessment of the interpretation of the lives of the 'subjects' is taking place. Thus, biographical work in ethnographic practice is beginning to take a more central place.

Recommended reading

Atkinson, P. (1990) *The Ethnographic Imagination: Textual Constructions of Reality*. London: Routledge. (An examination of the use of literary and rhetorical features of ethnographic texts that construct the social world to be read by the audience.)

Brewer, J. D. (2000) *Ethnography*. Buckingham: Open University Press. (This book is a comprehensive examination of ethnographic method, including the issue of reflexivity and data. It provides a strong advocacy of the method in the face of globalization theory and postmodern views.)

Coffey, A. (1999) *The Ethnographic Self: Fieldwork and the Representation of Identity*. London: Sage. (This text focuses on the role of the researcher in ethnography and how fieldwork affects the life of the researcher. It reviews a wide range of studies to investigate the complexities of field relations.)

Denzin, N. K. (1997) *Interpretive Ethnography*. London: Sage. (This book deals with recent developments in ethnography including epistemological issues, visual and poetic dimensions, performance, and narratives of the self.)

Ethnography (2000–). (This journal aims to be international and interdisciplinary and provide accounts of theoretically informed and reflexive fieldwork within the context of social critiques of 'late modern' economic, social, cultural and political changes.)

Okely, J. and Callaway, H. (eds) (1992) *Anthropology and Autobiography*. London: Routledge. (An examination of the role of the fieldworker with reference to gender, age, ethnicity and biography and provides a critique of traditional assumptions by raising questions of reflexivity and responsibility.)

(10) Conclusion

Qualitative research has undergone considerable development during the last twenty years or so and writers have identified various 'turns', 'moments' or similar changes in its concerns as new interpretive and methodological approaches have emerged (cf. Denzin and Lincoln 1994c, 2000a). Within these complex changes in qualitative research and the vociferous debates that have surrounded them, perhaps a less noticed trend has occurred – the study of individual lives through life stories, narratives, autobiography, and biography – which is now achieving prominence. The study of the fuller 'life' rather than glimpsing the individual through the selective snippets obtained by traditional methods has been gaining ground as part of a general biographical approach spanning a wide range of humanistic disciplines. The biographical 'trend' is also gathering pace in many countries, as witnessed by the expansion of oral history study and biographical work in sociology. Other evidence of this global expansion can be seen in the formation of the International Oral History Association, the strong activity of the Biography and Society research committee within the International Sociological Association, and the influence of the notion of narrative in the study of lives within psychology and other disciplines. What is astonishing is the degree to which biographical research is becoming established within a very varied range of empirical areas, even in some less promising fields for this type of approach. Just some of the major areas in which biographical study can be found are community history, family studies, migration, political change, education, work and careers, ageing, and health and medicine.

In the mid-1990s Denzin and Lincoln outlined a 'fifth moment' in qualitative research within which a number of former 'tensions' continued to operate: a 'critique of positivism and postpositivism that is coupled with ongoing self-critique and self-appraisal', 'crises of representation and legitimation', 'continued emergence of a cacophony of voices speaking with varying agendas', 'shifting scientific, moral, sacred, and religious discourses', and the 'influence of technology' (Denzin and Lincoln 1994a: 576). These tensions can be seen as present within the longer history of qualitative methods with differing intensities and levels of debate. They note the tendency to move from one 'intellectual fashion' to another and, while critique will continue to sharpen the 'basic strategies and techniques' of various methods, 'too much critique' will 'stifle' the 'multidisciplinary project called qualitative research' (Denzin and Lincoln 1994a: 577). Any sixth moment they said would have several themes: 'the voice and the presence of the Other . . . the social text; and the sacred, the humanistic, and the technological' (Denzin and Lincoln 1994a: 581). Thus, there would be multiple different or competing voices, a range of representational forms (visual, oral), and reflexive research practice. Latterly, Denzin and Lincoln have added a prediction of a seventh moment concerned with 'moral discourse' and with 'the development of sacred textualities' which calls on the social sciences and the humanities to be established as 'sites for critical conversations about democracy, race, gender, class, nation, freedom, and community' (Denzin and Lincoln 2000b: 1048).

What is clear is that in the future development of qualitative methodology, biographical research will have an important, expanding, even central, position. For example, in the recognition of multiple voices in research (of 'subjects' and fieldworker), the researcher as a biographical subject will certainly feature. Of course, researchers during the history of qualitative methods have been aware of their own experiences and feelings in the research practice, however, recent discussions have allowed such influences to be examined anew and more visibly. As Coffey argues, in ethnography the 'literary turn' has enabled the 'auto/biographical and the personal narrative/confessional' to be applied, and feminist and postmodernist influences have allowed the social world to be seen 'in terms of multiple perspectives and multiple selves' (Coffey 1999: 10).

Biographical research has had many influences on its conduct and concerns; for Miller these have 'coalesced' to a degree by which a number of common aspects can be seen. These include the concern with the complete individual life (or a major part of it) of the researched coupled with a commitment to methods which are processual, since the individual is to be related to time or past/present/future rather than a 'present orientation' (Miller 2000: 2). In addition, he says there is a commitment to replace the notion of the isolated individual with a figure within the social relations of the family and institutions such as work, health and education.

Disciplines

Biographical research is therefore taking place in disciplines or sub-disciplines across a wide span – within sociology, psychology, history, literary and cultural studies and substantive areas concerned with migration, the family, ageing, education, health, work, political change and others. This expansion of interest in the study of lives and the use of biographical material raises the immediate issue of whether there is really common ground – in epistemology, methodology, interpretation and theoretical framework: a shared approach. What is certainly apparent is the increasing cross-fertilization in many of these areas from discipline to discipline, for example on approaches to the question of memory, or the utilization of notions of narrative. A 'biographical approach' is hardly likely to come about which fully unites very different epistemological and methodological assumptions – on positivist, postpositivist, realist, narrative and other conceptions of the 'story', on the role of the researcher, or on the means of presentation (book, video, theatre, community publishing, internet, CD, or in some combination). The variety of materials to be included (written autobiography, life story interview, memos, poetry, novels and so on) will also be subject to debate. Further, it may be the case that some researchers within a discipline will have more in common in approach with those in another discipline and exhibit a dual identity, not wishing to be over-tied by a disciplinary traditionalism. In fact, one of the features of current biographical research is a pragmatism and eclecticism (which some would identify as a relative lack of methodological and theoretical rigour) in pursuing the collection, interpretation and presentation of lives (see Miller 2000: 156). Perhaps, as part of an emerging moment in qualitative research, the study of biography will recognize previous developments, and further critique past approaches (whether positivist, postpostivist, realist or other), but will not let intellectual fashions dismiss approaches and studies that have gone before. For example, as Denzin and Lincoln argue in relation to grounded theorization, while its 'postpositivist assumptions' will be criticized there will still be the procedure of constructing interpretations from the interactive context (Denzin and Lincoln 1994a; see Charmaz 2000). Biographical research cannot be fully united under one methodology or one theoretical approach but its practitioners will be aware of other ways of doing research and writing and should continue to be open to previous contributions and other possibilities.

The biographical turn

Given the rise of biographical research across the social or human disciplines perhaps the 'biographical turn' (see Chamberlayne et al. 2000) will be a confused and confusing development with multiple approaches to materials to be collected, methodological assumptions, theory construction and application, and modes of presentation. Some developments within or between disciplines, sub-disciplines or research areas will choose to be 'relatively autonomous' in practice and outlook while others will be much more 'boundary breaking', as in feminist contributions to biographical study. Perhaps we are witnessing an important social shift which for some will bring a revolution in thinking in human or social study: a type of social movement across the disciplines, and wider afield, in which the 'biographical' is given a fuller 'authenticity'. Within the practice of biographical research, the idea of the 'auto/biographical' is bringing a serious recognition of the limitations of 'conventional taxonomies' – past/present, self/other, memory/present and so on; in doing so, it brings epistemological and methodological challenges to bases of existing practices of social research as well as a means of placing the individual biography within, as Mills advocated, its interrelation with wider social structures (see Stanley 1993). But perhaps some caution needs to be exercised in this turn to biography. It may make binary oppositions and restrictions more visible and provide a possibility of overcoming them within sociological and other study (Miller 2000: 158), but biographical research is itself within a broader political context and formation of the 'biographical'. For Goodson, drawing on the 'storytelling' of major media: 'Is it not more likely then that new discourses and voices that empower the periphery at one and the same time fortify, enhance, and solidify the old centres of power? In short, are we not witnessing the old game of divide and rule?' (Goodson 1995: 98).

It is certainly clear that the portrayal of individual lives – the news human interest story, 'fly on the wall' 'real lives'; the soaps and docu-soaps, the fact–fiction reconstruction, the dating shows, the revelatory studio audience show, the newspaper celebrity obsession – appears to be expanding in intensity and in genre range and multiplicity. These developments raise important questions for biographical research relating to the ideological formation of popular conceptions of lives and life events – typifications, myths, stories, and narratives – that may reappear in the 'lives' that are collected. If in the 'postmodern'/'late modern' world we have less certainty regarding identity but more opportunity for its (multiple) construction, what will be the sources of all our stories?

Identity

In the face of debates about the 'fragmentation' of identity or 'multiple identities', with discussion often more in the realms of abstract theory rather than based on 'lives', the appropriateness of the study of biography becomes ever more apparent in seeing how identities are formed and grounded within spatial, organizational and other structures. Biographical research will increase its linkages with developments in a number of fields, for example by an increasing focus on 'narratives' of the body and sexuality. It is also probable that personal and family history research will continue to increase in popularity as a recreational pursuit. Another strong feature will be biographical work related to major social change – migration, nationalism, the aftermath of repressive regimes – and how memories are reshaped. Also, the need for an emphasis on the voices of the socially neglected or groups with identities that are socially repressed will remain. Finally, there is the pressing question to analyse through biographical work how identity formation can become a source of exclusion and violence, as witnessed in recent 'ethnic cleansing' and rising nationalist conflicts.

A number of features are evident in the 'rise' or re-emergence of biographical research:

Time

A vital theme in biographical research has been the question of 'time' (Roberts 1999a) – in the construction of narrative, in the way individuals move backwards and forwards between past/present/future in consciousness, in the models of research used in oral history, life cycle, career, and in age cohort studies. Lives, it is argued, should be studied 'over time'. This emphasis will become stronger in both the examination of individual lives and as part of the research process itself – with social action as retrospective and prospective as well as (and importantly) within the 'ongoing present'. Thus, longitudinal and retrospective research on biographies – whether as part of generation, cohort, community or group – will be developed further. But the 'timing' of experience will increasingly be conceptualized along with 'spatial dimensions', for instance in the development of individual identity formation, the symbolic mapping of place or 'home', and other dimensions of experience, which will probably be significant areas for research (see Roberts 1999b). Adam (1995) has drawn attention to the wider challenge of the 'temporal turn' to social science since it 'de-stabilises' the dualisms of the 'Enlightenment episteme': 'nature–culture, male–female, self–other, mind–matter, subject–object, continuity–change and local–global'. This challenge brings a complexity (and discomfort) which joins 'the personal and the global, the technological and the literary, the bodily and the scientific, totalizing tendencies and local particularities and coevalness and difference' (Adam 1995: 150). In our own personal conceptions of our biographical time we are aware of our own mortality but not our actual end; we also remember the 'past' but cannot live it again except in the imagery of recollection.

Memory

The question of memory has been part of traditional discussions in oral history and sociology in relation to its 'fallibility' in recollecting past experience and how this methodological difficulty can be minimized by, for instance, using other sources of information as confirmation (or rejection). More recently the nature of memory has begun to be subject to more intense investigation with, for example, a wider span of differing (and new) branches of psychology being consulted while, further afield, 'memory' has received increased attention in fields such as cultural studies. Attention has been drawn to how memories are reordered, selected, 'falsified' and constructed without resorting to a view that 'all is fiction' in narrative accounts. In addition, the operation of 'memory' in stories has been linked to how time is perceived. Stories, although constructed within and through the present, contain perspectives not only on the past but also on the future – a recognition that introduces existential considerations in cultural analysis and critique (see Robins 1995: 212).

Researcher's self

The biographical researcher, as any other human subject, has experiences set and interpreted within biographical and other forms of time – as researchers we interpret our own lives as we interpret the lives of others and in research our own biographical experience and feelings are involved. This emotional contact should not be seen as merely a hindrance in research but as (inescapably) part of the research relationships which should be expanded upon through the reflexive monitoring of our own self-involvement. While 'reflexive practice' has been a source of renewal across the range of the humanities it has had a number of definitions and forms, which require a reconfiguration (see G. E. Marcus 1994). The claims of reflexivity in research will also be further scrutinized and contested (see Lynch 2000; Pels 2000). The ethical dimensions of research will, of course, still remain and if anything become more complex: there are multiple responsibilities of the researcher, which centre on tensions between academic attachments and commitments to the researched. The researcher will continue to have multiple roles, as academic, adviser, advocate which bring the tensions that are inherent in biographical and other research. But many would go further and say there is an overriding commitment – not merely not to do harm, which is extremely important, but also to a 'democratic community' in which all voices are heard and taken into account. However, in releasing the voices of the unheard into the public sphere they enter into the vagaries of political processes whose consequences cannot be judged. Finally, biographical work is 'imaginative' – it is creative, image-laden, open, exploratory, reflexive and humanistic – and political. It is a practice that is not merely enacting a pre-scribed research role according to steps in a manual but one in which 'bio-ethnographers' are participatory, humanistic individuals within the 'worlds' of research and other arenas in which we dwell.

Methodology

Biographical research is primarily interested in the 'life'. Methodologically we usually see the research procedure as involving the collection of the 'oral' account by an audio-tape interview or, rather less so, the requested written autobiography – both according to some evaluative criteria. However, there is increasing recognition (for instance, due to the crossing of disciplinary boundaries) that 'lesser' forms of material that appear to be even further from traditional standards of 'evidence' (certainly as seen in sociology but much more accepted in some other disciplines), such as letters, diaries, logs and memoirs, among others (e.g. material artefacts), are to be included. Much of this variety has been subject to discussion since the 1930s but the variety of 'personal documents' and materials is being subject to renewed attention and usage. Questions of validity and reliability will also not disappear as debates on whether traditional criteria should be applied or some alternative criteria set, including ethical, moral or political evaluations, continue. The associated question of realism/referentiality and construction will no doubt remain a source for polarization in viewpoint and differences in the perceived purpose of biographical research (as a record of the past, as a current interpretation, or both). Most researchers, while more than merely aware of these debates, will continue their biographical research without the intensity of these issues unduly restraining their enthusiasm. Such issues and debates will be 'built in' – not dismissed but given cognisance (sometimes producing conflict but hope-fully adding to the sophistication of the 'field' rather than becoming a source of destructive opposition), and enter into the reflexive evaluation of research. Again, a pragmatic approach is hoped for which learns from previous approaches and veers toward rigour rather than dilettantism. As Atkinson and Coffey argue with reference to what they call 'radical textualism' in ethnographic writing, it 'is right to question a vulgar realism' that does not realize its own rhetorical devices and the 'textual conventions of realism', but 'such a recognition constitutes an extension of the ethnographic imagination rather than a radical threat to it' (Atkinson and Coffey 1995: 55).

New technology

Finally, the impact of fast-moving technical developments in audio and video recording, the linkage between the 'field' and the computer, the

Internet connections with subjects, sources, colleagues and the new possibilities for communicating research, the myriad forms of composing research in sound, picture, performance and narration produce excitement and, perhaps, trepidation in equal measure. The diversity of the 'research process' produces uncertainties regarding the relations with the researched, the materials to be collected, the form of composition of multiple voices and texts, the skills required to meet the technical and methodological challenges and so on. The traditional deductive conception of the research process was always a stylized model and qualitative researchers preferred some more rolling conception of the theory–data connection. Perhaps we are moving one step further (reflecting contemporary industrial–commercial–informational processes?) in research procedure to a 'model' in which all the elements of the process (theorization, collection, interpretation, writing) will take place more or less simultaneously? Biographical research will explore these new technological and procedural possibilities from its intra- and inter-disciplinary bases and sub-fields and within particular research studies; which will only be able to reflect a portion of the diversity of approaches. But there will be an awareness of other ways of doing things – even where they are not explored. Biographical research in the coming 'moment' is likely to be 'messy' and reflexive, experimental and feminist influenced, multimedia and multivocal but above all motivated to understand the lives of others and, in doing so, our own auto/biographies (see Marcus 1992; G. E. Marcus 1994).

Conclusion

It is a limitation only to conceive biographical research within various disciplines as variously in opposition to, or as only overlapping on, specific ideas of practice. Rather, the practices of biographical research should be seen more comprehensively as occupying unstable positions within a number of dimensions – object/subject; auto/biography; self/other; public/private; realist/constructionist and others – according to purpose, scope and conception of the individual life. The profound question of understanding and studying the individual life will be further complicated by new technology and techniques which will raise (and are raising) issues of methodological, theoretical and ethical importance. Are we entering an interactive, 'real'–cyber world of auto/biographies? Will even 'dead' individuals be brought to virtual, holographic life to speak and act anew, to interact via multimedia with researcher and audience(s)? Will all these participants interact in the past, present and 'future' and the separation between the contexts of biographical research and 'ordinary life' finally disappear?

Recommended reading

Chamberlayne, P., Bornat, J. and Wengraf, T. (eds) (2000) *The Turn to Biographical Methods in Social Science.* London: Routledge. (The first part of this book reviews issues in methodology and theory, including the 'biographical turn' in social science. The second half shows the application of biographical methods in a range of contexts, including older people, single mothers, locality, housing, with an emphasis on Britain and Germany.)

Denzin, N. K. and Lincoln, Y. S. (eds) ([1994]2000) *Handbook of Qualitative Research.* London: Sage. (A very comprehensive textbook which addresses major issues in qualitative research including major perspectives, strategies of inquiry, methods of collection, modes of analysis, interpretation, and the future of qualitative research. A number of chapters (in both editions) are relevant for life history, narrative, interviewing and documents.)

There are an increasing number of journals and newsletters at national and international level in biographical research. The following should be consulted for developments mainly within oral history and sociology.

Auto/Biography – Journal of the Auto/Biography Study Group, British Sociological Association.

Biography (USA).

Biography and Society Newsletter – Biography and Society, RC 38, International Sociological Association.

Bios: Zeitschrift fur Biographieforschung und Oral History (Germany).

The Narrative Study of Lives. London: Sage.

Oral History (UK) – Journal of the Oral History Society.

Oral History Review (USA).

Words and Silences – Bulletin of the International Oral History Association. The biannual conference proceedings of the association show the range of worldwide developments.

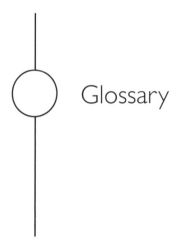

Glossary

The following is drawn, in part, from Hatch and Wisniewski's (1995a) and Denzin's (1989) very useful discussions of terms in the field.

Autobiography: An account by an individual of their life in written or oral form. Additional visual material may be given (photographs) and the life may be presented in the form of video or CD.

Biography: An account of an individual life written by another. It is the practice of writing about a person.

Biographical research: Research undertaken on individual lives employing autobiographical documents, interviews or other sources and presenting accounts in various forms (e.g. in terms of editing, written, visual or oral presentation, and degree of researcher's narration and reflexivity).

Epiphany: Points of difficulty in an individual's life which can challenge the individual's understanding of his or her life and may bring significant subsequent effects.

Hermeneutics: Hermeneutic method refers to the practice and theory of interpretation and understanding stemming from Scheleiermacher, Dilthey, Heidegger, Gadamer and others. The Hermeneutic circle concerns the circularity of all understanding – each textual reading adds to our knowledge and surpasses the initial interpretations and subsequent understandings.

Life history: The life history is based on the collection of a written or transcribed oral account requested by a researcher. The life story is subsequently edited, interpreted and presented in one of a number of ways – often in conjunction with other sources.

Life story: The account someone gives of his or her life to another. It is usually quite a full account across the length of life but may refer to a period or aspect of the life experience. When related by interview to the researcher it is the result of an interactive relationship.

Memory: This has been conceived in various ways to denote, for example, a location, a process, and/or a content (memories). A number of 'models' or types of memory are commonly described in psychology (short-term, long-term, flashbulb) including more recent attempts to provide a more social dimension (autobiographical memory). Collective or group memories have been discussed in a range of disciplines (e.g. cultural studies, oral history) and connected with the transmission of traditions, symbols and myths. A number of associated terms are commonly used, including reminiscence and recollection.

Narrative: Narrative is linked with time as a fundamental aspect of social action. It is held that we experience life through conceptions of the past, present and future. Narratives provide the organization for our actions and experiences.

Narrative analysis: Narrative analysis can refer to a method and its sources. A usual distinction is made between story and narrative – the former is the 'story' told by the individuals ('storied lives'), the latter denotes the means of inquiry.

Oral history: The practice of interviewing individuals on their past experiences of events with the intention of constructing an historical account.

Personal documents: These are usually taken to include non-formal or non-publicly produced documents such as personal letters and diaries or other private writing (logs, memoirs) not meant for public consumption.

Time: Time is inextricably part of our experience – how we organize and narrativize our interpretations of the myriad events that have occurred, and also our current life experience and anticipation of the future.

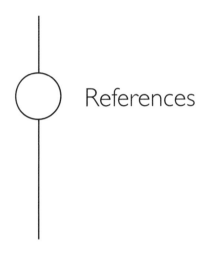

References

Ackroyd, P. (1991) *Dickens*. London: Minerva.

Ackroyd, P. (1997) *Milton in America*. London: Vintage.

Adam, B. (1990) *Time and Social Theory*. Cambridge: Polity.

Adam, B. (1995) *Timewatch: The Social Analysis of Time*. Cambridge: Polity.

Addison, R. B. (1999) A grounded hermeneutic editing approach, in B. F. Crabtree and W. L. Miller (eds) *Doing Qualitative Research*, 2nd edn. London: Sage.

Agar, M. (1995) Literary journalism as ethnography: exploring the excluded middle, in J. Van Maanen (ed.) *Representation in Ethnography*. London: Sage.

Ageing and Society (1996) Ageing, biography and practice, special issue, 16(6).

Alasuutari, P. (1995) *Researching Culture*. London: Sage.

Aldridge, J. (1993) The textual disembodiment of knowledge in research account writing, *Sociology*, 27(1): 53–66.

Alheit, P. (1994) Everyday time and life time: on the problems of healing contradictory experiences of time, *Time and Society*, 3(3): 305–19.

Allport, G. W. (1942) *The Use of Personal Documents in Psychological Science*. New York: SSRC.

Amit-Talai, V. and Knowles, C. (1996) *Re-Situating Identities*. Peterborough, Ontario: Broadview Press.

Anderson, L. (1997) *Women and Autobiography in the Twentieth Century – Remembered Futures*. London: Harvester Wheatsheaf.

Anderson, L. (2001) *Autobiography*. London: Routledge.

Angell, R. (1945) A critical review of the development of the personal document method in sociology, 1920–40, in L. Gottschalk, C. Kluckhohn and R. Angell (eds) *The Use of Personal Documents in History, Anthropology and Sociology.* New York, NY: SSRC.

Atkinson, P. (1990) *The Ethnographic Imagination.* London: Routledge.

Atkinson, P. and Coffey, A. (1995) Realism and its discontents: on the crisis of cultural representation in ethnographic texts, in B. Adam and S. Allan (eds) *Theorizing Culture: An Interdisciplinary Critique after Postmodernism.* London: UCL Press.

Atkinson, P. and Hammersley, M. (1994) Ethnography and participant observation, in N. K. Denzin and Y. S. Lincoln (eds) *Handbook of Qualitative Research.* London: Sage.

Atkinson, R. (1998) *The Life Story Interview.* London: Sage.

Auto/Biography (1996) Review of Richard Holmes' *Footsteps: Adventures of a Romantic Biographer*, 4(2/3): 144–5.

Baddeley, A. D. (1994) Memory, in C. C. French and A. M. Coleman (eds) *Cognitive Psychology.* London: Longman.

Baddeley, A. D. (1999) *Essentials of Human Memory.* Hove: Psychology Press.

Baker, P. J. (1973) The life histories of W. I. Thomas and Robert E. Park, *American Journal of Sociology*, 79(2): 243–60.

Barnard, D., Towers, A., Boston, P. and Lambrinidou, Y. (2000) *Crossing Over: Narratives of Palliative Care.* Oxford: Oxford University Press.

Barthes, R. (1977) *Roland Barthes by Roland Barthes.* New York, NY: Hill and Wang.

Bean, P. and Melville, J. (1990) *Lost Children of the Empire.* London: Unwin Hyman.

Becker, H. S. (1963) *Outsiders.* New York, NY: The Free Press.

Becker, H. S. (1966) Introduction, in C. R. Shaw, *The Jack-Roller: A Delinquent Boy's Own Story.* Chicago, IL: University of Chicago Press.

Becker, H. S. (1970) The life history, in P. Worsley (ed.) *Modern Sociology: Introductory Readings.* Harmondsworth: Penguin.

Bellaby, P. (1991) Histories of sickness: making use of multiple accounts of the same process, in S. Dex. (ed.) *Life and Work History Analyses.* London: Routledge.

Benmayor, R. (1991) Testimony, action research, and empowerment: Puerto Rican women and popular education, in S. B. Gluck and D. Patai (eds) *Women's Words: The Feminist Practice of Oral History.* London: Routledge.

Benmayor, R. and Skotnes, A. (eds) (1994*) Migration and Identity: International Yearbook of Oral History and Life Stories*, III. Oxford: Oxford University Press.

Berger, A. A. (1997) *Narratives in Popular Culture, Media and Everyday Life.* London: Sage.

Berger, P. L. (1966) *Invitation to Sociology.* Harmondsworth: Penguin.

Berger, P. L. and Berger, B. (1975) *Sociology: A Biographical Approach*, 2nd edn. New York, NY: Basic Books.

Berger, P. L. and Luckmann, T. (1971) *The Social Construction of Reality.* Harmondsworth: Penguin.

Bernard, H. R. (1995) *Research Methods in Anthropology: Qualitative and Quantitative approaches*, 2nd edn. Walnut Creek CA: AltaMira Press.

Bertaux, D. (ed) (1981) *Biography and Society.* London: Sage.

Bertaux, D. (1983) The bakers of France, *History Today*. June, 33: 33–7.

Bertaux, D. (1991) From methodological monopoly to pluralism in the sociology of social mobility, in S. Dex (ed.) *Life and Work History Analyses*. London: Routledge.

Bertaux, D. and Bertaux-Wiame, I. (1981) Life stories in the baker's trade, in D. Bertaux (ed.) *Biography and Society*. London: Sage.

Bertaux, D. and Delcroix, C. (2000) Case histories of families and social processes: enriching sociology, in P. Chamberlayne, J. Bornat and T. Wengraf (eds) *The Turn to Biographical Methods in Social Science*. London: Routledge.

Bertaux, D. and Thompson, P. (eds) (1993a) *Between Generations: Family Models, Myths and Memories: International Yearbook of Oral History and Life Stories*. II. Oxford: Oxford University Press.

Bertaux, D. and Thompson, P. (1993b) Introduction, in D. Bertaux and P. Thompson (eds) *Between Generations*. Oxford: Oxford University Press.

Bertaux, D. and Thompson, P. (eds) (1997) *Pathways to Social Class: A Qualitative Approach to Social Mobility*. Oxford: Clarendon Press.

Beverley, J. (2000) Testimonio, subalternity, and narrative authority, in N. K. Denzin and Y. S. Lincoln (eds) *Handbook of Qualitative Research*, 2nd edn. London: Sage.

Bios (1990) Special Issue – The History of Oral History: Development, Present State, and Future Prospects.

Birch, E. L. (1994) *Black American Women's Writing*. London: Harvester Wheatsheaf.

Blake, D. (1995) Student teachers remember their schooling: an approach through oral history, *Oral History*, 23(2): 71–5.

Blatchford, R. (ed.) (2001) *The Genealogical Services Directory: Family and Local History Handbook*. York: GR Specialist Information Services.

Blaxter, M. (1993) Why do victims blame themselves?, in A. Radley (ed.) *Worlds of Illness: Biographical and Cultural Perspectives on Health and Disease*. London: Routledge.

Bloom, L. R. and Munro, P. (1995) Conflicts of selves: nonunitary subjectivity in women administrators' life history narratives, in J. A. Hatch and R. Wisniewski (eds) *Life History and Narrative*. London: Falmer Press.

Blumenfeld-Jones, D. (1995) Fidelity as a criterion for practicing and evaluating narrative inquiry, in J. A. Hatch and R. Wisniewski (eds) *Life History and Narrative*. London: Falmer Press.

Blumer, H. ([1939]1969) An Appraisal of Thomas and Znaniecki's *The Polish Peasant in Europe and America*, in H. Blumer *Symbolic Interactionism*. Englewood Cliffs, NJ: Prentice-Hall.

Bornat, J. (1994a) Introduction, in J. Bornat (ed.) *Reminiscence Reviewed*. Buckingham: Open University Press.

Bornat, J. (1994b) Is oral history auto/biography?, *Auto/Biography*, 3(1/2): 17–30.

Bornat, J. (1994c) Recording oral history, in M. Drake and R. Finnegan (eds) *Sources and Methods for Family and Community Historians: A Handbook*. Cambridge: Cambridge University Press.

Bornat, J. (ed.) (1994d) *Reminiscence Reviewed*. Buckingham: Open University Press.

Bornat, J. (1998) Oral history as a social movement, in R. Perks and A. Thomson (eds) *The Oral History Reader*. London: Routledge.

Boyne, R. and Rattansi, A. (1990) The theory and politics of postmodernism, in R. Boyne and A. Rattansi (eds) *Postmodernism and Society*. London: Macmillan.

Brewer, J. D. (2000) *Ethnography*. Buckingham: Open University Press.

Brewer, W. F. (1986) What is autobiographical memory?, in D. C. Rubin (ed.) *Autobiographical Memory*. Cambridge: Cambridge University Press.

Brown, N. R., Shevell, S. K. and Rips, L. J. (1986) Public memories and their personal context, in D. C. Rubin (ed.) *Autobiographical Memory*. Cambridge: Cambridge University Press.

Brown, R. H. (1978) History and hermeneutics: Wilhelm Dilthey and the dialectics of interpretive method, in R. H. Brown and S. M. Lyman (eds) *Structure, Consciousness and History*. Cambridge: Cambridge University Press.

Browne, J. (1995) *Charles Darwin: Voyaging*. London: Jonathan Cape.

Bruner, J. (1986) *Actual Minds, Possible Worlds*. Cambridge, MA: Harvard University Press.

Bruyn, S. T. (1966) *The Human Perspective in Sociology*. Englewood Cliffs, NJ: Prentice-Hall.

Bryman, A. (1988) *Quantity and Quality in Social Research*. London: Unwin Hyman.

Bryman, A. and Burgess, R. G. (eds) (1994a) *Analyzing Qualitative Data*. London: Routledge.

Bryman, A. and Burgess, R. G. (1994b) Developments in qualitative data analysis: an introduction, in A. Bryman and R. G. Burgess (eds) *Analyzing Qualitative Data*. London: Routledge.

Bryman, A. and Burgess, R. G. (eds) (1999) *Qualitative Research*, 4 vols. London: Sage.

Bryman, A., Bytheway, B., Allatt, P. and Keil, T. (eds) (1987) *Rethinking the Life Cycle*. London: Macmillan.

Bulmer, M. (1983) *The Polish Peasant in Europe and America*: a neglected classic, *New Community*, X(3): 470–6.

Bulmer, M. (1984) *The Chicago School of Sociology*. Chicago, IL: University of Chicago Press.

Burgess, E. W. (1925) What social case records should contain to be useful for sociological interpretation, *Social Forces*, 76: 524–32.

Burgess, R. G. (1982) Personal documents, oral sources and life histories, in R. G. Burgess (ed.) *Field Research: A Sourcebook and Field Manual*. London: Unwin Hyman.

Burnett, J. (1994) *Useful Toil*. London: Routledge.

Byatt, A. S. (2000a) *The Biographer's Tale*. London: Chatto and Windus.

Byatt, A. S. (2000b) *On Histories and Stories: Selected Essays*. London: Chatto and Windus.

Bytheway, B. (1993) Ageing and biography: The letters of Bernard and Mary Berenson, *Sociology*, 27(1): 153–65.

Calder, A. and Sheridan, D. (eds) (1984) *Speak For Yourself: A Mass-Observation Anthology*, 1937–49. London: Jonathan Cape.

Chamberlain, M. and Thompson, P. (1998a) Introduction, in M. Chamberlain and P. Thompson (eds) *Narrative and Genre*. London: Routledge.

Chamberlain, M. and Thompson, P. (eds) (1998b) *Narrative and Genre*. London: Routledge.

Chamberlayne, P. and King, A. (2000) *Cultures of Care: Biographies of Carers in Britain and the two Germanies*. Bristol: Polity Press.

Chamberlayne, P., Bornat, J. and Wengraf, T. (eds) (2000) *The Turn to Biographical Methods in Social Science*. London: Routledge.

Charmaz, K. (1995) Grounded theory, in J. A. Smith, R. Harré and L. Van Langenhove (eds) *Rethinking Methods in Psychology*. London: Sage.

Charmaz, K. (2000) Grounded theory: objectivist and constructivist methods, in N. K. Denzin and Y. S. Lincoln (eds) *Handbook of Qualitative Research*, 2nd edn. London: Sage.

Chivers, T. (1997) Phenomenology for life review, *Auto/Biography*, 1,2,3: 77–86.

Clandinin, D. J. and Connelly, F. M. (1994) Personal Experience Methods, in N. K. Denzin and Y. S. Lincoln (eds) *Handbook of Qualitative Research*. London: Sage.

Clausen, J. A. (1998) Life reviews and life stories, in J. Z. Giele and G. H. Elder Jr, *Methods of Life Course Research: Qualitative and Quantitative Approaches*. London: Sage.

Clayton, T. and Craig, P. (2000) *Finest Hour*. London: Hodder & Stoughton.

Clifford, D. (1995) Methods in oral history and social work, *Oral History*, 23(2): 65–70.

Clifford, J. and Marcus, G. E. (eds) (1986) *Writing Culture*. Berkeley, CA: University of California Press.

Coffey, A. (1999) *The Ethnographic Self: Fieldwork and the Representation of Identity*. London: Sage.

Coffey, A. and Atkinson, P. (1996) *Making Sense of Qualitative Data*. London: Sage.

Cohen, A. P. (1992) Self-conscious anthropology, in J. Okely and H. Callaway (eds) *Anthropology and Autobiography*. London: Routledge.

Cohen, G. (ed.) (1987) *Social Change and the Life Course*. London: Tavistock.

Cohen, G. (1989) *Memory in the Real World*. Hove: Lawrence Erlbaum.

Coleman, P. (1994) Reminiscence within the study of ageing, in J. Bornat (ed.) *Reminiscence Reviewed*. Buckingham: Open University Press.

Coleman, P. G. (1991) Ageing and life history: the meaning of reminiscence in late life, in S. Dex (ed.) *Life and Work History Analyses*. London: Routledge.

Collini, S. (1993) *Public Moralists: Political Thought and Intellectual Life in Britain, 1850–1930*. Oxford: Clarendon Press.

Connell, R. (1995) *Masculinities*. London: Polity.

Connerton, P. (1992) *How Societies Remember*. Cambridge: Cambridge University Press.

Conway, M. A. (1990) *Autobiographical Memory: An Introduction*. Milton Keynes: The Open University.

Conway, M. A. (1992) A structural model of autobiographical memory, in M. A. Conway, D. C. Rubin, H. Spinnler and W. A. Wagenaar (eds) *Theoretical Perspectives on Autobiographical Memory*. Dordrecht, the Netherlands: Kluwer Academic Publishing.

Conway, M. A., Rubin, D. C., Spinnler, H. and Wagenaar, W. A. (eds) (1992) *Theoretical Perspectives on Autobiographical Memory*. Dordrecht, the Netherlands: Kluwer Academic Publishing.

Corner, J. and Harvey, S. (eds) (1991) *Enterprise and Heritage*. London: Routledge.

Cortazzi, M. (1993) *Narrative Analysis*. London: Falmer Press.

Coser, L. A. (1977) *Masters of Sociological Thought*, 2nd edn. New York, NY: Harcourt Brace Jovanovich.

Cotterill, P. and Letherby, G. (1993) Weaving stories: personal auto/biographies in feminist research, *Sociology*, 27(1): 67–79.

Coupland, N. and Nussbaum, J. F. (eds) (1993) *Discourse and Lifespan Identity*. London: Sage.

Crabtree, B. F. and Miller, W. L. (1999) Using codes and code manuals, in B. F. Crabtree and W. L. Miller (eds) *Doing Qualitative Research*, 2nd edn. London: Sage.

Crossley, M. (2000a) Deconstructing autobiographical accounts of childhood sexual abuse: some critical reflections, *Feminism and Psychology*, 10(1): 73–90.

Crossley, M. (2000b) *Introducing Narrative Psychology: Self, Trauma and the Construction of Meaning*. Buckingham: Open University Press.

Crossley, M. (2000c) Narrative psychology, trauma and the study of self/identity, *Theory and Psychology*, 10(4): 527–46.

Current Sociology (1995) Special Issue: *Biographical Research*, 43(2/3).

Curtis, T. (ed.) (1986) *Wales: The Imagined Nation*. Bridgend: Poetry Wales Press.

Darwin, C. ([1839]1997) *The Voyage of the Beagle*. Ware: Wordsworth.

Davies, C. B. (1994) *Black Women, Writing and Identity: Migrations of the subject*. London: Routledge.

Davis, J. (1992) Tense in ethnography: some practical considerations, in J. Okely and H. Callaway (eds) *Anthropology and Autobiography*. London: Routledge.

Davis, K. (1994) *Reshaping the Female Body: The Dilemma of Cosmetic Surgery*. London: Routledge.

Davis, K. (ed.) (1997) *Embodied Practices*. London: Sage.

Day Sclater, S. (1998) Creating the self: stories as transitional phenomena, *Auto/Biography*, VI (1/2): 85–92.

Dentith, S. (ed.) (1995) *Bakhtinian Thought: An Introductory Reader*. London: Routledge.

Denzin, N. K. (1970) *The Research Act in Sociology*. London: Butterworth.

Denzin, N. K. (1989*) Interpretive Biography*. London: Sage.

Denzin, N. K. (1995) Stanley and Clifford: undoing an interactionist text, *Current Sociology*, 43(2/3): 115–23.

Denzin, N. K. (1997) *Interpretive Ethnography*. London: Sage.

Denzin, N. K. and Lincoln, Y. S. (1994a) The fifth moment, in N. K. Denzin and Y. S. Lincoln (eds) (1994) *Handbook of Qualitative Research*. London: Sage.

Denzin, N. K. and Lincoln, Y. S. (eds) (1994b) *Handbook of Qualitative Research*. London: Sage.

Denzin, N. K. and Lincoln, Y. S. (1994c) Introduction: entering the field of qualitative research, in N. K. Denzin and Y. S. Lincoln (eds) *Handbook of Qualitative Research*. London: Sage.

Denzin, N. K. and Lincoln, Y. S. (eds) (2000a) *Handbook of Qualitative Research*, 2nd edn. London: Sage.

Denzin, N. K. and Lincoln, Y. S. (2000b) The seventh moment: out of the past, in N. K. Denzin and Y. S. Lincoln (eds) *Handbook of Qualitative Research*, 2nd edn. London: Sage.

Desmond, A. and Moore, J. (1991) *Darwin*. London: Michael Joseph.

Dex, S. (1991a) Life and work history analyses, in S. Dex (ed.) *Life and Work History Analyses*. London: Routledge.

Dex, S. (ed.) (1991b) *Life and Work History Analyses*. London: Routledge.

Dickens, C. ([1853]1971) *Bleak House*. Harmondsworth: Penguin.

Dollard, J. (1935) *Criteria for the Life History*. New Haven, CT: Yale University Press.

Donnachie, I. (1994) Landscapes, buildings and physical artifacts, in M. Drake and R. Finnegan (eds) *Sources and Methods for Family and Community Historians: A Handbook*. Cambridge: Cambridge University Press.

Downes, D. and Rock, P. (1995) *Understanding Deviance*, 2nd edn. Oxford: Clarendon Press.

Driessen, H. (1998) Introduction: trends, genres and cases in self-revelation, *Focaal*, 32: 7–13.

Dunaway, D. K. (1996) Introduction: the interdisciplinarity of oral history, in D. K. Dunaway and W. K. Baum (eds) *Oral History: An Interdisciplinary Anthology*, 2nd edn. Walnut Creek, CA: AltaMira Press.

Dunaway, D. K. and Baum, W. K. (eds) (1996) *Oral History: An Interdisciplinary Anthology*, 2nd edn. Walnut Creek, CA: AltaMira Press.

Eakin, P. J. (1985) *Fictions in Autobiography: Studies in the Art of Self-Invention*. Princeton, NJ: Princeton University Press,

Eakin, P. J. (1999a) Autobiography and the value structures of ordinary experience: Marianne Gullestad's *Everyday Life Philosophers*, in R. Josselson and A. Lieblich (eds) *The Narrative Study of Lives*, 6. London: Sage.

Eakin, P. J. (1999b) *How Our Lives Become Stories*. London: Cornell University Press.

Eichler, M. (1997) Feminist methodology, *Current Sociology*, 45(2), April: 9–36.

Elder, G. (1981) History and the life course, in D. Bertaux (ed.) *Biography and Society*. London: Sage.

Ellis, C. and Bochner, A. P. (2000) Autoethnography, personal narrative, reflexivity: researcher as subject, in N. K. Denzin and Y. S. Lincoln (eds) *Handbook of Qualitative Research*, 2nd edn. London: Sage.

Erben, M. (1993) The problem of other lives: social perspectives on written biography, *Sociology*, 27(1): 15–25.

Erben, M. (1996) The purposes and processes of biographical method, in R. Usher and D. Scott (eds) *Understanding Educational Research*. London: Routledge.

Erben, M. (ed.) (1998a) *Biography and Education: A Reader*. London: Falmer Press.

Erben, M. (1998b) Biography and research method, in M. Erben (ed.) *Biography and Education: A Reader*. London: Falmer Press.

Erben, M. (1998c) Introduction, in M. Erben (ed.) *Biography and Education: A Reader*. London: Falmer Press.

Evans, G. E. (1993) *The Crooked Scythe*. London: Faber and Faber.

Evans, M. (1993) Reading lives: how the personal might be social, *Sociology*, 27(1): 5–13.

Evans, M. (1999) *Missing Persons*. London: Routledge.

Evans, M. and Lunn, K. (1997) *War and Memory in the Twentieth Century*. Oxford: Berg.

Eysenck, M. W. (1993) *Principles of Cognitive Psychology*. Hove: Lawrence Erlbaum Associates.

Faraday, A. and Plummer, K. (1979) Doing life histories, *Sociological Review*, 27(4): 773–98.

Featherstone, M., Hepworth, M. and Turner, B. S. (1991) *The Body: Social Processes and Cultural Theory*. London: Sage.

Feldman, M. S. (1995) *Strategies for Interpreting Qualitative Data*. London: Sage.

Fetterman, D. M. (1998) *Ethnography: Step by Step*, 2nd edn. London: Sage.

Finnegan, R. (1992) *Oral Traditions and the Verbal Arts*. London: Routledge.

Finnegan, R. (1996a) A note on oral tradition and historical evidence, in D. K. Dunaway and W. K. Baum (eds) *Oral History: An Interdisciplinary Anthology*, 2nd edn. Walnut Creek, CA: AltaMira Press.

Finnegan, R. (1996b) Personal narratives and urban theory in Milton Keynes, *Auto/Biography*, 4(2/3): 13–25.

Finnegan, R. (1998) *Tales of the City: A Study of Narrative and Urban Life*. Cambridge: Cambridge University Press.

Fischer-Rosenthal, W. and Rosenthal, G. (1997) Daniel Bertaux's complaints or against false dichotomies in biographical research, in *Biography and Society Newsletter*: 5–11, ISA Research Committee, 38: 5–11.

Fisher, B. M. and Strauss, A. L. (1979) Interactionism, in T. Bottomore and R. Nisbet (eds) *A History of Sociological Analysis*. London: Heinemann.

Forster, J. (1874) *The Life of Charles Dickens*. London.

Fortier, A.-M. (2000) *Migrant Belongings*. Oxford: Berg.

Forster, M. (1996) *Hidden Lives*. Harmondsworth: Penguin.

Forster, M. (1999) *Precious Lives*. London: Vintage.

Francis, H. (1984) *Miners against Fascism: Wales and the Spanish Civil War*. London: Lawrence and Wishart.

Frank, L. (1984) *Charles Dickens and the Romantic Self*. London: University of Nebraska Press.

Fraser, R. (1984) *In Search of a Past*. London: Verso.

Freeman, M. (1993) *Rewriting the Self: History, Memory, Narrative*. London: Routledge.

Frisch, M. (1990) *A Shared Authority: Essays on the Craft and Meaning of Oral and Public History*. Albany, NY: State University of New York Press.

Frisch, M. (1998) Oral history and *Hard Times*: a review essay, in R. Perks and A. Thomson (eds) *The Oral History Reader*. London: Routledge.

Fussell, P. (2000) *The Great War and Modern Memory*. Oxford: Oxford University Press.

Geertz, C. (1973) *The Interpretation of Cultures*. New York, NY: Basic Books.

Geertz, C. (1988) *Works and Lives*. Stanford, CA: Stanford University Press.

Gergen, K. J. (1999) *An Invitation to Social Constructionism*. London: Sage.

Gergen, M. M. and Gergen, K. J. (1984) The social construction of narrative accounts, in K. J. Gergen and M. M. Gergen (eds) *Historical Social Psychology*. Hillside, NJ: Erlbaum.

Giele, J. Z. and Elder, G. H. Jr (1998a) Life course research: development of a field, in J. Z. Giele and G. H. Elder Jr. (eds) *Methods of Life Course Research: Qualitative and Quantitative Approaches*. London: Sage.

Giele, J. Z. and Elder G. H. Jr (eds) (1998b) *Methods of Life Course Research: Qualitative and Quantitative Approaches*. London: Sage.

Glaser, B. G. and Strauss, A. L. (1967) *The Discovery of Grounded Theory: Strategies for Qualitative Research*. Chicago, IL: Aldine Press.

Glaser, B. G. and Strauss, A. L. (1970) The discovery of grounded theory, in P. Worsley (ed.) *Modern Sociology: Introductory Readings*. Harmondsworth: Penguin.

Gluck, S. (1996) What's so special about women? Women's oral history, in D. K. Dunaway and W. K. Baum (eds) *Oral History: An Interdisciplinary Anthology*, 2nd edn. Walnut Creek, CA: AltaMira Press.

Gluck, S. B. and Patai, D. (1991a) Introduction, in S. B. Gluck and D. Patai (eds) *Women's Words: The Feminist Practice of Oral History*. London: Routledge.

Gluck, S. B. and Patai, D. (eds) (1991b) *Women's Words: The Feminist Practice of Oral History*. London: Routledge.

Goffman, E. (1968) *Asylums*. Harmondsworth: Penguin.

Golby, J. (1994) Autobiographies, letters and diaries, in M. Drake and R. Finnegan (eds) *Sources and Methods for Family and Community Historians: A Handbook*. Cambridge: Cambridge University Press.

Goldthorpe, J. H. (1980) *Social Mobility and Class Structure in Modern Britain*. Oxford: Clarendon Press.

Goodey, J. (2000) Biographical lessons for criminology, *Theoretical Criminology*, 4(4): 473–98.

Goodson, I. F. (ed.) (1992) *Studying Teachers' Lives*. London: Routledge.

Goodson, I. F. (1995) The story so far: personal knowledge and the political, in J. A. Hatch and R. Wisniewski (eds) *Life History and Narrative*. London: Falmer Press.

Goodson, I. F. and Sikes, P. (2001) *Life History Research in Educational Settings*. Buckingham: Open University Press.

Gottschalk, L. (1945) The historian and the historical document, in L. Gottschalk, C. Kluckhohn, and R. Angell (eds) *The Use of Personal Documents in History, Anthropology and Sociology*. New York: SSRC.

Gottschalk, L., Kluckhohn, C. and Angell, R. (eds) (1945) *The Use of Personal Documents in History, Anthropology and Sociology*. New York: SSRC.

Grele, R. J. (ed.) (1985) *Envelopes of Sound: The Art of Oral History*. Chicago, IL: Precedent.

Grele, R. J. (1990) The development, cultural peculiarities and state of oral history in the United States, *Bios*, Special Issue The History of Oral History – Development, Present State, and Future Prospects, pp. 3–15.

Grele, R. J. (1991) *Envelopes of Sound: The Art of Oral History*, 2nd edn. New York: Praeger.

Grele, R. J. (1996) Directions for oral history in the United States, in D. K. Dunaway and W. K. Baum (eds) *Oral History: An Interdisciplinary Anthology*, 2nd edn. Walnut Creek, CA: AltaMira Press.

Grele, R. J. (1998) Movement without aim: methodological and theoretical problems in oral history, in R. Perks and A. Thomson (eds) *The Oral History Reader*. London: Routledge.

Gubrium, J. F. and Holstein, J. A. (1995) Biographical work and new ethnography, in R. Josselson and A. Lieblich (eds) *The Narrative Study of Lives: 3*. London: Sage.

Gullestad, M. (1995) The intimacy of anonymity: reflections on a Norwegian life story competition, *Oral History*, 23(2): 51–9.

Gullestad, M. (1996) *Everyday Life Philosophers*. Oslo: Scandinavian University Press.

Haines, K. (1993) Review: Martyn Hammersley, *What's Wrong with Ethnography?*, *Sociology*, 27(2): 345–6.

Hale, S. (1991) Feminist method, process, and self-criticism: interviewing Sudanese women, in S. B. Gluck and D. Patai (eds) *Women's Words: The Feminist Practice of Oral History*. London: Routledge.

Hammersley, M. (1990) *The Dilemma of Qualitative Method*. London: Routledge.

Hammersley, M. (1992a) On feminist methodology, *Sociology*, 26(2): 187–206.

Hammersley, M. (1992b) *What's Wrong with Ethnography?* London: Routledge.

Hammersley, M. and Atkinson, P. (1989) *Ethnography: Principles in Practice*. London: Routledge.

Hankiss, A. (1981) Ontologies of the self: on the mythological rearranging of one's life history, in D. Bertaux (ed) *Biography and Society*. London: Sage.

Hardwick, M. and Hardwick, M. (1990) *The Charles Dickens Encyclopedia*. London: Futura.

Harper, D. (1994) On the authority of the image, in N. K. Denzin and Y. S. Lincoln (eds) *Handbook of Qualitative Research*. London: Sage.

Harper, D. (2000) Reimagining visual methods: Galileo to *Neuromancer*, in N. K. Denzin and Y. S. Lincoln (eds) *Handbook of Qualitative Research*, 2nd edn. London: Sage.

Hastrup, K. (1992) Writing ethnography, in J. Okely and H. Callaway (eds) *Anthropology and Autobiography*. London: Routledge.

Hatch, J. A. and Wisniewski, R. (1995a) Life history and narrative: questions, issues, and exemplary works, in J. A. Hatch and R. Wisniewski (eds) *Life History and Narrative*. London: Falmer Press.

Hatch, J. A. and Wisniewski, R. (eds) (1995b) *Life History and Narrative*. London: Falmer Press.

Hattersley, R. (1999) *Blood and Fire: William and Catherine Booth and their Salvation Army*. London: Little, Brown.

Hawthorn, J. (1987) *Unlocking the Text*. London: Edward Arnold.

Henriques, J., Hollway, W., Urwin, C., Venn, C. and Walkerdine, V. (1984) *Changing the Subject*. London: Methuen.

Heron, L. (ed.) (1985) *Truth, Dare or Promise: Girls Growing Up in the Fifties*. London: Virago Press.

Hewison, R. (1987) *The Heritage Industry*. London: Methuen.

Hibbert, C. (2000) *The Making of Charles Dickens*. Harmondsworth: Penguin.

Hobsbawm, E. (1997) *On History*. London: Weidenfeld and Nicolson.

Hobsbawm, E. and Ranger, T. (eds) (1983) *The Invention of Tradition*. Cambridge: Cambridge University Press.

Hodder, I. ([1994]2000) The interpretation of documents and material culture, in N. K. Denzin and Y. S. Lincoln (eds) *Handbook of Qualitative Research*, original and 2nd edns. London: Sage.

Hoffman, A. (1996) Reliability and validity in oral history, in D. K. Dunaway and W. K. Baum (eds) *Oral History: An Interdisciplinary Anthology*, 2nd edn. Walnut Creek, CA: AltaMira Press.

Hoggart, R. (1958) *The Uses of Literacy*. Harmondsworth: Penguin.

Hoggart, R. (1968) Richard Hoggart, in R. Goldman (ed.) *Breakthrough*. London: Routledge & Kegan Paul.

Hollway, W. and Jefferson, T. (1999) Gender, generation, anxiety and the reproduction of culture, in R. Josselson and A. Lieblich (eds) *The Narrative Study of Lives*, 6. London: Sage.

Hollway, W. and Jefferson, T. (2000) *Doing Qualitative Research Differently.* London: Sage.

Holmes, R. (1985) *Footsteps.* London: Flamingo.

Holmes, R. (1994) *Dr Johnson and Mr Savage.* London: Flamingo.

Holmes, R. (2000) *Sidetracks.* London: HarperCollins.

Holroyd, M. (2000) *Basil Street Blues.* London: Abacus.

Holstein, J. A. and Gubrium, J. F. (1994) Phenomenology, ethnomethodology, and interpretive practice, in N. K. Denzin and Y. S. Lincoln (eds) *Handbook of Qualitative Research.* London: Sage.

Horowitz, I. L. (1970a) Introduction, in I. L. Horowitz (ed.) *Sociological Self-Images: A Collective Portrait.* Oxford: Pergamon.

Horowitz, I. L. (ed.) (1970b) *Sociological Self-Images: A Collective Portrait.* Oxford: Pergamon.

Howkins, A. (1994) Inventing Everyman: George Ewart Evans, oral history and national identity, *Oral History,* 22(2): 26–32.

Humphries, S. and Gordon, P. (1993) *A Labour of Love: The Experience of Parenthood in Britain, 1900–1950.* London: Sidgwick and Jackson.

Humphries, S. and Hopwood, B. (2000) *Green and Pleasant Land.* London: Channel 4 Books.

Hunter, I. M. L. (1964) *Memory,* revised edn. Harmondsworth: Penguin.

Hutcheon, L. (1989) *The Politics of Postmodernism.* London: Routledge.

Hyvärinen, M. (1998) Thick and thin narratives: thickness of description, expectation, and causality, *Cultural Studies: A Research Volume,* 3: 149–74.

Ingham, P. (1992) *Dickens, Women and Language.* Hemel Hempstead: Harvester Wheatsheaf.

Inglis, R. (1990) *The Children's War: Evacuation 1939–45.* London: Fontana.

Jennings, H. and Madge, C. (eds) ([1937]1987) *May the Twelfth: Mass-Observation Day-Survey 1937.* London: Faber and Faber.

Johnson, J. C. (1990) *Selecting Ethnographic Informants.* London: Sage.

Johnson, R., McLennan, G., Schwarz, B. and Sutton, D. (eds) (1982) *Making Histories: Studies in History-writing and Politics.* London: Hutchinson.

Jones, B. and Williams, C. (1999a) *B. L. Coombes.* Cardiff: University of Wales Press.

Jones, B. and Williams, C. (eds) (1999b) *With the Dust Still in His Throat: An Anthology of Writing by B. L. Coombes.* Cardiff: University of Wales Press.

Jones, G. R. (1983) Life history methodology, in G. Morgan (ed.) *Beyond Method.* London: Sage.

Josselson, R. (1995) Imagining the real: empathy, narrative, and the dialogic self, in R. Josselson and A. Lieblich (eds) *The Narrative Study of Lives,* 3. London: Sage.

Josselson, R. and Lieblich, A. (eds) (1993) *The Narrative Study of Lives,* 1. London: Sage.

Josselson, R. and Lieblich, A. (eds) (1995) Introduction, in R. Josselson and A. Lieblich (eds) *The Narrative Study of Lives,* 3. London: Sage.

Josselson, R. and Lieblich, A. (eds) (1999) *The Narrative Study of Lives: Making Meaning of Narratives,* 6. London: Sage.

Jovchelovitch, S. and Bauer, M. W. (2000) Narrative interviewing, in M. W. Bauer and G. Gaskell (eds) *Qualitative Research with Text, Image and Sound.* London: Sage.

Kenna, M. E. (1992) Changing places and altered perspectives: research on a Greek island in the 1960s and in the 1980s, in J. Okely and H. Callaway (eds) *Anthropology and Autobiography*. London: Routledge.

Khubova, D., Ivankiev, A. and Sharova, T. (1992) After Glasnost: oral history in the Soviet Union, in L. Passerini (ed.) *Memory and Totalitarianism*. Oxford: Oxford University Press.

Kirk, J. and Miller, M. L. (1986) *Reliability and Validity in Qualitative Research*. London: Sage.

Kluckhohn, C. (1945) The personal document in anthropological science, in L. Gottschalk, C. Kluckhohn and R. Angell (eds) *The Use of Personal Documents in History, Anthropology and Sociology*. New York, NY: SSRC.

Laing, R. D. and Cooper, D. G. (1971) *Reason and Violence*, 2nd edn. London: Tavistock.

Lea, M. and West, L. (1995) Motives, mature students, the self and narrative, in J. Swindells (ed.) *The Uses of Autobiography*. London: Taylor and Francis.

Leach, E. (1970) *Lévi-Strauss*. London: Fontana.

Lee, R. M. (2000) *Unobtrusive Methods in Social Research*. Buckingham: Open University Press.

Lejeune, P. (1989) *On Autobiography*. Minneapolis, MN: University of Minnesota Press.

Lemert, E. M. (1967) *Social Deviance, Social Problems and Social Control*. New York: Prentice-Hall.

Lewis, O. (1961) *The Children of Sanchez: Autobiography of a Mexican family*. New York: Random House.

Leydesdorff, S. (1992) A shattered silence: the life stories of survivors of the Jewish proletariat of Amsterdam, in L. Passerini (ed.) *Memory and Totalitarianism*. Oxford: Oxford University Press.

Leydesdorff, S., Passerini, L. and Thompson, P. (eds) (1996) *Gender and Memory: International Yearbook of Oral History and Life Stories*, IV. Oxford: Oxford University Press.

Lieblich, A., Tuval-Mashiach, R. and Zilber, T. (1998) *Narrative Research*. London: Sage.

Lowenthal, D. (1985) *The Past is a Foreign Country*. Cambridge: Cambridge University Press.

Lumley, R. (ed.) (1988) *The Museum Time-Machine*. London: Routledge.

Lynch, M. (2000) Against reflexivity as academic virtue and source of privileged knowledge, *Theory, Culture & Society*, 17(3), June: 26–54.

McAdams, D. (1997) *The Stories We Live By: Personal Myths and the Making of the Self*. London: Guilford Press.

Mandelbaum, D. (1982) The study of life history, in R. G. Burgess (ed.) *Field Research: a Sourcebook and Field Manual*. London: Unwin Hyman.

Mangabeira, W. C. (ed.) (1996) Trend report: qualitative sociology and computer programs: advent and diffusion of computer-assisted qualitative data analysis software (CAQDAS), *Current Sociology*, 44(3), Winter: 279–321.

Mann, C. (1994) 'How did I get here?' Educational life histories of adolescent girls doing A-Levels, *Auto/Biography*, 3(1/2): 59–70.

Mann, C. (1998a) Family fables, in M. Chamberlain and P. Thompson (eds) *Narrative and Genre*. London: Routledge.

Mann, C. (1998b) Adolescent girls reflect on educational choices, in M. Erben (ed.) *Biography and Education: A Reader*. London: Falmer Press.

Manning, P. K. and Cullum-Swan, B. (1994) Narrative, content, and semiotic analysis, in N. K. Denzin and Y. S. Lincoln (eds) *Handbook of Qualitative Research*. London: Sage.

Marcus, G. (1992) Past, present and emergent identities: requirements for ethnographies of late twentieth-century modernity worldwide, in S. Lash and J. Friedman (eds) *Modernity and Identity*. Oxford: Blackwell.

Marcus, G. E. (1994) What comes (just) after 'post'?: the case of ethnography, in N. K. Denzin and Y. S. Lincoln (eds) *Handbook of Qualitative Research*. London: Sage.

Marcus, L. (1994) *Auto/biographical Discourses: Theory, Criticism, Practice*. Manchester: Manchester University Press.

Marcus, L. (1995) The face of autobiography, in J. Swindells (ed.) *The Uses of Autobiography*. London: Taylor and Francis.

Martin, R. R. (ed.) (1995) *Oral History in Social Work: Research, Assessment and Intervention*. London: Sage.

Martins, H. (1974) Time and theory in sociology, in J. Rex (ed.) *Approaches to Sociology*. London: Routledge.

Mascuch, M. (1997) *Origins of the Individualist Self: Autobiography and Self-Identity in England, 1591–1791*. Cambridge: Polity.

Matthews, F. H. (1977) *Quest for an American Sociology: Robert E. Park and the Chicago School*. Montreal: McGill-Queens University Press.

Matza, D. (1964) *Delinquency and Drift*. New York: Wiley.

Matza, D. (1969) *Becoming Deviant*. New Jersey: Prentice-Hall.

Maynard, M. and Purvis, J. (eds) (1994) *Researching Women's Lives from a Feminist Perspective*. London: Taylor and Francis.

Mead, G. H. (1932) *The Philosophy of the Present*. La Salle, IL: Open Court.

Mead, G. H. ([1934]1967) *Mind, Self and Society*. Chicago, IL: University of Chicago Press.

Mead, G. H. (1964) *On Social Psychology*, Chicago, IL: University of Chicago Press.

Merton, R. (1988) Some thoughts on the concept of sociological autobiography, in M. W. Riley (ed.) *Sociological Lives*. Newbury Park, CA: Sage.

Miller, N. and Morgan, D. (1993) Called to account: the CV as an autobiographical practice, *Sociology*, 27(1): 133–43.

Miller, R. L. (2000) *Researching Life Stories and Family Histories*. London: Sage.

Mills, C. W. (1966) *Sociology and Pragmatism*. New York, NY: Oxford University Press.

Mills, C. W. (1970) *The Sociological Imagination*. Harmondsworth: Penguin.

Mintz, S. (1996) The anthropological interview and the life history, in D. K. Dunaway and W. K. Baum (eds) *Oral History: An Interdisciplinary Anthology*, 2nd edn. Walnut Creek, CA: AltaMira Press.

Mitchell, W. J. T. (ed.) (1981) *On Narrative*. Chicago, IL: University of Chicago Press.

Morgan, D. (1998) Sociological imaginings and imagining sociology: bodies, auto/biographies and other mysteries, *Sociology*, 32(4): 647–63.

Morgan, G. (ed.) (1983) *Beyond Method*. London: Sage.

Morris, P. (1978) Models of long-term memory, in M. M. Gruneberg and P. Morris (eds) *Aspects of Memory*. London: Methuen.

Morris, P. and Gruneberg, M. M. (eds) (1994) *Theoretical Aspects of Memory*, 2nd edn. London: Routledge.

Muller, J. H. (1999) Narrative approaches to qualitative research in primary care, in B. F. Crabtree and W. L. Miller (eds) *Doing Qualitative Research*, 2nd edn. London: Sage.

Mumby, D. K. (ed.) (1993) *Narrative and Social Control*. London: Sage.

Munslow, A. (2000) *The Routledge Companion to Historical Studies*. London: Routledge.

Murray, K. (1989) The construction of identity in the narratives of romance and comedy, in J. Shotter and K. J. Gergen (eds) *Texts of Identity*. London: Sage.

Neisser, U. (1982) Snapshots or benchmarks?, in U. Neisser (ed.) *Memory Observed: Remembering in Natural Contexts*. San Francisco, CA: W. H. Freeman and Co.

Nevins, A. (1996) Oral history: how and why it was born, in D. K. Dunaway and W. K. Baum (eds) *Oral History: An Interdisciplinary Anthology*, 2nd edn. Walnut Creek, CA: AltaMira Press.

Newcomb, M. (1989) *The Imagined World of Charles Dickens*. Columbus, OH: Ohio State University Press.

Niethammer, L. (1992) Where were *you* on 17 June? A niche in memory, in L. Passerini (ed.) *Memory and Totalitarianism*. Oxford: Oxford University Press.

Norris, C. (1991) *Deconstruction: Theory and Practice*, revised edn. London: Routledge.

Oakley, A. (1998) Gender, methodology and people's ways of knowing, *Sociology*, 32(4): 707–31.

Okely, J. (1992) Anthropology and autobiography: participatory experience and embodied knowledge, in J. Okely and H. Callaway (eds) *Anthropology and Autobiography*. London: Routledge.

Okely, J. (1994) Thinking through fieldwork, in A. Bryman and R. G. Burgess (eds) *Analyzing Qualitative Data*. London: Routledge.

Okely, J. and Callaway, H. (eds) (1992) *Anthropology and Autobiography*. London: Routledge.

Olesen, V. L. (2000) Feminisms and qualitative research at and into the millennium, in N. K. Denzin and Y. S. Lincoln (eds) *Handbook of Qualitative Research*, 2nd edn. London: Sage.

Olney, J. (1972) *Metaphors of Self: The Meaning of Autobiography*. Princeton, NJ: Princeton University Press.

Olney, J. (ed.) (1980) *Autobiography: Essays Theoretical and Critical*. Princeton, NJ: Princeton University Press.

Oral History (1989) Reminiscence Special, 17(2).

Oral History (1995) Health and Welfare, 23(1).

O'Rand, A. M. (1998) The craft of life course studies, in J. Z. Giele and G. H. Elder Jr. (eds) *Methods of Life Course Research: Qualitative and Quantitative Approaches*. London: Sage.

Parker, T. (1971) *The Frying Pan*. London: Panther.

Parker, T. (1985) *The People of Providence*. Harmondsworth: Penguin.

Parker, I. (1992) *Discourse Dynamics: Critical Analysis for Social and Individual Psychology*. London: Routledge.

Parker, T. (1988) *Red Hill: A Mining Community*. London: Coronet.

Parker, Z. (1998) PhD Students and the auto/biographies of their learning, in M. Erben (ed.) *Biography and Education*. London: Falmer Press.

Passerini, L. (1979) Work ideology and consensus under Italian Fascism, *History Workshop*, 8: 82–108.

Passerini, L. (1990) Mythbiography in oral history, in R. Samuel and P. Thompson (eds) *The Myths We Live By*. London: Routledge.

Passerini, L. (1992a) Introduction, in L. Passerini (ed.) *Memory and Totalitarianism*. Oxford: Oxford University Press.

Passerini, L. (ed.) (1992b) *Memory and Totalitarianism: International Yearbook of Oral History and Life Stories*, I. Oxford: Oxford University Press.

Pels, D. (2000) Reflexivity: one step up, *Theory, Culture & Society*, 17(3), June: 1–25.

Peneff, J. (1990) Myths in life stories, in R. Samuel and P. Thompson (eds) *The Myths We Live By*. London: Routledge.

Perakyla, A. (1997) Reliability and validity in research based on transcripts, in D. Silverman (ed.) *Qualitative Research: Theory, Method, and Practice*. London: Sage.

Perks, R. (1999) Oral History Websites, *Oral History*, 27(2): 87–9.

Perks, R. (2000) Listening to the past, *History Today*, 50(11): 36–7.

Perks, R. and Thomson, A. (1998a) Introduction, in R. Perks and A. Thomson (eds) *The Oral History Reader*. London: Routledge.

Perks, R. and Thomson, A. (eds) (1998b) *The Oral History Reader*. London: Routledge.

Personal Narratives Group (eds) (1989) *Interpreting Women's Lives: Feminist Theory and Personal Narratives*. Bloomington, IN: Indiana University Press.

Petras, J. W. (ed.) (1968) *George Herbert Mead: Essays on His Social Philosophy*. Columbia University, NY: Teachers College Press.

Plummer, K. (1983) *Documents of Life*. London: George Allen and Unwin.

Plummer, K. (1992) *Modern Homosexualities: Fragments of Lesbian and Gay Experiences*. London: Routledge.

Plummer, K. (1995a) Life Story Research, in J. A. Smith, R. Harré and L. Van Langenhove (eds) *Rethinking Methods in Psychology*. London: Sage.

Plummer, K. (1995b) *Telling Sexual Stories: Power, Change and Social Worlds*. London: Routledge.

Plummer, L. (2001) *Documents of Life, 2*. London: Sage.

Polkinghorne, D. E. (1988) *Narrative Knowing and the Human Sciences*. Albany, NY: State University of New York Press.

Polkinghorne, D. E. (1995) Narrative configuration in qualitative analysis, in J. A. Hatch and R. Wisniewski (eds) *Life History and Narrative*. London: Falmer Press.

Pollock, K. (1993) Attitude of mind as a means of resisting illness, in A. Radley (ed.) *Worlds of Illness: Biographical and Cultural Perspectives on Health and Disease*. London: Routledge.

Popular Memory Group (1982) Popular memory: theory, politics, method, in R. Johnson, G. McLennan, B. Schwarz and D. Sutton (eds) *Making Histories: Studies in History-writing and Politics*. London: Hutchinson.

Portelli, A. (1981) The peculiarities of oral history, *History Workshop*, 12: 96–107.

Portelli, A. (1990) Uchronic dreams: working-class memory and possible worlds, in R. Samuel and P. Thompson (eds) *The Myths We Live By*. London: Routledge.

Portelli, A. (1991) *The Death of Luigi Trastulli and Other Stories: Form and Meaning in Oral History*. Albany, NY: State University of New York Press.

Portelli, A. (1998) Oral history as genre, in M. Chamberlain and P. Thompson (eds) *Narrative and Genre*. London: Routledge.

Porter, R. (2000) *Enlightenment*. Harmondsworth: Allen Lane.

Potter, J. and Wetherell, M. (1994) Analyzing discourse, in A. Bryman and R. G. Burgess (eds) *Analyzing Qualitative Data*. London: Routledge.

Pryce, W. T. R. (1994) Photographs and picture postcards, in M. Drake and R. Finnegan (eds) *Sources and Methods for Family and Community Historians: A Handbook*. Cambridge: Cambridge University Press.

Radley, A. (1993a) The role of metaphor in adjustment to chronic illness, in A. Radley (ed.) *Worlds of Illness: Biographical and Cultural Perspectives on Health and Disease*. London: Routledge.

Radley, A. (ed.) (1993b) *Worlds of Illness: Biographical and Cultural Perspectives on Health and Disease*. London: Routledge.

Radstone, S. (ed.) (2000) *Memory and Methodology*. Oxford: Berg.

Rapaport, L. (1997) *Jews in Germany after the Holocaust*. Cambridge: Cambridge University Press.

Read, P. (1998) Presenting voices in different media: print, radio and CD-ROM, in R. Perks and A. Thomson (eds) *The Oral History Reader*. London: Routledge.

Reed-Danahay, D. (ed.) (1997) *Auto/Ethnography: Rewriting the Self and the Social*. Oxford: Berg.

Reinharz, S. (1992) *Feminist Methods in Social Research*. Oxford: Oxford University Press.

Richardson, L. (1995) Narrative and sociology, in J. Van Maanen (ed.) *Representation in Ethnography*. London: Sage.

Ricoeur, P. (1981) Narrative time, in W. J. T. Mitchell (ed.) *On Narrative*. Chicago, IL: University of Chicago Press.

Ricoeur, P. (1984, 1985, 1988) *Time and Narrative*, 3 vols. Chicago, IL: University Chicago Press.

Riessman, C. K. (1993) *Narrative Analysis*. London: Sage.

Riley, M. W. (ed.) (1988) *Sociological Lives*. London: Sage.

Riley, M. W. (1998) A life course approach: autobiographical notes, in J. Z. Giele and G. H. Elder Jr (eds) *Methods of Life Course Research: Qualitative and Quantitative Approaches*. London: Sage.

Ritchie, D. A. (1995) *Doing Oral History*. New York: Twayne.

Ritchie, D. A. (2001) When history goes public: recent experiences in the United States, *Oral History*, 29(1): 92–7.

Roberts, B. (1977) G. H. Mead: the theory and practice of his philosophy, *Ideology and Consciousness*, Autumn, 2: 81–106.

Roberts, B. (1996) Dickens, Mr Jarndyce and the autobiographical statement, *Auto/Biography*, 4(2/3): 81–91.

Roberts, B. (1998) An auto/biographical account of educational experience, in M. Erben (ed.) *Biography and Education*. London: Falmer Press.

Roberts, B. (1999a) Some thoughts on time perspectives and auto/biography, *Auto/Biography*, VII(1/2): 21–5.

Roberts, B. (1999b) Time, biography and ethnic and national identity formation, in K. J. Brehony and N. Rassool (eds) *Nationalisms Old and New*. Basingstoke: Macmillan.

Roberts, B. (1999c) Welsh identity in a former mining valley: social images and imagined communities, in R. Fevre and A. Thompson (eds) *Nation, Identity and Social Theory: Perspectives from Wales*, first published in *Contemporary Wales*, Vol. 7, 1995. Cardiff: University of Wales Press.

Robins, T. (1995) Remembering the future: the cultural study of memory, in B. Adam and S. Allan (eds) *Theorizing Culture: An Interdisciplinary Critique after Postmodernism*. London: UCL Press.

Robinson, J. A. (1986) Autobiographical memory: a historical prologue, in D. C. Rubin (ed.) *Autobiographical Memory*. Cambridge: Cambridge University Press.

Rogers, L. K., Leydesdorff, S. and Dawson, G. (eds) (1999) *Trauma and Life Stories: International Perspectives*. London: Routledge.

Roos, J. P. (1994) The true life revisited: autobiography and referentiality after the 'posts', *Auto/Biography*, 3(1/2): 1–16.

Rose, D. (1990) *Living the Ethnographic Life*. London: Sage.

Rosenthal, G. (1991) German war memories: narrability and the biographical and social functions of remembering, *Oral History*, 19(2): 34–41.

Rosenthal, G. (1993) Reconstruction of life stories: principles of selection in generating stories for narrative biographical interviews, in R. Josselson and A. Lieblich (eds) *The Narrative Study of Lives*, I. London: Sage.

Rosenthal, G. (ed.) (1998) *The Holocaust in Three Generations: Families of Victims and Perpetrators of the Nazi Regime*. London: Cassell.

Rosenwald, G. C. and Ochberg, R. L. (eds) (1992) *Storied Lives: The Cultural Politics of Self-understanding*. New Haven, CT and London: Yale University Press.

Rowland, P. (ed.) (1997) *Charles Dickens: My Early Times*, revised edn. London: Arum Press.

Rubin, D. C. (ed.) (1986a) *Autobiographical Memory*. Cambridge: Cambridge University Press.

Rubin, D. C. (1986b) Introduction, in D.C. Rubin (ed.) *Autobiographical Memory*. Cambridge: Cambridge University Press.

Russell, D. (1997) An oral history project in mental health nursing, *Journal of Advanced Nursing*, 26: 489–95.

Rustin, M. (1999) A biographical turn in social science?, in *Sostris Working Paper*, 6. London: Centre for Biography in Social Policy. University of East London.

Sage, L. (2000) *Bad Blood*. London: Fourth Estate.

Salmon, P. (1985) *Living in Time: A New Look at Personal Development*. London: Dent.

Samuel, R. (1994) *Theatres of Memory*, Vol. 1. London: Verso.

Samuel, R. and Thompson, P. (1990a) Introduction, in R. Samuel and P. Thompson (eds) *The Myths We Live By*. London: Routledge.

Samuel, R. and Thompson, P. (eds) (1990b) *The Myths We Live By*. London: Routledge.

Sangster, J. (1998) Telling our stories: feminist debates and the use of oral history, in R. Perks and A. Thomson (eds) *The Oral History Reader*. London: Routledge.

Sarbin, T. (ed.) (1986) *Narrative Psychology: The Storied Nature of Human Conduct*. New York: Praeger.

Sartre, J.-P. (1968) *Search for a Method*. New York: Vintage.

Schlicke, P. (ed.) (1999) *Oxford Reader's Companion to Dickens*. Oxford: Oxford University Press.

Schrager, S. (1998) What is social in oral history?, in R. Perks and A. Thomson (eds) *The Oral History Reader*. London: Routledge.

Schutz, A. (1971) *Collected Papers, I: The Problem of Social Reality*, edited by M. Natanson. The Hague: Martinus Nijhoff.

Schütze, F. (1992) Pressure and guilt: the experience of a young German soldier in World War II and its biographical implication, *International Sociology*, 7(2): 187–208 and (3)347–67.

Scott, D. (1998) Fragments of a life: recursive dilemmas, in M. Erben (ed.) *Biography and Education*. London: Falmer Press.

Scott, D. and Usher, R. (eds) (1996) *Understanding Educational Research*. London: Routledge.

Scott, J. (1990) *A Matter of Record*. Cambridge: Polity.

Shaw, C. R. ([1930]1966) *The Jack-Roller: A Delinquent Boy's Own Story*, revised edition. Chicago, IL: University of Chicago Press.

Sherbakova, I. (1992) The Gulag in memory, in L. Passerini (ed.) *Memory and Totalitarianism*. Oxford: Oxford University Press.

Sheridan, D. (ed.) (1985) *Among You Taking Notes . . .: The Wartime Diary of Naomi Mitchison, 1939–1945*. London: Gollancz.

Sheridan, D. (1993) Writing to the Archive: Mass-Observation as autobiography, *Sociology*, 27(1): 27–40.

Sheridan, D. (2000) *Wartime Women: A Mass-Observation Anthology*. London: Phoenix Press.

Shilling, C. (1993) *The Body and Social Theory*. London: Sage.

Shilling, C. and Mellor, P. (1994) Embodiment, auto/biography and carnal knowing, *Auto/Biography*, 3(1/2): 115–28.

Silverman, D. (1993) *Interpreting Qualitative Data*. London: Sage.

Silverman, D. (1997) Towards an aesthetics of research, in D. Silverman (ed.) *Qualitative Research: Theory, Method and Practice*. London: Sage.

Sim, S. (ed.) (1998) *Postmodern Thought*. Cambridge: Icon Books.

Sisman, A. (2000) *Boswell's Presumptuous Task*. London: Hamish Hamilton.

Skultans, V. (1997) *The Testimony of Lives*. London: Routledge.

Skultans, V. (1998a) Remembering Latvian childhood and the escape from history, *Auto/Biography*, VI(1/2): 5–13.

Skultans, V. (1998b) Remembering time and place: a case study in Latvian narrative, *Oral History*, 26(1): 55–63.

Slater, M. (1996) *Dickens' Journalism*, Vol. 2. London: Dent.

Slim, H. and Thompson, P. with Bennett, O. and Cross, N. (1998) Ways of listening, in R. Perks and A. Thomson (eds) *The Oral History Reader*. London: Routledge.

Smith, D. (1988) *The Chicago School: A Liberal Critique of Capitalism*. Basingstoke: Macmillan.

Smith, G. (1998) Mega-memories on CD-Rom, *Oral History*, 26(1): 93–5.

Smith, L. M. (1994) Biographical method, in N. K. Denzin and Y. S. Lincoln (eds) *Handbook of Qualitative Research*. London: Sage.

Smith, P. M. (2001) *Transnational Urbanism*. Oxford: Blackwell.

Snodgrass, J. (1982) *The Jack-Roller at Seventy: A Fifty-Year Follow-up.* Lexington, MA: Lexington Books.

Sontag, S. (ed.) (1983) *Barthes: Selected Writings.* London: Fontana.

Sociology (1993) Special Issue: Biography and Autobiography in Sociology, 27(1).

Sparkes, A. (1993) Reciprocity in critical research? Some unsettling thoughts, in G. Shacklock and J. Smyth (eds) *Being Reflexive in Critical Educational and Social Research.* London: Falmer Press.

Sparkes, A. C. (1994a) Life histories and the issue of voice: reflections on an emerging relationship, *International Journal of Qualitative Studies in Education,* 7(2): 165–83.

Sparkes, A. C. (1994b) Self, silence and invisibility as a beginning teacher, *British Journal of Sociology of Education,* 15(1): 93–118.

Sparkes, A. C. (1997a) An elite body, illness, and the fragmentation of self: a collaborative exploration, *Auto/Biography,* 1,2,3: 27–37.

Sparkes, A. C. (1997b) Ethnographic fiction and representing the absent other, *Sport, Education and Society,* 2(1): 25–40.

Sparkes, A. (1997c) Narrating the fragile male body/self: an alchemy of disruptive, fragmented and emotionally charged moments, *Auto/Biography,* 1,2,3: 115–29.

Spradley, J. P. (1979) *The Ethnographic Interview.* London: Holt, Rinehart and Winston.

Stanley, L. (ed.) (1984) *The Diaries of Hannah Cullwick.* New Jersey: Rutgers University Press.

Stanley, L. (1992) *The Auto/Biography I: The Theory and Practice of Feminist Auto/biography.* Manchester: Manchester University Press.

Stanley, L. (1993) On auto/biography in sociology, *Sociology,* 27(1): 41–52.

Stanley, L. (1994a) Introduction: lives and works and auto/biographical occasions, *Auto/Biography,* 3(1/2): i–ii.

Stanley, L. (1994b) Sisters under the skin? Oral histories and auto/biographies, *Oral History,* 22(2): 88–9.

Stanley, L. and Morgan, D. (1993) Introduction, *Sociology,* 27(1): 1–4.

Stanley, L. and Wise, S. (1990) Method, methodology and epistemology in feminist research processes, in L. Stanley (ed.) *Feminist Praxis: Research, Theory and Epistemology in Feminist Sociology.* London: Routledge.

Stanley, L. and Wise, S. (1993) *Breaking Out Again: Feminist Ontology and Epistemology,* 2nd revised edn. London: Routledge.

Starr, L. (1996) Oral History, in D. K. Dunaway and W. K. Baum (eds) *Oral History: An Interdisciplinary Anthology,* 2nd edn. Walnut Creek, CA: AltaMira Press.

Steedman, C. (1986) *Landscape for a Good Woman.* London: Virago.

Stern, F. (1992) Antagonistic memories: the post-war survival and alienation of Jews and Germans, in L. Passerini (ed.) *Memory and Totalitarianism.* Oxford: Oxford University Press.

Stone, G. P. and Farberman, H. A. (1970) Introduction, in G. P. Stone and H. A. Farberman (eds) *Social Psychology through Symbolic Interaction.* Waltham, MA: Xerox College.

Strachey, L. ([1918]1948) *Eminent Victorians.* Harmondsworth: Penguin.

Strauss, A. and Corbin, J. (1994) Grounded theory methodology: an overview, in N. K. Denzin and Y. S. Lincoln (eds) *Handbook of Qualitative Research.* London: Sage.

Stuart, M. (1993) 'And how was it for you, Mary?' Self, identity and meaning for oral historians, *Oral History*, 21(2): 80–3.

Swindells, J. (1995a) Introduction, in J. Swindells (ed.) *The Uses of Autobiography*. London: Taylor and Francis.

Swindells, J. (ed.) (1995b) *The Uses of Autobiography*. London: Taylor and Francis.

Tedlock, B. (2000) Ethnography and ethnographic representation, in N. K. Denzin and Y. S. Lincoln (eds) *Handbook of Qualitative Research*, 2nd edn. London: Sage.

Temple, B. (1994) The message and the medium: oral and written accounts of lives, *Auto/Biography*, 3(1/2): 31–42.

Temple, B. (1995) Telling tales: accounts in the journeys of British Poles, *Oral History*, 23(2): 60–4.

Temple, B. (1996) Time travels: time, oral histories and British–Polish identities, *Time and Society*, 5(1): 85–96.

Temple, B. (1997) Watch your tongue: issues in translation and cross-cultural research, *Sociology*, 31(3): 607–18.

Thomas, W. I. and Znaniecki, F. ([1918–20]1958) *The Polish Peasant in Europe and America*, 2 vols. New York, NY: Dover Press.

Thompson, P. (1983) Oral history and the historian, *History Today*, 33: June: 24–8.

Thompson, P. (1988) *The Voice of the Past*, 2nd edn. Oxford: Oxford University Press.

Thompson, P. (1992) Preface, in L. Passerini (ed.) *Memory and Totalitarianism*. Oxford: Oxford University Press.

Thompson, P. (1993) Family myth, models, and denials in the shaping of individual life paths, in D. Bertaux and P. Thompson (eds) *Between Generations*. Oxford: Oxford University Press.

Thompson, P. (1994) Tony Parker – writer and oral historian, *Oral History*, 22(2): 64–73.

Thompson, P. (1995) Letters, *Oral History*, 23(2): 27–8.

Thompson, P. (2000) *The Voice of the Past*, 3rd. edn. Oxford: Oxford University Press.

Thompson, P. and Burchardt, N. (eds) (1982) *Our Common History: The Transformation of Europe*. London: Pluto.

Thompson, P., Itzin, C. and Abendstern, M. (1990) *I Don't Feel Old: The Experience of Later Life*. Oxford: Oxford University Press.

Thomson, A. (1994) *Anzac Memories: Living with the Legend*. Oxford: Oxford University Press.

Thomson, A. (1995) Writing about learning: using Mass-Observation educational life-histories to explore learning through life, in J. Swindells (ed.) *The Uses of Autobiography*. London: Taylor and Francis.

Thomson, A. (1998) Anzac memories: putting popular memory theory into practice in Australia, in R. Perks and A. Thomson (eds) *The Oral History Reader*. London: Routledge.

Thomson, A., Frisch, M. and Hamilton, P. (1994) The memory and history debates: some international perspectives, *Oral History*, 22(2): 33–43.

Tierney, W. G. (2000) Undaunted courage: life history and the postmodern challenge, in N. K. Denzin and Y. S. Lincoln (eds) *Handbook of Qualitative Research*, 2nd edn. London: Sage.

Tomalin, C. (1991) *The Invisible Woman: The Story of Nelly Ternan and Charles Dickens*. Harmondsworth: Penguin.

Tonkin, E. (1990) History and the myth of realism, in R. Samuel and P. Thompson (eds) *The Myths We Live By*. London: Routledge.

Tonkin, E. (1995) *Narrating Our Pasts: The Social Construction of Oral History*. Cambridge: Cambridge University Press.

Toolan, M. J. (1988) *Narrative: A Critical Linguistic Introduction*. London: Routledge.

Townsend, C. and Townsend, E. (1990) *War Wives: A Second World War Anthology*. London: Grafton.

Tremblay, M.-A. (1982) The key informant technique: a non-ethnographic application, in R. G. Burgess (ed.) *Field Research: A Sourcebook and Field Manual*. London: Unwin Hyman.

Turner, B. S. (1984) *The Body and Society: Explorations in Social Theory*. Oxford: Blackwell.

Turner, R. (1967) Introduction, in R. Turner (ed.) *Robert E. Park on Social Control and Collective Behavior*. Chicago, IL: Chicago University Press.

Tyler, S. A. (1986) Post-modern ethnography: from document of the occult to occult document, in J. Clifford and G. Marcus (eds) *Writing Culture*. Berkeley, CA: University of California Press.

Usher, R. (1998) The story of the self: education, experience and autobiography, in M. Erben (ed.) *Biography and Education*. London: Falmer Press.

Van Dijk, T. A. (1997) *Discourse as Structure and Process*. London: Sage.

Van Maanen, J. (1988) *Tales of the Field: On Writing Ethnography*. Chicago, IL: University of Chicago Press.

Van Maanen, J. (1995a) An end to innocence: the ethnography of ethnography, in J. Van Maanen (ed.) *Representation in Ethnography*. London: Sage.

Van Maanen, J. (ed.) (1995b) *Representation in Ethnography*. London: Sage.

Vansina, J. (1973) *Oral Tradition: A Study of Historical Methodology*. Harmondsworth: Penguin.

Vidich, A. J. and Lyman, S. M. (1994) Qualitative methods: their history in sociology and anthropology, in N. K. Denzin and Y. S. Lincoln (eds) *Handbook of Qualitative Research*. London: Sage.

Walder, D. (1995) The genre approach, in D. Walder (ed.) *The Realist Novel*. London: Routledge/The Open University.

Walkerdine, V. and Lucey, H. (1989) *Democracy in the Kitchen: Regulating Mothers and Socialising Daughters*. London: Virago.

Wallot, J.-P. and Fortier, N. (1998) Archival science and oral sources, in R. Perks and A. Thomson (eds) *The Oral History Reader*. London: Routledge.

Ward, A. and Jenkins, A. (1999) Collecting the life-stories of graduates: evaluating students' educational experiences, *Oral History*, 27(2): 77–86.

Wells, H. G. (1934) *Experiment in Autobiography*, Vol. 1. London: Victor Gollancz/Cresset Press.

Wengraf, T. (2001) *Qualitative Research Interviewing: Biographic Narrative and Semi-Structured Methods*. London: Sage.

White, H. (1973) *Metahistory*. Baltimore, MD: Johns Hopkins University Press.

White, H. (1987) *The Content of the Form*. Baltimore, MD: The Johns Hopkins University Press.

White, J. (1981) Beyond autobiography, in R. Samuel (ed.) *People's History and Socialist Theory*. London: Routledge and Kegan Paul.

Whyte, W. F. ([1943]1955) *Street Corner Society*, 2nd edn. Chicago, IL: University of Chicago Press.

Whyte, W. F. (1970) Reflections on my work, in I. L. Horowitz (ed.) *Sociological Self-images: A Collective Portrait*. Oxford: Pergamon Press.

Whyte, W. F. (1992) In defence of *Street Corner Society, Journal of Contemporary Ethnography*, 21(1): 52–68.

Widdicombe, S. and Wooffitt, R. (1995) *The Language of Youth Subcultures*. Hemel Hempstead: Harvester Wheatsheaf.

Williams, R. (1958) *Culture and Society*. Harmondsworth: Penguin.

Williams, R. (1961) *The Long Revolution*. Harmondsworth: Penguin.

Williams, R. (1977) *Marxism and Literature*. Oxford: Oxford University Press.

Winter, J. (1995) *Sites of Memory, Sites of Mourning*. Cambridge: Cambridge University Press.

Wolff, K. H. (1979) Phenomenology and sociology, in T. Bottomore and R. Nisbet (eds) *A History of Sociological Analysis*. London: Heinemann.

Words and Silences: Bulletin of the International Oral History Association (1998) 1(3).

Worpole, K. (1981) A ghostly pavement: the political implications of local working-class history, in R. Samuel (ed.) *People's History and Socialist Theory*. London: Routledge and Kegan Paul.

Wright, P. (1985) *On Living in an Old Country*. London: Verso.

Young, J. (1993) *The Texture of Memory: Holocaust Memorials and Meaning*. New Haven, CT: Yale University Press.

Yow, V. R. (1994) *Recording Oral History: A Practical Guide for Social Scientists*. London: Sage.

Zeitlin, I. M. (1973) *Rethinking Sociology*. Englewood Cliffs, NJ: Prentice-Hall.

Index

accuracy
   problem of reliability in oral history,
      104–7
   see also reliability; validity
Ackroyd, P., *Dickens*, 66–9
Adam, B., time, 82, 140, 171
ageing, and the life story, 25–8
'Ageing and life history: the meaning of
   reminiscence in late life'
   (Coleman), 26–7
Aldridge, J., memory, 77
Alheit, P., 82
Allport, G. W., 45
   forms of life history, 47
   use of diaries, 64–5
Althusser, L., 4
ambiguity, 57
analytic induction, 8–9, 10–11
' "And how was it for you, Mary?" Self,
   identity and meaning for oral
   historians' (Stuart), 108
Angell, R.
   personal documents in sociology, 19
   see also Gottschalk, L.
anthropology, *see* ethnography

Anthropology and Autobiography
   (Okely and Callaway), 162–4
anti-history, 102
*Anzac Memories: Living with the
   Legend* (Thomson), 146
Atkinson, P.
   story and *discours*, 161
   with A. Coffey
      anthropological texts, crisis of
         representation, 160
      methodology, 173
      reflexivity, 8
Atkinson, R., 22
   data and theory, 21
   evaluation, 39–40
   interpretations of life stories,
      13
   life story, 3
   The Life Story Interview, 40
   meanings in life histories, 20
authorship, 61
   place of, 55–6
'Auto/biographical account of
   educational experience, An'
   (Roberts), 86

Auto/biographical Discourses: Theory, Criticism, Practice (Marcus), 58
Auto/Biography I: The Theory and Practice of Feminist Auto/biography, The (Stanley), 75
auto/biography, 4, 30–1, 52–72, 176
  anthropology, 162–4
  case studies, 66–9, 88–91
  and education, 88–91
  feminism, 59, 77–8
  fiction and non-fiction, 69–71
  genre, 56–60
  hermeneutics and phenomenology, 80–2
  individual and society, 88
  intertextuality, 78–9
  and oral history, 53–4, 75–6, 79
  personal artefacts, 62–6
  postmodernism, 61, 76–7
  researcher as auto/biographer, 84–7
  researcher-researched relationship, 87–8
  and sociology, 73–92
  time, 82–4
  see also life histories; researchers
auto/biographical I, 86–7
autobiographical memory, 136–7

Baddeley, A. D., working memory, 135
Baker, P. J., 'The life histories of W. I. Thomas and Robert E. Park', 35
Bakhtin, M. M., 62, 71
Barthes, R., 4
  myth, 124, 125
  rhetorical forms, 127
  Roland Barthes by Roland Barthes, 61
Basil Street Blues (Holroyd), 55
Baum, W. K., with D. K. Dunaway, oral history, 96
Becker, H. S.
  functions of life history, 19
  life stories within sociology, 6, 18
Becoming Deviant (Matza), 41
Benn, T., diary, 63–4
Berger, P., 36
Bernard, H. R., 152
  coding, 11
  participant observation, 153
Bertaux, D., 49, 73
  Biography and Society, 47

with P. Thompson
  Between Generations: Family Models, Myths and Memories, 110–13
  intergenerational transmission of memory, 145
Between Generations: Family Models, Myths and Memories (Bertaux and Thompson), 110–13
Biographer's Tale, The (Byatt), 70
biographical research, 176
biography, 30–1, 176
  and autobiography, 52–72
  biographical turn, 3–6, 169–70
  ethnography, 157
  see also auto/biography; life histories
Biography and Society (Bertaux), 47
Black Women, Writing and Identity (Davies), 59
Bleak House (Dickens), 68
Blumer, H., 13
  on *The Polish Peasant*, 44, 45
body, and sexuality, 29–30
Bornat, J.
  interpretation in oral history, 100, 105
  oral history and auto/biography, 75
Boswell, J., *Life of Johnson*, 53, 54, 63
Boswell's Presumptuous Task (Sisman), 53
Brewer, J. D., research roles, 153
British Sociological Association, on biography and autobiography, 73
Brown, N. R., with S. K. Shevell and L. J. Rips
  autobiographical memory, 141–2
  'Public memories and their personal context', 138
Bruner, J., 118
Bruyn, S. T., 161
Bryman, A.
  analytic induction, 10
  qualitative research, 3
  with R. G. Burgess
    language, 14
    research methods, 8
Bulmer, M., on *The Polish Peasant*, 45
Burgess, R. G., with A. Bryman
  language, 14
  research methods, 8

Butler, R., reminiscence, 131
Byatt, A. S., historical novel, 70
Bytheway, B., gerontology, 28

Callaway, H., with J. Okely,
    Anthropology and Autobiography,
    162–4
career, theory of deviance, 40–1
case history, and case study, 38
case studies
    Anthropology and Autobiography
        (Okely and Callaway), 162–4
    auto/biography and education, 88–91
    *Between Generations: Family
        Models, Myths and Memories*
        (Bertaux and Thompson), 110–13
    Dickens (Ackroyd), 66–9
    The Jack-Roller (Shaw), 45–6
    Memory and Totalitarianism
        (Passerini), 142–4
    The Polish Peasant (Thomas and
        Znaniecki), 42–5
    *Tales of the City: A Study of
        Narrative and Urban Life*
        (Finnegan), 128–30
case study, and case history, 38
Chamberlain, M., with P. Thompson
    fiction and non-fiction, 70
    genre, 56
'Changing places and altered
    perspectives: research on a Greek
    island in the 1960s and in the
    1980s' (Kenna), 163
Charmaz, K., grounded theory, 9,
    10–11
Chicago interactionism, 4, 7
Chicago School, 20, 33–4
    career and deviance, 40–1
    use of private letters, 63
*Children of Sanchez: Autobiography
    of a Mexican family, The* (Lewis),
    155
Children's War: Evacuation, The
    (Inglis), 65
Chivers, T., life review and life-plan, 131
chronology, *see* time
Clandinin, D. J., with F. M. Connelly
    field texts, 2
    narrative and story, 117
    time, 124

Clark, A., 63
Clausen, J. A.
    life review, 131
    myths and self-conception, 126
Clifford, J., with G. E. Marcus,
    ethnographic writing, 161
coding, 11
Coffey, A.
    characters in ethnographic research,
        155
    literary turn in ethnography, 168
    narrative elements in ethnography,
        158
    researcher's memory, 148
    with P. Atkinson
        anthropological texts, crisis of
            representation, 160
        methodology, 173
        reflexivity, 8
cognitive psychology, memory, 135
Cohen, A. P., self-conscious
    anthropology, 164
Cohen, G., autobiographical memory,
    retrieval process, 137–8
Coleman, P. G., 'Ageing and life
    history: the meaning of
    reminiscence in late life', 26–7
communal projects, oral history,
    22–3
Connelly, F. M., with D. J. Clandinin
    field texts, 2
    narrative and story, 117
    time, 124
'Construction of identity in the
    narratives of romance and comedy,
    The' (Murray), 126
constructionism, and realism, 7–8
Conway, M. A., memories as
    dynamically constructed, 137
corroboration, 40
Cortazzi, M., structure of narrative,
    121
Coser, L. A., on *The Polish Peasant*, 45
Crabtree, B. F., with W. L. Miller,
    coding, 11
*Crooked Scythe: An Anthology of Oral
    History, The* (Evans), 98
Cullum-Swan, B., with P. K. Manning,
    narratives and stories, 118
Current Sociology, 73

data
  and methodology, 37–40
  and theory, 6–13, 21
David Copperfield (Dickens), 69
Davies, C. B., *Black Women, Writing
  and Identity*, 59
Davis, K., cosmetic surgery, 29
De Man, P., philosophy and literature,
  55
*Death of Luigi Trastulli and Other
  Stories: Form and Meaning in Oral
  History, The* (Portelli), 101
declarative memory, 135
deconstructionism, 5
  meanings in opposition, 55
delinquency
  delinquent careers, 41
  The Jack-Roller, 11, 19, 45–6
Delinquency and Drift (Matza), 41
Dentith, S., intertextuality, 78–9
Denzin, N. K., 22, 73
  biographical research, 1
  data and method, 38
  on *The Jack-Roller*, 46, 48
  lives as narrative fictions, 49
  use of diaries, 64–5
  validity, 39
  with Y. S. Lincoln
    grounded theory, 10
    interpretations from interactive
      context, 169
    interpretive paradigms, 14
    qualitative research, 5, 168
deviance, career theory of, 40–1, 50
Dex, S.
  biography in education, 23
  lives and structures, 131
dialogic relationship, 71
diaries, 63–4
Dickens (Ackroyd), 66–9
Dickens, C., 67–9
Dilthey, W., 4, 80
disciplines, 22–3
discours, and story, 161
discourse, 118–19
displacement, narrative, 116
Doing Qualitative Research Differently
  (Hollway and Jefferson), 123
Dollard, J.
  criteria for life history, 47–8

  use of life history, 45
Dunaway, D. K.
  influence of postmodernism, 100
  oral history, 97, 98
  with W. K. Baum, oral history, 96

Eakin, P. J., autobiography in the
  present, 60
education
  and auto/biography, 88–91
  biography in, 23–4
Elder, G. H. Jr
  life stage, 132
  with J. Z. Giele, life course, 130–1
Eminent Victorians (Strachey), 54
emplotted narrative, narrative analysis,
  122
empowerment
  narrative, 116
  oral history as, 96–7
Enlightenment, 4
epiphany, 176
Erben, M.
  biography in education, 23
  hermeneutics and phenomenology, 80
  individual and society, 74
  method and purpose of study, 12
  text, 77
  time, 123
ethics, oral history, 104
ethnography, 151–66
  case study, 162–4
  fieldwork, 152
  informants, 154–7
  interpretation of life histories, 49
  literary turn, 168
  methodology, 153–4
  myth, 164
  oral traditions, 164–5
  reflexivity, 157–60
  research roles, 152–3
  text, 160–2
European Sociological Association, 74
evaluation, 39
Evans, G. E., 97
  *The Crooked Scythe: An Anthology
    of Oral History*, 98
Evans, M.
  code of biography, 54
  grand narratives, 77, 88

Everyday Life Philosophers (Gullestad), 61
experience, and narration, 81
experiential, 6

family
  family mysteries, 142
  group memories, 144–5
  intergenerational transmission of stories, 110–13
feminism, 21, 28–9
  and auto/biography, 59, 77–8
  ethics in oral history, 104
  ethnography, 153
  hidden ideologies in narrative, 124
  oral history as feminist encounter, 107
  personal documents, 65
  see also gender
Fetterman, D. M., life history and ethnography, 156
fiction
  and memory, 139
  and non-fiction in auto/biography, 67–71
field texts, 2
fieldwork, 152
Finnegan, R.
  influences on oral history, 96
  Tales of the City: A Study of Narrative and Urban Life, 128–30
Fischer-Rosenthal, W., with G. Rosenthal, hermeneutics, 81
flashbulb memory, 136
Forster, M., 67
Foucault, M., 29
Francis, H., 62
Frank, L., on Dickens, 68
free association, 21, 123
Freeman, M.
  memory and rewriting the self, 127
  Rewriting the Self: History, Memory, Narrative, 139
Frisch, M., 144
  memory, 140–1
  oral history, 99, 101–2
  power, 107
  A Shared Authority: Essays on the Craft and Meaning of Oral and Public History, 102

see also Thomson A.
functionalism, 4, 35

Geertz, C., fictive characteristics of ethnographic writing, 160–1
gender
  and auto/biographies, 58, 90
  see also feminism
generations, intergenerational transmission of stories, 110–13
genre, auto/biography, 56–60
Gergen, K. J., with M. M. Gergen
  narrative forms, 124
  time, 126
Gergen, M. M., with K. J. Gergen
  narrative forms, 124
  time, 126
gerontology, 28
Giddens, A., 29
Giele, J. Z., with G. H. Elder Jr, life course, 130–1
Glaser, B. G., with A. L. Strauss, grounded theory, 9
Gluck, S. B.
  oral history as collaborative production, 96
  oral history as empowerment, 96–7
  oral history as feminist encounter, 107
  types of oral history, 95
  with D. Patai, *Women's Words: The Feminist Practice of oral History*, 29
Golby, J., autobiography, 58
Goodson, I. F.
  life story, 5–6
  media, divide and rule, 170
Gottschalk, L., with C. Kluckhohn and R. Angell, 45
Gramsci, A., 4
Green and Pleasant Land (Humphries and Hopwood), 110
Grele, R. J.
  ethics in oral history, 104
  ideological context of oral history, 141
  interviewing, 106
  need for more conscious history, 102
  oral history, 98, 99

oral history as cultural narrative, 106–7
Griffin, S., researcher telling his/her own story, 127
grounded theory, 9–11
Gubrium, J. F., with J. A. Holstein, biographical work in ethnography, 157
Gullestad, M., *Everyday Life Philosophers*, 61

Hamilton, P., *see* Thomson, A.
Hammersley, M., grounded theory, 9
Hastrup, K., memory and recollection, 134
Hatch, J. A., with R. Wisniewski, truth, 6
Hawthorn, J.
  genre, 56
  on Sillitoe, 69–70
health, life story giving as therapeutic, 25–8
hermeneutics, 176
  and phenomenology, 80–2
histoire, 161
historical novel, 70
  see also fiction
history
  as literary genre, 57
  and myth, 125, 142, 165
Hoffman, A., accuracy in oral history, 105
Hoggart, R., *The Uses of Literacy*, 71
Hollway, W., with T. Jefferson
  Doing Qualitative Reseach Differently, 123
  producing meanings, 21
Holmes, R., *Sidetracks*, 54
Holroyd, M., 54
  Basil Street Blues, 55
Holstein, J. A., with J. F. Gubrium, biographical work in ethnography, 157
Hopwood, B., with S. Humphries, *Green and Pleasant Land*, 110
Horowitz, I. L.
  process of becoming a sociologist, 37, 50
  subjectivity in sociology, 84–5

Humphries, S., with B. Hopwood, *Green and Pleasant Land*, 110
Hunter, I. M. L., long-term memory, 135–6
Husserl, E., 4
Hutcheon, L., 61
  postmodern representation, 49
Hyvärinen, M., narrative and time, 125–6

identity, 170–1
  and narrative, 86
ideological context, oral history, 141
ideologies, hidden in narrative, 124
immigrants, 42
indexing, record of events by thematic knowledge, 137
individual
  auto/biographical writing and creation of self, 75–7
  and social sciences, 4–5
  and social structures, 34–7
  and society, 47, 60, 74, 88
individuality, 4, 21–2
Inglis, R., 64
  The Children's War: Evacuation, 65
interactive process, 20–1
interdisciplinarity, oral history, 96
intergenerational transmission, memory, 112, 145
internal consistency, 39–40
International Oral History Association, 25, 167
International Sociological Association, 74, 167
interpretation, 78, 100
  ethnography, 154
  life history, 46–50
  oral history, 105
intertextuality, 78–9
interview, oral history, 94
interviewer, role, 106
interviews
  relation between interviewer and interviewee, 107–8
  relevance of, 25
  science and art of, 40
  see also researchers
introspection, 4

Jack-Roller, The (Shaw), 11, 19, 45–6
Jefferson, T., with W. Hollway
Doing Qualitative Research Differently, 123
producing meanings, 21
Josselson, R.
meaning constructed through social discourse, 118
narrative analysis, 115
narrative as a meaning-making system, 138–9
narrative as process, 120
narrative psychology, 121
with A. Lieblich
The Narrative Study of Lives, Making Meanings of Narratives, 120
use of psychology in narrative analysis, 119–20

Kenna, M. E., 'Changing places and altered perspectives: research on a Greek island in the 1960s and in the 1980s', 163
Kluckhohn, C., 154
see also Gottschalk, L.
knowledge, 49
Kohli, M., 82
Kristeva, J., 78

Landscape for a Good Woman (Steedman), 59
Lejeune, P., autobiography, 60
letters, use of, 62–3
Lévi-Strauss, C., myth, 124–5
Lewis, O.
The Children of Sanchez: Autobiography of a Mexican family, 155
work criticized, 154–5
Lieblich, A.
with R. Josselson
The Narrative Study of Lives, Making Meanings of Narratives, 120
use of psychology in narrative analysis, 119–20
with R. Tuval-Mashiach and T. Zilber

holistic and categorical approaches to narrative study, 122
narrative, 117
life course, 130–1
life histories, 3, 33–50, 177
case studies, 42–6
data and method, 37–40
deviance, 40–1
elderly, 25–8
and ethnography, 156, 157
individual and society, 34–7
interpretation, 46–50
and life passage, 132
as perfect sociological material, 44
of sociologists, 35–7
as therapy, 25–8
see also auto/biography
'Life histories of W. I. Thomas and Robert E. Park, The' (Baker), 35
Life of Johnson (Boswell), 53, 54, 63
life passage, and life history, 132
life review, reminiscence, 131
life story, 3, 5–6, 177
Life Story Interview, The (Atkinson), 40
life-plan, 131
Lincoln, Y. S., with N. K. Denzin
grounded theory, 10
interpretations from interactive context, 169
interpretive paradigms, 14
qualitative research, 5, 168
literary narrative, 129
literary turn, 168
literature, relation to philosophy, 55
Living the Ethnographic Life (Rose), 159
Lundberg, G. A., life history not scientific, 43

Mandelbaum, D., life passage and life history, 132
Mann, C., adolescent girls, case study, 89–91
Manning, P. K., with B. Cullum-Swan, narratives and stories, 118
Marcus, G. E.
reflexivity in ethnography, 159–60
with J. Clifford, ethnographic writing, 161
Marcus, L.

Auto/biographical Discourses: Theory, Criticism, Practice, 58
autobiography, 57–8
Matza, D.
Becoming Deviant, 41
Delinquency and Drift, 41
Mead, G. H., 41
reality of social life, 19
symbolic interactionism, 35
time, 82
meanings
individuals as creators of, 6
narrative as meaning-making system, 138–9
produced by researcher and researched, 21
media, 103
Mellor, P., with C. Shilling, cognitive priority, 4
memories, 127, 172, 177
and autobiography, 134–49
case study, 142–4
family, 144–5
oral history, 107
recollection and selectivity, 147–8
relationship between public and private, 145–6
selectivity, 77, 147–8
social transmission, 140–2
and trauma, 143
Memory and Totalitarianism (Passerini), 142–4
Merton, R., sociological autobiography, 50
methodology, 173
and data, 6–13, 21, 37–40
ethnography, 153–4
memories, recollection and selectivity, 147–8
Millennium Memory Bank, 103
Miller, R. L.
approaches to life stories, 14–15
biographical research, 168
grounded theory, 10
objective hermeneutics, 81
Researching Life Stories and Family Histories, 121
Miller, W. L., with B. F. Crabtree, coding, 11
Mills, C. W., 46, 170

sociological imagination, 18, 36, 80
Milton Keynes, Finnegan's *Tales of the City*, 128–30
Mintz, S., ethnography, position of researcher, 158
Mitchell, W. T., narrative theory, 116
'more history', 102
Morgan, D., auto/biography, 85
Morgan, G., sociologists' lives, 50
motivation, 55
Muller, J. H., narrative in qualitative tradition, 117
Murray, K., 'The construction of identity in the narratives of romance and comedy', 126
myth
family, 110–13
and history, 125, 142, 165
narrative analysis, 124–8
oral traditions, 164
see also subjectivity

Narrating Our Pasts: The Social Construction of Oral History (Tonkin), 165
narration, and experience, 81
narrative, 177
and identity, 86
oral history as cultural narrative, 106–7
and time, 83–4
narrative analysis, 5, 115–33, 177
case study, 128–30
life course, life review, life plan and life passage, 130–2
myth, 124–8
psychology, 118, 119–21
time and plot, 123–4
Narrative Analysis (Riessman), 122
narrative approach, life stories, 15
narrative fiction, lives as, 49
Narrative Study of Lives, Making Meanings of Narratives, The (Josselson and Lieblich), 120
Neisser, U., flashbulb memory, 136
neo-positivist approach, life stories, 15
neutrality, realist tale, 48
Nevins, A., 97
Niethammer, L., memory, 143
novels, *see* fiction

objective hermeneutics, 81
objectivity
  Chicago School, 46
  and subjectivity, 19–20
  see also accuracy; reliability; validity
Okely, J., with H. Callaway,
  Anthropology and Autobiography,
  162–4
Olney, J., 56
On Narrative (Mitchell), 116
open questions, 123
oral history, 22–3, 24–5, 93–113, 177
  and auto/biography compared, 52–3,
  75–6, 79
  case study, 110–13
  ethics, 104
  origins of, 97–9
  political issues, 107–10
  reliability of accounts, 104–7
  subjectivity, 106–7
oral traditions, ethnography, 164–5

paradigmatic reasoning, analysis of
  narratives, 122
Park, R. E., 71
  formalism, 41
  life histories, 33, 35
Parker, T., 97
  Red Hill: A Mining Community, 100
participant observation, 153
Passerini, L., 99, 100
  Memory and Totalitarianism, 142–4
  myth, 125
  myth and history, 142
  subjectivity in oral history, 107
  'Work ideology and consensus under
  Italian fascism', 101
past, as narratives of historians, 125
Patai, D., with S. B. Gluck, *Women's
  Words: The Feminist Practice of
  Oral History*, 29
Peneff, J.
  myth in oral traditions, 164
  myths, 126–7
personal documents, 62–6, 177
personal knowledge, 5–6
persuasion, 40
Petras, J. W., time, 82
phenomenology, and hermeneutics,
  80–2

philosophy, relation to literature, 55
photographs, 66
plot, and time in narrative, 123–4
Plummer, K., 49, 73
  analytic induction, 9
  documents of life, 19–20
  life history method 37–8
  *Telling Sexual Stories: Power,
  Change and Social Worlds*, 30
  validity, 38–9
*Polish Peasant in Europe and America,
  The* (Thomas and Znaniecki),
  11–12, 13, 34, 42–5, 63
political standpoint, oral history,
  107–10
Polkinghorne, D. E.
  data and theory, 11
  incomplete plot, 124
  narrative analysis and analysis of
  narratives, 122
  narrative enquiry, 116
Popular Memory Group, 106
  oral history movement, 108–9
  public and private memories, 146,
  147
Portelli, A., 98, 99, 100, 142
  credibility in oral history, 105
  *The Death of Luigi Trastulli and
  Other Stories: Form and Meaning
  in Oral History*, 101
  genre, 59
  oral history as composite genre, 94
Porter, R., *Enlightenment*, 4
postmodern representation, 49
postmodernism, 4–5
  authorship, 55–6
  autobiography, 61
  construction of self in
  auto/biography, 76–7
  ethnography, 160
  history as literary genre, 57
  intertextuality, 78–9
  oral history, 100
Potter, J., with M. Wetherell, discourse,
  118
power, 87
  oral history, 107
  and textual analysis, 119
presentation, 23
process, 19

progressive-regressive method, 7, 36
psychology, and narrative analysis, 118,
    119–21
public memories, construction and
    impact on private memories,
    145–6
'Public memories and their personal
    context' (Brown, Shevell and Rips),
    138

qualitative research, 2–3, 5, 8, 168

Radley, A., *Worlds of Illness:
    Biographical and Cultural
    Perspectives on Health and
    Disease*, 27
realism, and constructionism, 7–8
realist approach, life stories, 14–15
reality, and fiction, 67–71
recall, 136
'Reciprocity in critical research? Some
    unsettling thoughts' (Sparkes), 24
recollection, 134, 141
    and selectivity, 147–8
    see also memories
reconstruction, 81
Red Hill: A Mining Community
    (Parker), 100
'Reflections on my work' (Whyte), 36
reflexivity, 8, 78
    ethnography, 157–60
    see also self
Reformation, 4
Reinharz, S.
    feminist researchers, 77
    interpretation, 78
    types of feminist oral history, 95
reliability
    oral history, 96
    and validity, 38–9
    see also accuracy; objectivity; validity
'Remembering Latvian childhood and
    the escape from history' (Skultans),
    141
reminiscence, 26–7
    life review, 131
representation, 49
    and intertextuality, 78–9
researchers
    as auto/biographer, 84–7

ethnography, position of researcher,
    158
    feminist, 77
    and meanings, 21
    memory, 148
    relationship with researched, 87–8
    and researched, 84–8
    researcher's memory, 148
    researcher's self, 172–3
    role of, 13–14
    telling his/her own story, 127
    see also auto/biography; interviews
*Researching Life Stories and Family
    Histories* (Miller), 121
*Rewriting the Self: History, Memory,
    Narrative* (Freeman), 139
rhetorical forms, 127
Richardson, L., sociology and
    narrative, 127–8
Ricoeur, P.
    myth, 125
    plot, 124
    time, 82, 83–4
Riessman, C. K.
    Narrative Analysis, 122
    narrative analysis, 117–18
    structure of narrative, 121
Riley, M. W., life stage, 132
Rips, L. J., *see* Brown, N. R.
Ritchie, D. A., oral history practice,
    93–4, 95
Roberts, B.
    'An auto/biographical account of
        educational experience', 86
    on Dickens, 68
    'Some thoughts on time perspectives
        and auto/biography', 83
    time, 123
Robins, T., self-narration and self-
    creation, 147
Roland Barthes by Roland Barthes
    (Barthes), 61
Rose, D., *Living the Ethnographic Life*,
    159
Rosenthal, G.
    family transmission of memory, 145
    narrative analysis, 121
    with W. Fischer-Rosenthal,
        hermeneutics, 81
Rowland, P., on Dickens, 69

Rubin, D. C., memory as
  reconstruction, 137

Samuel, R., with P. Thompson
  myths, 125
  vagaries of recollection, 141
Sartre, J.-P., 4
  progressive-regressive method, 7, 36
Saturday Night and Sunday Morning
  (Sillitoe), 69
Schutz, A., 4, 7
  phenomenology, 7, 36
  time, 82–3
Schütze, F., 82
scientific criteria
  and life histories, 46
  see also accuracy; objectivity; validity
Scott, D., 80
  individual and society, 91
Scott, J.
  authenticity of personal documents, 65
  autobiography, 57
script, 131, 142
self
  construction of in auto/biography,
    75–7
  myths, 126
  narrative and memory, 127–8
  researcher's self, 172–3
  see also reflexivity
self-conception, and myths, 126
selfhood, narrative and memory, 127–8
sensory memory, 135
sequentiality, 81
sexuality, 29–30
*Shared Authority: Essays on the Craft
  and Meaning of Oral and Public
  History, A* (Frisch), 102
Shaw, C. R.
  delinquent careers, 41
  The Jack-Roller, 11, 19, 45–6
Sheridan, D., 55
Shevell, S. K., *see* Brown, N. R.
Shilling, C., with P. Mellor, cognitive
  priority, 4
short-term memory, 135
Sidetracks (Holmes), 54
Sillitoe, A., 69
Silverman, D., experiential, 6
Sisman, A., *Boswell's Presumptuous
  Task*, 53

'Sisters under the skin? Oral histories
  and auto/biographies' (Stanley), 86
Skultans, V., 'Remembering Latvian
  childhood and the escape from
  history', 141
small scale, 88
Smith, L. M., 67
  ambiguity, 57
  autobiography, 60
Smith, P. M., ethnography, participants
  as interpreters, 157
social sciences, individual, 4–5
society
  and the individual, 34–7
  and individual, 47, 60, 74, 88
sociological imagination, 18, 36, 80
sociology, 22
  and auto/biography, 73–92
  diaries, 64
  letters, 63
  life histories as material, 44
  life histories of sociologists, 35–7
  life history within, 33–50
  life stories within, 6, 18
  and narrative, 127–8
  sociological imagination, 18, 36, 80
  subjectivity in, 84–5
  use of personal documents, 19
'Some thoughts on time perspectives
  and auto/biography' (Roberts), 83
Sparkes, A. C.
  body and sexuality, 30
  interactive process, 21
  'Reciprocity in critical research?
    Some unsettling thoughts', 24
  solidarity and change, 91
Stanley, L., 77, 86
  *The Auto/Biography I: The Theory
    and Practice of Feminist
    Auto/biography*, 75
  auto/biography, 74
  autobiographical I, 86, 87
  biographical research, 3–4
  'Sisters under the skin? Oral histories
    and auto/biographies', 86
  textual politics, 75–6
  time, 84
  understanding present through
    history, 78
  with D. Morgan, 73, 74, 79
  with S. Wise

feelings and emotions, 87
feminist theory, 78
Starr, L., oral history, 97
Steedman, C., *Landscape for a Good Woman*, 59
story, 48, 129
  and *discours*, 161
  and narrative, 117
  see also narrative
Strachey, L., *Eminent Victorians*, 54
Strauss, A. L., with B. G. Glaser, grounded theory, 9
Street Corner Society (Whyte), 156
Stuart, M., ' "And how was it for you, Mary?" Self, identity and meaning for oral historians', 108
subjectivity
  meaning of personal life, 35
  and objectivity, 19
  oral history, 106–7
  see also myth
Swindells, J.
  individual and society, 60
  literary autobiography 30–1
  The Uses of Autobiography, 31
  women in autobiographical writing, 58
symbolic interactionism, 35

Tales of the City: A Study of Narrative and Urban Life (Finnegan), 128–30
television, faction and docu-soap, 64
Telling Sexual Stories: Power, Change and Social Worlds (Plummer), 30
Temple, B.
  autobiographical I, 86–7
  interpretation and representation, 79
  'Time travels: time, oral histories and British-Polish identities', 85
Terkel, S., trauma and memory, 144
text, ethnography, 160–2
textual analysis, 119
textual politics, 75–6
thematic knowledge, indexing of specific events, 137
theory, and data, 6–13, 21, 37–40, 44
therapy, life history giving as, 25–8
Thomas, W. I.
  life histories, 35
  life history, 33

with F. Znaniecki, 19
  The Polish Peasant in Europe and America, 11–12, 13, 34, 42–5, 63
Thompson, P., 122
  ageing and the life story, 25–6
  intergenerational transmission of memory, 145
  memory and family mysteries 142
  oral history, 98, 99, 103
  remembering as mutual process, 148
  stories transmitted across generations, 112
  with D. Bertaux
    Between Generations: Family Models, Myths and Memories, 110–13
    intergenerational transmission of memory, 145
  with M. Chamberlain
    fiction and non-fiction, 70
    genre, 56
  with R. Samuel
    myths, 125
    vagaries of recollection, 141
Thomson, A.
  Anzac Memories: Living with the Legend, 146
  with M. Frisch and P. Hamilton, ethics in oral history, 99, 104
time, 82, 140, 171, 177
  auto/biography, 82–4
  and myth, 125–6
  and plot in narrative, 123–4
  'Time travels: time, oral histories and British-Polish identities' (Temple), 85
Tonkin, E.
  myth, 125
  Narrating Our Pasts: The Social Construction of Oral History, 165
Toolan, M. J.
  fabrication in narrative, 116
  time, 124
totalitarianism, and memory, 142–4
Townsend, C., with E. Townsend, *War Wives: A Second World War Anthology*, 65
Townsend, E., with C. Townsend, *War Wives: A Second World War Anthology*, 65
trauma, and memory, 143–4

truth, 6
Tuval-Mashiach, R., *see* Lieblich, A.

Uses of Autobiography, The
(Swindells), 31
Uses of Literacy, The (Hoggart) 71
Usher, R., time, 84

validity
internal and external, 39
oral history, 105
and reliability, 38–9
see also accuracy; objectivity;
reliability
Van Maanen, J.
ethnography, phases in research
practice, 160
interpretation, 48–9
Vansina, J., oral traditions, 164
verstehen, 4, 7, 80
videos (home), 66
voice, 21

*War Wives: A Second World War
Anthology* (Townsend and
Townsend), 65
Weber, M., *verstehen*, 4, 7, 80
Wells, H. G., 62
Wetherell, M., with J. Potter, discourse,
118
White, H.
history as narrative, 57
narratives of historians, 125
Whyte, W. F.
'Reflections on my work', 36
reflexivity, 158

Street Corner Society, 156
Widdicombe, S., with R. Wooffitt,
discourse, 119
Williams, R., genre, 56
Wise, S., with L. Stanley
feelings and emotions, 87
feminist theory, 78
Wisniewski, R., with J. A. Hatch, truth,
6
*Women's Words: The Feminist Practice
of Oral History* (Gluck and Patai),
29
Wooffitt, R., with S. Widdicombe,
discourse, 119
'Work ideology and consensus under
Italian fascism' (Passerini), 101
working memory, 135
*Worlds of Illness: Biographical and
Cultural Perspectives on Health
and Disease* (Radley), 27
writing conventions, 8

Yow, V. R., 22
autobiography and oral history, 53
ethics in oral history, 104
oral history, 93, 94, 95–6
role of interviewer, 106
use of interviews, 25

Zilber, T., *see* Lieblich, A.
Znaniecki, F.
analytic induction, 8
with W. I. Thomas, 19
*The Polish Peasant in Europe and
America*, 11–12, 13, 34, 42–5, 63

Learning Resources
Centre